Theological Ethics

SCM CORE TEXT

Theological Ethics

Edward Dowler

scm press

© Edward Dowler 2011

Published in 2011 by SCM Press
Editorial office
13–17 Long Lane,
London, EC1A 9PN, UK

SCM Press is an imprint of Hymns Ancient & Modern Ltd
(a registered charity)
13A Hellesdon Park Road
Norwich NR6 5DR, UK

www.scm-canterburypress.co.uk

British Library Cataloguing in Publication data

A catalogue record for this book is available
from the British Library

Scripture quotations are from the New Revised Standard Version
copyright 1989 by the Division of Christian Education of the
National Council of Churches of Christ in the USA.
Used by permission. All rights reserved.

978-0-334-04199-3

Typeset by Regent Typesetting, London
Printed and bound by
CPI Antony Rowe, Chippenham, Wiltshire

Contents

Preface

Manners morals and ethics are caught, not taught.

I've been justified by faith and I keep the Ten Commandments.
Why do I need any of this?

While I have considerable sympathy with both of these comments, one of which was habitually made by my grandmother and the other by a former student, I nonetheless offer this book as an introduction to some central themes in theological ethics.

In the first section, I aim to give a basic orientation in the subject by exploring some of the key concepts in the Christian moral tradition. The second section discusses some of the contrasts and controversies that have made this subject the contested field that it undoubtedly has been and still is. In the final section, I take a necessarily rather selective look at what seem to me to be some of the most important modern perspectives on themes that have already been explored. Some objectives for the book may be briefly outlined.

First, I hope to be readable. My aim is that this book should stretch and challenge readers who are relatively new to this subject, and yet be kind to them, by explaining ideas patiently and carefully, without heavy academic name-dropping, skipping around from point to point, or use of unnecessarily technical language.

Second, I hope to be appropriately biblical. The course of lectures, delivered at theological colleges in Oxford, which originally gave rise to this book, included a lecture on Ethics and the Bible. Some readers may be disconcerted that the book contains no chapter bearing such a title, but the reason for this is that I think Christian theological ethics should engage at all times with the Scriptures, and not consign them to a solitary chapter.

Third, I hope to be appropriately historical. Throughout the book, I try to place the concepts that are explored in their context. Needless to say, ideas about Ethics, or any other subject, do not occur in a vacuum, and it is important to understand something of how they came to be as they are, and how they relate to one another.

Fourth, perhaps unusually for a book on this subject, I hope to pay attention to the literary qualities of the writers in this field. One of the reasons why the ideas of many of them have been influential is because they present (to borrow a phrase from Matthew Arnold) 'the best that has been thought and said' about this subject, and they often do so in beautiful and compelling ways. I have tried to bring this out by paying attention to the way in which their arguments are constructed, and by quoting directly from them. I hope this means that readers will be able to move on quickly from reading what I have written to the primary texts that I discuss.

Fifth, I have tried to be, for want of a better word, relevant. At the time of writing, there are a number of deep disputes within the Church on ethical matters. This book will certainly not resolve any of these, but I hope it may contribute to a clearer understanding of how we think about theological ethics, which is necessary prior to the consideration of specific issues. In any case, I have tried throughout the book to show how concepts that may seem abstract and theoretical do in fact relate to contemporary ethical issues.

Sixth, throughout the book, I aim to be charitable. Although I write from the perspective of Christian theology, and primarily engage with the themes that the mainstream tradition of moral thought has believed to be important, I nonetheless aim to present a variety of views, and to see the good in the different approaches that I discuss.

Finally, as a Christian teacher and pastor, I hope that some of what I say may not only explain to readers some ideas about ethics, but also have the capacity to inspire them with a deeper sense of both the challenges and the gifts that God gives to those who seek to live the Christian moral life.[1] If anything here can help to build up even one person in the theological virtues of faith, hope and love, then, so far as I am concerned, nothing will have been wasted.

Edward Dowler

Clay Hill, Enfield, February 2011

---

1 'The Christian Moral Life' was the title of my first Ethics course, taught by Professor Timothy Sedgwick at the (now defunct) Seabury Western Theological Seminary in Evanston, USA. Professor Sedgwick, an inspiring teacher, used the term frequently, as I do in this book. Although the term is singular, I hope the text will show that I do not want to imply by using it that there is some sort of rigid blueprint for life that is lived in response to God's gift and his call. Thanks be to God, the Christian moral life can take many and various forms.

Acknowledgements

I would like to thank my publisher, Natalie Watson at SCM Press, for her support and encouragement.

I am grateful to my former colleagues at St Stephen's House, Oxford, and to the students who attended my Ethics course, both there and at Wycliffe Hall. Without their suggestions, insights, comments and questions I could never even have begun to write about this subject.

Most of all, I would like to thank my wife, Anna for supporting me and being patient with me, both while I have been writing this book, and at all other times.

PART ONE

Key Concepts

1

Sin and Grace

Augustine and Pelagius

The incident of the pears

Theft receives certain punishment by your law (Exodus 20:15) Lord and by the law written in the hearts of men (Rom 2:14) which not even iniquity itself destroys ... I wanted to carry out an act of theft and did so, driven by no kind of need other than my inner lack of any sense of or feeling for, justice. Wickedness filled me. I stole something which I had in plenty and of much better quality. My desire was to enjoy not what I sought by stealing but merely the excitement of thieving and the doing of what was wrong. There was a pear tree near our vineyard laden with fruit, though attractive neither in colour nor taste. To shake the fruit off the tree and carry off the pears, I and a gang of naughty adolescents set off late at night after (in our usual pestilential way) we had continued our game in the streets. We carried off a huge load of pears. But they were not for our feasts but merely to throw to the pigs. Even if we ate a few, nevertheless our pleasure lay in doing what was not allowed. Such was my heart, O God, such was my heart. You had pity on it when it was at the bottom of the abyss. Now let my heart tell you what it was seeking there in that I became evil for no reason. I had no motive for my wickedness except wickedness itself. It was foul and I loved it. I loved the self-destruction, I loved my fall, not the object for which I had fallen but my fall itself. My depraved soul leaped down from your firmament to ruin. I was seeking not to gain any thing by shameful means but shame for its own sake.

Augustine of Hippo, Confessions 2.4.9, trans. H. Chadwick

In a famous passage from his spiritual autobiography, the *Confessions*, Saint Augustine (AD 354–430), Bishop of Hippo in North Africa and 'father of the western Church', draws a far-reaching account of the human condition out of an incident in which he and a group of teenage friends stole pears from a neighbour's tree. Our first reaction to Augustine's analysis of this trivial youthful misdemeanour might be to agree with the American justice Oliver Wendell Holmes who commented to his friend Harold Laski, 'Rum thing to see a man making a mountain out of robbing a pear tree in his teens.' But if we do find the story, as it is told in the *Confessions*, absurdly over-solemn, then this perhaps gives Augustine his point. For his reflections on stealing the pears make it clear that sinful desires and inclinations are so deeply rooted in human life that they permeate all of it, even the most apparently trivial incidents. And, Augustine would claim, this is not simply his own observation, since in the book of Genesis itself, much is also made of Adam and Eve illicitly eating a piece of fruit (Gen. 3), while Jesus himself has a story about a young man who craves food that is only fit for pigs (Luke 15.15–16). The incident of the pears reveals that both Adam and the prodigal son lurk below the surface identity of an apparently ordinary African youth, doing normal adolescent things with his friends.

Samuel Taylor Coleridge used the expression 'motiveless malignity' to describe the evil perpetrated by Iago in Shakespeare's play *Othello* and, for Augustine, the frightening fact about human sinfulness is precisely its motiveless quality. He is at pains to tell us that there was no real reason for his theft of the pears, no rational explanation for what he and his friends did that night. They could not have justified their action on the grounds that they were hungry, since they were not. Neither were their eyes bigger than their stomachs, as might have been the case if they had been left alone in a shop full of enticing sweets, but the pears were 'attractive neither in colour nor in taste'. The incident reveals, as Augustine recounts it, that human beings love to do what is wrong simply because it is wrong, and seek shame 'for its own sake'.

For Augustine, then, human nature is fundamentally skewed and disordered, a fact that may be apprehended in virtually all of our thoughts and actions, however trivial. Such a bias towards willing and doing what is wrong may be compared with the game of bowls or the French pétanque. In this game, even if the ball is thrown in an absolutely straight direction, its inbuilt bias will cause it to veer off track. Similarly, in Augustine's view, even when human beings are consciously determined to act rightly, their distorted desires tend to lead them radically off course. 'All this life of ours,' he writes, 'is a weakness; and a long life is nothing else but a prolonged weakness.'[1]

In Augustine's view, human beings experience grave difficulty both in knowing and doing the good. So far as the former of these is concerned, human moral vision has been, in Augustine's view, clouded and darkened by sin. But even when we can clearly see what is good, we nonetheless still find it hard to do it. Looking into ourselves, we find that we are deeply divided and conflicted, that our motives are constantly mixed, and that we are frequently unable to do even the good things that we sincerely intend and wish. Augustine frequently quotes some words of Saint Paul in the letter

---

1 Augustine, *Sermon* 30.2.

4

to the Romans; words that he believes echo frighteningly in each of our lives: 'I do not understand my own actions. For I do not do what I want, but I do the very thing that I hate ... I do not do the good I want, but the evil I do not want is what I do' (Rom. 7.15–19).

Throughout his writings and sermons, Augustine, who was not only a theologian and polemicist, but first and foremost the pastor of a local congregation, shines a spotlight on the weakness of human beings, the distortions and divisions that exist within us, and the enormous complexity that attends our deepest motivations and intentions. He powerfully depicts the experience of being gripped by passionate but often contradictory desires: 'it was no iron chain imposed by anyone else that fettered me, but the iron of my own will'.[2] In his account of the battle he experienced inside his own will on the eve of his conversion to Christianity, he writes, 'I neither wanted it wholeheartedly nor turned from it wholeheartedly. I was at odds with myself, and fragmenting myself.'[3] Even if our inner motivations are clear to God 'to whom all hearts are open and all desires known',[4] they often remain frighteningly opaque even to ourselves: 'I am become a question to myself', he writes, 'and therein lies my downfall.'[5]

Augustine finds the explanation of these problems in the story of Adam in the book of Genesis: 'this disintegration was occurring without my consent ... it was not I who brought it about, but the sin that dwelt within me as penalty for that other sin committed with greater freedom; for I was a son of Adam'.[6] In Augustine's view, Adam was created perfectly free to do as he willed, either for good or evil. But when Adam sinned, he transmitted his original sin to his descendants who already existed in his seed: that is the entire human race. In the aftermath of Adam's sin, human beings no longer enjoy the freedom that their first ancestor had at the beginning but are, because of his original sin and our seminal identity with him, preprogrammed to go wrong. Thus, sin resides in us innately and from the moment of our conception, permeating our every thought and action. A favourite proof text for this view comes from the Psalms: 'indeed I was born guilty, a sinner when my mother conceived me' (Ps. 51.5). Even babies, who are too young to make conscious moral choices, are nevertheless infected with original sin so that, in Augustine's view, they too need to be baptized. After all, who could be more selfish than a baby? 'I have watched and experienced for myself,' Augustine writes, 'the jealousy of a small child: he could not even speak, yet he glared with livid fury at his fellow-nursling.'[7]

---

2 Augustine, *Confessions* 8.5.10.
3 Augustine, *Confessions* 8.10.22.
4 Collect for Purity, Book of Common Prayer.
5 Augustine, *Confessions* 10.33.50.
6 Augustine, *Confessions* 8.10.22.
7 Augustine, *Confessions* 1.7.11.

Many objections have been raised to some of the biological and historical details of Augustine's description of original sin, especially since his exegesis of a crucial New Testament passage about our seminal identity with Adam (Rom. 5.12) notoriously rests on a mistranslation of Paul's words in the Latin translation of the Bible with which he was working.[8] However, despite such difficulties, Augustine's dramatic and profound insights into the nature of human psychology have remained a compelling account of human moral agency, in which either knowing the good or willing ourselves to do it is rarely straightforward, and often deeply problematic.

Pelagius

Augustine's account of original sin certainly failed to convince his greatest adversary in a life full of argument and controversy. The British monk Pelagius (c. 354–c. 420), memorably described by Saint Jerome (347–420) as 'a fat booby bloated on Scotch porridge', was in fact a stern ascetic who advocated a programme of spiritual renewal and moral discipline in order to reform what he saw as an increasingly lax church, tending more and more to adopt the corrupt moral norms of the Roman Empire, into which he feared it would become assimilated. Around AD 413, Pelagius wrote a letter to Demetrias, a wealthy young woman who, shortly before she was due to get married, had decided to become a nun. In it, Pelagius describes the human condition in terms that contrast starkly with those of Augustine:

> In our case, God himself, that eternal Majesty, that ineffable and inestimable Sovereignty, has sent us the holy Scriptures as the crown of his truly adorable precepts; and, so far from receiving them at once with joy and veneration, and taking the commands of so illustrious a sovereign for a high privilege (especially as there is no thought of advantage for him who gives the command, but only of profit for him who obeys it) on the contrary, with hearts full of scorn and slackness, like proud and worthless servants, we shout in God's face and say, 'It's hard! It's difficult! We can't! We are but men, encompassed by the frailty of the flesh!' What blind folly! What rash profanity! We make the God of knowledge guilty of twofold ignorance: of not knowing what he has made and of not knowing what he has commanded. God wished to bestow on his rational creation the privilege of doing good voluntarily, and the power of free choice, by implanting in man the possibility of choosing either side; and so he gave him, as his own characteristic, the power of being what he wished to be;

---

8 Augustine, relying on his Latin text, refers to Adam as the one '*in whom* all have sinned', but the original Greek text of Romans does not attribute the problem to Adam in such a strong sense: 'death spread to all *because* all have sinned'; see Augustine, *Against two Letters of the Pelagians*, 7; Bonner (1986), pp. 372–3.

so that he should be naturally capable of good and evil, that both should be within his power, and that he should incline his will towards one or the other.

Pelagius, *Letter to Demetrias*, 16.2, trans. B. R. Rees

Whereas Augustine in his description of the incident of the pears wrestles with the mystery of his mixed motivations and the recalcitrance of a human will that seems to impel us in the wrong direction, even when we would rationally choose otherwise, it is evident from this letter that Pelagius is impatient of such tortuous complexities. In his view, the particular characteristic of human beings as moral agents is that we are endowed with absolute freedom of choice: 'the possibility of choosing either side'. As we have seen, in Augustine's view, Adam enjoyed this freedom before the Fall, but, as a consequence of his sin, it has been irrevocably lost thereafter both for Adam and for the descendants who were 'in him'. By contrast, although Pelagius would accept that human beings are weakened by factors such as the individual slothfulness of each one of us, our accumulated bad habits, and the unfortunate examples that others set us, he does not accept Augustine's view that we are innately and inescapably predisposed towards sin. Rather, having been given the law, we are simply required to obey it without making excuses. The Scriptures tell us what God requires of us, and our task is to get on and do it.

We can see from Pelagius's letter to Demetrias that, in his view, Augustine's understanding of this subject seems first of all to imply an impoverished view of human agency: indoctrination with a strong sense of our helplessness and inability in the face of original sin will lead us to give up on our own abilities. We will too easily say 'It's hard. It's difficult. We can't,' whereas we should instead redouble our efforts to lead good and holy lives. Writing at a time when Christianity was becoming respectable in the Roman Empire, Pelagius was concerned that Christians might use the moral teaching of Augustine's *Confessions* to exonerate themselves from following the rigorous moral standards that would distinguish them from others in society. If being good is impossible, why even try?

A second criticism implicit in the letter to Demetrias is that Augustine holds a diminished view of God's wisdom: to claim that we are unable to do what God has commanded implies that God does not know what he is doing. But, argues Pelagius, the God who made us in the first place, and who gave us the law through Moses and Jesus, knows what he is doing: 'no one knows better the true measure of our strength than he who has given it to us nor does anyone understand better how much we are able to do than he who has given us this very capacity of ours to be able'.[9] Since he has said that human beings should reflect his own holiness (Lev. 19.2) and that we

---

9 Pelagius, *Letter to Demetrias*, 16.3.

should be perfect as our heavenly Father is perfect (Matt. 5.48), who are we to say that these things are somehow not possible?

Anthropology and theology

Pelagius, then, is far more positive than Augustine about the capacity of human beings to make good moral choices. He admits, at least in possibility, a brighter view of ourselves, in which we are essentially self-determining moral beings, able to know what is good and then to get on and do it. By contrast, Augustine's pessimism on this subject has often seemed unattractive. A disturbing example of this may be found in his dealings with the Donatists, the name given to members of a rival church in North Africa which had split away from the mainstream Catholic Church in the aftermath of the persecution under the Emperor Diocletian (244–311), over the Catholic Church's perceived leniency to those who had lapsed. Early on in his time as a bishop, Augustine had hoped that the Donatists would become reunited with the Catholic Church through persuasion rather than fear. As time went on, however, he came to the conclusion that compulsion would indeed be the best means of achieving this end.[10] To some extent, Augustine's change of mind was caused by his observation of the high success rate of the Roman authorities in persuading Donatists to become Catholics – unsurprisingly high, given that their property, livelihoods and even lives often depended upon it. But this empirical evidence was backed up by his anthropology: Augustine's assessment of the human condition under original sin persuaded him that, in the words of Peter Brown, 'men needed firm handling'.[11] His low estimate of human moral capabilities made him able to support the imperial policy of coercion, which he justified by the chilling use of Jesus' words in the parable of the great feast: 'Compel them to come in' (Luke 14.23).

However, when assessing the argument between Augustine and Pelagius, it would be wrong to make too simple a contrast between Augustine's somewhat dark and gloomy vision of humanity and what has sometimes wrongly been portrayed as Pelagius's sunny liberal optimism. For Pelagius was essentially a stern ascetic. He advocated a quasi-monastic existence for all Christians, and emphasized the terrifying consequences of moral laxity. If human beings possess the unclouded capacity to see the good and the unfettered capacity to do it, then they can be held entirely responsible if they fail. For Pelagius, as for many in the early Church, it was barely possible for sins committed after baptism to be forgiven. As a consequence, Pelagius puts far more emphasis on hell fire and punishment than does Augustine: 'after so many notices drawing your attention to virtue; after the giving of the law, after the Prophets, after the gospels, after the apostles, I just do

---

10 See Augustine, *Letter* 93.
11 Brown (1967), pp. 236–7.

not know how God can show indulgence to you if you wish to commit a crime'.[12]

Augustine by contrast is far more able to present a compelling account of the nature and extent of God's grace. Since sin is original, and stretches back to its origin in the sin of Adam, individual human beings cannot entirely be blamed for it. Since each of us is effectively pre-programmed to go wrong, then it follows that we cannot be entirely responsible, as we would be if we, like Adam, had a completely free choice in the matter. Thus, in the comparison between Pelagius and Augustine, we see that when the focus changes from anthropology to theology, from talking about human beings to talking about God, a sort of reversal takes place:

	Augustine	Pelagius
Anthropology	–	+
Theology	+	–

Augustine's low view of human nature; his belief in its inherent wickedness and weakness leads him to set a very high premium on God's grace. For if we are in the hopeless and helpless state that Augustine thinks we are in, then we have all the more need for Christ's saving work and for God's help every minute of the day to save us from falling into the sin which is so utterly ingrained in our nature. Augustine often quotes Jesus' words in John's Gospel, 'apart from me you can do nothing' (John 15.5) to assert our total reliance on a gracious God for any good actions that we might do. In the words of H. F. Lyte's famous hymn 'Abide with Me',

I need thy presence every passing hour;
What but thy grace can foil the tempter's power?

The *Confessions* depict to us just such a God, who is indeed abundantly gracious: constantly present and active in the life of an individual man; constantly working to save him from the slough of sin into which, left to his own unaided efforts, he would inevitably fall, even after he has been baptized.

Conversely, Pelagius's higher view of our capabilities and our ability to get things right on our own finds its counterpart in a pessimistic view of God. God is not, as for Augustine, a perpetually present companion, but a stern lawgiver, who tells us what we need to know and do and then leaves us to get on with it, only returning in order to judge how successfully or otherwise we have performed. In a famous section of the *Confessions*, Augustine asks

---

12 Quoted in Brown (1967), p. 371.

9

God to 'Give what you command, and then command whatever you will.'[13] Pelagius would certainly have believed God free to command whatever he wills, but he took grave exception to Augustine saying that God should give what he commands: that if God requires something from us, then he must also graciously give us the strength to do it.

For Pelagius, the grace of God operates, as it were, externally. God has endowed us at our creation with free will. Christians have been washed clean from sin by baptism. Moses and Jesus have revealed the moral law. In Pelagius's view, all the grace we need has been dispensed through these channels. In contrast, Augustine would certainly agree that grace operates in these ways, but for him it also has a crucial inner dimension as daily help and strengthening, and not just law and doctrine. Grace is 'an internal and secret power, wonderful and ineffable by which God operates in our hearts' and, as Bonner puts it, 'not only the endowment given to us as created beings made in the image of God, but ... the ministration of the Holy Spirit, assisting our wills and actions'.[14] We need this grace every minute of the day to initiate the good within us and to carry it through to fruition. If we don't have it, we are lost: 'we cannot conquer the temptations of this life without God's help, by the exercise of our wills alone'.[15]

Freedom

> That is the trouble with freeing people: relatively easy to know what you're freeing them *from*; much more difficult to know what you're freeing them *for*.[16]

The argument between Augustine and Pelagius has further implications for the way in which we think about the nature of human freedom. The theme of freedom is prominent in the New Testament, and particularly in the letters of Saint Paul, who reminds the Galatians, whom he believes to be in danger of giving up their Christian liberty, that 'for freedom Christ has set us free' (Gal. 5.1). To the Romans, Paul writes of the eschatological age when the creation will obtain 'the freedom of the glory of the children of God' (Rom. 8.21). The precise nature of Christian freedom is central to the dispute between Augustine and Pelagius, and their attitudes towards it are radically different. For Pelagius, freedom consists in the opportunity for self-determination, self-actualization and choosing our own path. Human beings in their moral actions are essentially free because we are equally poised between good and evil, with 'the possibility of choosing either side'. By contrast, for Augustine, to be free is to be liberated through God's grace

---

13 Augustine, *Confessions* 10.29.40; cf. *The Gift of Perseverance* 20.53.
14 Bonner (1986), p. 360.
15 Augustine, *Exposition of Psalm* 89.4.
16 Andrew Marr, quoted from the BBC TV series, *The Making of Modern Britain*.

from the necessity of sinning, from the constraining power of the sin that dwells within us (cf. Rom. 7.23). 'The beginning of freedom,' he tells his congregation, 'is to be free from crime ... such as murder, adultery, fornication, theft, fraud, sacrilege and so forth. Once one is without these crimes (and every Christian should be without them), one begins to lift up one's head toward freedom.'[17]

Echoing the perspective of Pelagius, many have questioned whether the freedom that Augustine describes is really freedom at all. Augustine was often to quote Proverbs 8.35 (Septuagint), 'the will is prepared by God'. God's actions predate our merits and every good deed that we do must be attributed to him. Augustine often asks his congregation Paul's rhetorical question, 'what do you have that you did not receive?' (1 Cor. 4.7) As Augustine sees it, God's grace is irresistible. As Rist summarizes his approach, 'fallen man is totally subject to the acts of God'. This is a view that, towards the end of his life, Augustine pressed to its conclusions in his works *On the Predestination of the Saints* and *On the Gift of Perseverance*. In some of the more extreme statements of it, human beings can seem little more than puppets, incapable themselves of free choice, but continually overwhelmed either by original sin or, if God has chosen that it be so, by God's grace.[18]

In response to this, however, Augustine would argue that the grace of God acts within the hearts of men and women, so as to make them delight in God's commandments, and thus start to obey the commandments not under duress, but freely and willingly. One of his favourite New Testament verses is Romans 5.5: 'God's love has been poured into our hearts through the Holy Spirit that has been given to us.' Grace does not *disem*power human agents, obliterating their wills and taking away their freedom, but *em*powers them, enabling them freely to love God and neighbour, and to do good works that express such love. For all his stress on human limitations, Augustine was clear that it was part of the basic, observable structure of human psychology that we, unlike inanimate objects, do have a will, and that we are not simply governed by necessity.[19] Thus, when the Holy Spirit bestows grace on human beings, enabling them to love and to do the good, this does not simply make them passive recipients: 'they are acted upon that they may act, not that they may themselves do nothing'.[20]

This dispute between Augustine and Pelagius about the nature of freedom has far-reaching repercussions for ethics, since any understanding of morality presupposes a basic level of freedom: if human actions were completely predetermined, and if we were entirely unable to make choices, and to determine to some degree the direction of our lives, then the whole notion of right and wrong would be meaningless. Freedom is of course very high-

---

17 Augustine, *Tractates on the Gospel of John* 41.10.
18 For further discussion of this subject, see Rist (1994), chapter 5.
19 See Augustine, *On the Freedom of the Will* 3.1.2.
20 Augustine, *On Admonition and Grace* 2.4.

ly prized in modern Western society. Taking their cue from the American Declaration of Independence, with its stress on 'life, liberty and the pursuit of happiness', many people would regard freedom as being an absolute and transcendent good. Ironically, perhaps, such an emphasis on the importance of freedom often goes hand in hand with a simultaneous sense that the lives and decisions of modern men and women are, to a large extent, determined by factors outside their control, such as their genetic make-up, upbringing, or economic circumstances. As O'Donnell comments, 'We are a culture blithe in our praise for freedom and our missionary zeal to share freedom with others, but at the same time obsessed with a series of discourses – political, ethical, medical – about the conflicts and limits of freedom ... We act as though we are free, but we beg off the consequences of our actions by pleading incapacity.'[21] Moreover, as the newspaper extract below argues, it is questionable whether the enormous amount of choice available to affluent people in the West necessarily makes for human flourishing.

Modern life is making us miserable because we have too much choice, claims new research.

From the foods we eat, to the television channels we watch, to the schools we send our children to and the career we choose to pursue, society has never offered us so much variety.

But while the ability to choose is generally a good thing, too much freedom of choice is crippling us with indecision and making us unhappy, claims the new research. People can become paralysed by too much variety and wracked with uncertainty and regret about whether they have made the right decision. Ultimately they can be less satisfied by the choices they have made.

The study believes that the problem is that when you have too much choice, you become obsessed about what your decision will say about you. Then when you have made the choice you worry that it is wrong. Choice can also foster selfishness and a lack of empathy because it can focus people on their own preferences and on themselves at the expense of what is good for society as a whole.

Professor Hazel Rose Markus, the author from Stanford University's Department of Psychology, said: "We cannot assume that choice, as understood by educated, affluent Westerners, is a universal aspiration, and that the provision of choice will necessarily foster freedom and well-being.

"Even in contexts where choice can foster freedom, empowerment, and independence, it is not an unalloyed good. Choice can also produce a numbing uncertainty, depression, and selfishness."

---

21 O'Donnell (2005), pp. 329–30.

The authors looked at a body of research into the cultural ideas surrounding choice. They found that among non-Western cultures and among working-class Westerners, freedom and choice are less important or mean something different than they do for the university-educated people. Professor Markus said: "And even what counts as a 'choice' may be different for non-Westerners than it is for Westerners. Moreover, the enormous opportunity for growth and self-advancement that flows from unlimited freedom of choice may diminish rather than enhance subjective well-being." Professor Markus said her study, which focused on Americans, applied to all middle-class Westerners. She said: "Americans live in a political, social, and historical context that advances personal freedom, choice, and self-determination above all else. Contemporary psychology has proliferated this emphasis on choice and self-determination as the key to healthy psychological functioning."

Richard Alleyne, *Independent*, 21 January 2010

In line with such insights, it seems that we should question whether freedom is simply the ability to do whatever we choose, and that our freedom is greatest when we have multiplied the number of possibilities open to us.[22] Rather, as Oliver O'Donovan argues, choices always take place within certain limits and if there were no limits, there could be no meaningful choices, and therefore no freedom. Moreover, when we make choices, we necessarily impose new limits on ourselves, and these limits then govern the context in which our future choices will be made. 'Decision,' O'Donovan writes, 'depends upon existing limits and imposes new ones. Limit is the very material with which freedom works.'[23] An illustration of this point may be found in Shakespeare's play, *King John*, in which one of the citizens comments in the following terms about the wedding of the Dauphin and Blanche of Spain:

He is the half part of a blessed man,
Left to be finished by such as she;
And she a fair divided excellence,
Whose fulness of perfection lies in him.
O, two such silver currents, when they join,
Do glorify the banks that bound them in.[24]

The citizen points out that the marriage into which Blanche and the Dauphin are entering will necessarily create limits upon them. Just as the banks of a

---

22 See O'Donovan (1994), p. 107.
23 O'Donovan (1994), p. 108.
24 Shakespeare, *King John*, Act 2, Scene 1, 437–42. I owe this comparison to Stephen Batty.

river bind it in, channel it in a particular direction, and enable it to flow more freely and forcefully, so, the married state will impose limits on Blanche and the Dauphin, but these limits will not simply curtail their freedom, but focus and energize it, so that it can flow more forcefully in a particular direction. The banks (that is, in this instance, the married state) are glorified by the strongly flowing river, because if there were no banks, there could be no river.

A further problem about understanding freedom as the maximizing of choices is that not everyone can be absolutely free all of the time since the freedom exercised by one person will sometimes inevitably interfere with those claimed by another. This point was made in relation to the issue of assisted suicide by the Archbishop of Canterbury, Rowan Williams in an address to the General Synod of the Church of England in 2010. Williams argued that a relaxation of British law in relation to assisted suicide might lead to pressure being placed on sick or elderly people to end their lives: 'the freedom of one person to utilise in full consciousness a legal provision for assisted suicide brings with it a risk to the freedom of others not to be manipulated or harassed or simply demoralised when in a weakened condition'. As Williams sees it, we are faced here not with a simple scenario in which everybody is simply able to be free, but rather, with a competing and complex 'balance of freedoms' which must be carefully worked out in order to avoid injustice.

Many of these later debates are foreshadowed by the seminal argument between Augustine and Pelagius on the nature of freedom. True freedom, in Augustine's understanding of it, is not so much the ability to choose what we want, unfettered by any constraint, but freedom from the power of sin. What is important is not so much that we should be free from all constraints, but that we should be free for excellence, for happiness, for flourishing.

> Christian freedom as St Paul spells it out is always freedom from isolation
> – from the isolation of sin separating us from God, and the isolation of
> competing self-interest that divides us from each other. To be free is to be
> free for relation; free to contribute what is given to us into the life of the
> neighbour, for the sake of their formation in Christ's likeness, with the
> Holy Spirit carrying that gift from heart to heart and life to life.[25]

Sexuality and the body

(Headstone) ... walked with a bent head hammering at one fixed idea. It had been an immovable idea since he first set eyes upon her. It seemed to him as if all that he could restrain in himself he had restrained, and

---

25 Rowan Williams, *Archbishop's Presidential Address to the General Synod of the Church of England*, February, 2010. This section draws on McCoy (2004), pp. 45–53.

the time had come – in a rush, in a moment – when the power of self-command had departed from him. Love at first sight is a trite expression quite sufficiently discussed; enough that in certain smouldering natures like this man's, that passion leaps into a blaze, and makes such head as fire does in a rage of wind, when other passions, but for its mastery, could be held in chains.[26]

Augustine displays in his writing a very vivid understanding of the power of sexual desire and its capacity, as he expresses it in one of his later writings, to 'swamp the mind'.[27] It is likely that he would have entirely recognized Dickens's description in the passage quoted above of the school master, Bradley Headstone, caught in the grips of his passion for the somewhat insipid Lizzie Hexam, a passion that Headstone can neither understand nor control. Indeed Augustine himself was notoriously subject to such feelings. In a passage from the third book of the *Confessions* paraphrased by T. S. Eliot, he writes of himself as a young man, 'enamoured with the idea of love', seeking the delights of this major city with its cosmopolitan atmosphere and relaxed sexual mores:

> To Carthage then I came
> Burning, burning, burning, burning
> O Lord Thou pluckest me out
> O Lord thou pluckest
> burning.[28]

Augustine lived at a time when commentators both within and outside the Church habitually expressed strongly negative attitudes to the body, sexual desire and indeed physical existence generally. The Neoplatonist philosopher Porphyry, an important influence on Augustine, famously held that 'the body is to be fled by all'. Augustine himself was deeply influenced as a young man by the Manichee sect, whose religion erected a strict set of dualistic divisions, such as those between light and darkness, the Old Testament and the New, believers and outsiders. In particular, the Manichees recoiled from all the physical aspects of human existence. Indeed, the central task of their 'elect' was to consume brightly coloured vegetables such as tomatoes and peppers, and then belch so as to liberate the particles of light contained in them from their corrupt material casing.

Critics of Augustine, from the scourge of his later years, Julian of Eclanum (c. 386–455), until today have accused Augustine himself of hiding deep-seated Manichaean distaste for the body under a veneer of orthodox

---

26 Charles Dickens, *Our Mutual Friend* (Oxford: Oxford University Press), p. 341.
27 Augustine, *Against Julian* 4.7.
28 T. S. Eliot, *The Waste Land*, 307–11 from T. S. Eliot (1969), *The Complete Poems and Plays* (London: Faber and Faber); cf. Augustine, *Confessions* 3.1.1.

Christianity. In fairness to Augustine, it is clear that as he matured as a Christian, he grew also in his appreciation of the importance of physical existence. In this, he was strongly influenced by his reflection on scriptural texts such as Ephesians 5.29, 'No one hates his own flesh' and, in particular, by the Christian doctrine of the resurrection of the body. In contrast to Porphyry, Augustine tells his congregation in a sermon that 'I do not want my flesh to be removed from me for ever, as if it were something alien to me, but that it be healed, a whole within me.'[29] The most serious aspect of the human predicament is not for Augustine that we are condemned to bodily life, but that our wills are divided and disordered. He reflects in the *Confessions* on his ability to bring his body under control, while his mind and will remain divided: 'the mind commands the body and is instantly obeyed; the mind commands itself, and meets resistance'.[30]

Moreover, as the title of his work *On the Good of Marriage* suggests, Augustine had a positive view of the institution of marriage that contrasts strongly with negative assessments of it, and indeed of women in general, held by contemporaries such as Jerome. The married state is a good one, although it is a lesser good than virginity: 'marriage and fornication', he writes, 'are not two evils, one of which is worse, but marriage and continence are two goods, one of which is better'. Augustine's reading of Genesis leads him to conclude that 'God instituted marriage from the beginning':[31] it was given prior to original sin, and with it the sexual intercourse that would replenish and populate the earth.

However, although sexual intercourse itself did belong to the life that God created for men and women in the beginning, it was sexual intercourse with a crucial difference. In the Garden of Eden, sex was free of lust in a way that it no longer is after the Fall: 'if sin had not come into being, therefore, marriage, because worthy of the felicity of Paradise, would have produced children to be loved, but without the shame of lust'.[32] According to Augustine, Adam, in his unfallen state, would have been an entirely coordinated being, who enjoyed perfect mastery over his body, including the sexual organs that are now so recalcitrant. 'We move our hands and feet,' he writes, 'to perform their tasks when we so will ... why, then, with respect to the procreation of children, should we not believe that the sexual organs could have been as obedient to the will of mankind as other members are, if there had been no lust, which arose in retribution for the sin of disobedience?'[33] But for Adam's descendants after the Fall, this perfect control of the sexual organs has been lost, just as the Fall has damaged our control of our bodies more generally. In an entertaining passage in the *City*

---

29 Augustine, *Sermon* 30.4, quoted in Rist (1994), p. 92.
30 Augustine, *Confessions* 8.9.21.
31 Augustine, *City of God* 14.21.
32 Augustine, *City of God* 14.23.
33 Augustine, *City of God* 14.23.

of God, Augustine argues that, despite this loss of control, the remnants of our unfallen condition endure in the ability of some people to move their ears, others to be able to bring their scalp down to their eyebrows and still others, he claims somewhat improbably, to perspire at will and sing out of their anuses.[34]

Thus, although our central problem is weakness of the will rather than having a corrupt body, a key aspect of this weakness is that it undermines the soul's capacity to do what it ought to do, which is to govern and direct the body. Augustine regards sex as the paradigmatic case study of the will's inability to exert proper rational direction over the body. The phenomenon of sexual desire epitomizes the words of Paul that express the entire human condition: 'I do not do the good I want, but the evil I do not want is what I do' (Rom. 7.19). Augustine shows a profound appreciation for the ability of sexual desire to generate feelings that run so deeply that they are not able simply to be suppressed, Pelagius-style, by the exercise of free choice. As Banner writes,

> We will not come to terms with certain phenomena in human sexual life – amongst them the awfully widespread phenomena of child abuse, rape, addiction to pornography, and the like – if 'bad choices' remains our principal analytic tool. We shall never come to terms with these phenomena, that is to say, while we think that 'choosing better' is the solution to our predicament; our real predicament lies in enthrallment to bad choices and thus in an inability to choose well.[35]

For all his deep understanding of the power and the dynamics of human sexuality, and for all that he viewed it more favourably than most of his contemporaries, Augustine can be criticized for insisting that, in the aftermath of Adam's fall, sex is always infected with the sin of concupiscence: lust or immoderate desire. This is evident in his contrast between the controlled and rational sexual activity of the Garden of Eden and sexual activity as it now is in a fallen world, in which desire will *always* overwhelm those involved, and militate against their right use of reason.[36] For fallen human beings, even sexual acts that pass the strictest moral criteria are nevertheless marked by some degree of concupiscence: 'the weakness of carnal generation is from the transgression of original sin'.[37] Because, according to the New Testament, Christ's own conception was not caused by sexual intercourse, he alone is free from this taint. Thus, despite the psychological profundity of Augustine's understanding of sexual desire, and despite his being more positive than many of his contemporaries in his attitudes to the body and to

---

34 See Augustine, *City of God* 14.25.
35 Banner (2008), p. 37.
36 See Banner (1999), p. 300.
37 Augustine, *On the Merits and Remission of Sins* 2.15.

sexuality, he nonetheless introduces what Henry Chadwick describes as a 'powerful and toxic theme' into later Christian theology,[38] by insisting that sex and sin are always coterminous for fallen human beings.

Questions for discussion

How would you assess the relative strengths and weaknesses of the arguments of Augustine and Pelagius about sin and grace?

How would you define freedom?

What connections do you think can be drawn between the dispute between Augustine and Pelagius and modern controversies among Christians about sexual ethics?

Case study: crime and punishment

Jason is an eighteen-year-old boy who has grown up on a deprived inner-city estate. Jason has never known his father, but has been brought up by his mother and her succession of boyfriends, with whom she has had difficult and often violent relationships. Throughout his life, Jason has always attended schools in which teachers have struggled to maintain discipline and his academic achievement has been low. Jason is already familiar to the police for a large number of crimes on his housing estate, including vandalism and petty theft. In his latest appearance in a magistrate's court, his lawyer argued in his defence that antisocial behaviour could be expected of somebody who had been brought up in a world where so many things seemed to be against him.

Questions for discussion

How you would assess the moral aspects of Jason's situation?

How do you think it relates to the dispute between Augustine and Pelagius?

Commentary

Those who take a sterner view of Jason's predicament might instinctively side with Pelagius in his insistence that moral choices are not predetermined, but that it is entirely up to him as a mature moral agent to act

---

38 Chadwick (1986), p. 114.

rightly and to take responsibility for what he does. If Jason's actions were simply the result of his social conditioning, then it would be expected that everyone brought up in similar conditions would also become criminals, but the fact that they do not shows that Jason alone is responsible for his actions. As a free human being, he possesses what Pelagius describes to Demetrias as 'the power of being what he wished to be', and he is manifestly misusing it.

Others would be inclined to be more sympathetic to Jason. They would emphasize his difficult family circumstances and the grim conditions in which he has been brought up, and argue that these are bound to have influenced his capacity for making good moral decisions. They will stress that Jason primarily needs rehabilitation into society and that simply to punish him will be useless and counter-productive. This more lenient view of Jason's predicament coincides with Augustine's strong insistence that when we make moral choices, we do not always do so in a cool, objective way but rather we are subject to a variety of forces that impel us in particular directions, and are often beyond our control.

This latter view finds echoes in the work of a variety of modern thinkers, many of whom may seem very different from Augustine, but who nonetheless argue, like him, that pervasive forces outside our control (e.g. sexual factors [Freud] or economic factors [Marx]) govern much of what we do, even when we are unaware of them and believe ourselves to be acting in complete freedom.[39] The more extreme version of such views (often described as Determinism) can, if stretched to the limit, entirely evacuate the idea of free will from moral decision making, and make human beings seem little more than puppets: precisely the criticism that Augustine received from some of his Pelagian critics.

---

39 On Augustine and Freud, see Brown (1967), p. 366.

2

Natural Law

Background to natural law theories

> Theft receives certain punishment by your law (Exodus 20:15) Lord and by the law written in the hearts of men (Rom 2:14) which not even iniquity itself destroys.

> *Confessions* 2.4.9

Augustine knew that stealing the pears was wrong for two reasons. First of all, it was declared to be wrong by the direct law of God in the biblical commandment not to steal. Second, however, he claims that stealing is known to be wrong through our innate sense of morality: the law that is 'written in the hearts of men'. It is this latter source of moral guidance that is often described as 'natural law'. This extract indicates that Augustine believes that these two sources of moral instruction accompany and complement one another. Moreover, although, in Augustine's view, original sin causes us to have a clouded and darkened vision of the good, he takes care to point out that it does not entirely obliterate human beings' innate capacity for moral discernment. Natural law theories, of which there are a wide range, hold in common the belief that the reality of how things are in ourselves and in the world around us will give us important clues about the way we ought to act; that, as Fergus Kerr puts it, 'in some sense or other the basic principles of morals and legislation are objective, accessible to reason and based on human nature'.[1]

Biblical sources

While no natural law theory can be drawn fully-formed either from the Old or the New Testament, nonetheless, an embryonic sense of them may be found in the following two areas of biblical reflection:

---

1 Kerr (2002), p. 98.

Reflection on creation

The heavens are telling the glory of God; and the firmament proclaims
his handiwork
Day to day pours forth speech, and night to night declares knowledge.
There is no speech, nor are there words; their voice is not heard;
yet their voice goes out through all the earth, and their words to the ends
of the earth.

Psalm 19.1–4

The opening verses of Psalm 19 tell of the glory of God's creation. Every
part of this creation continually conveys messages about God's glory which,
although inarticulate in the sense that they are not expressed in human language, are nevertheless extraordinarily eloquent and far-reaching. As the
psalm moves on, its focus changes from God's gift in creation to his gift of
the Torah:

The law of the Lord is perfect, reviving the soul;
the decrees of the Lord are sure, making wise the simple;
the precepts of the Lord are right, rejoicing the heart;
the commandment of the Lord is clear, enlightening the eyes.

Psalm 19.7–8

Although some commentators have seen this shift of perspective as an
indication that Psalm 19 is in fact two psalms conflated into one, most
acknowledge that, underlying the contrast in this psalm, there lies a deeper
unity. While, in its opening verses, the psalm speaks of what has often
been described as the *general* revelation of God's goodness that all creation
gives, the latter verses speak in a complementary way of the more specific
special revelation which is to be found in the Torah. As it has sometimes
been expressed, the opening verses speak of knowledge of God that can be
acquired through the *Book of Nature*; the latter of the knowledge that is
gained through the *Book of Scripture*.[2]

In line with this psalm, and with the Wisdom tradition that pervades not
only the Psalms, but also many other parts of the Old Testament, natural
law theories presuppose that, since the universe has been created by God,
it is not just neutral matter governed by impersonal laws, but a good creation, that contains beauty, order and purpose in its very structure: 'you have
arranged all things by measure and number and weight' (Wisd. 11.20). Thus,
moral rules and principles are not just random, arbitrary instructions imposed on human beings by God from outside, but rather they reflect God's
own design of the universe, created through his Word (see John 1.1), and

---

2 See Holmgren (2000), chapters 3 and 4.

ordered by the divine Wisdom which 'reaches mightily from one end of the earth to the other, and ... orders all things well' (Wisd. 8.1). Moreover, God has given human beings a unique capacity to apprehend the goodness that is inherent in creation, and also to live in a way that consciously acknowledges and respects it. As Barton puts it, 'Wisdom is essentially the ability to live one's life in accordance with ... (cosmic) order, at both the physical and the moral level: to be skilful in one's occupation, sensible and sagacious in one's decisions, and moral in one's whole way of life.'[3]

A crucial, although controversial, New Testament passage for natural law theories further reinforces this point. Writing to the Romans, Saint Paul encapsulates the sense both of the capacity of the world to disclose the nature of God, and also the capacity of human beings to perceive it: 'ever since the creation of the world [God's] eternal power and divine nature, invisible though they are, have been understood and seen through the things he has made' (Rom. 1.20; cf. Wisd. 13.1–9). Paul's words in this key text for natural law theories suggest that the created world points us to the power and goodness of the God who made it, and that it does so in a way that is clear for all to see.

Reflection on Jews and Gentiles

Such reflections upon the accessibility of knowledge about God's power and goodness relates to a further strand of biblical reflection about the judgement that is made on those who have not been directly given the divine law. For, if all people are at some level able to perceive God's physical and moral patterning of creation, then even those who have not explicitly been given the Torah should possess an innate understanding of what is good and right and, as a corollary to this, be able to be held responsible if they fail to live up to it.

Both ancient and modern commentators have remarked on the way that this is implied in a passage near the start of the book of Amos, where, in a series of thundering oracles, the prophet condemns in the same formula the shortcomings of a variety of Israel's neighbouring states in the ancient Near East, and concludes with a very similar condemnation of Judah and Israel themselves:

Thus says the Lord:
For three transgressions of Damascus, and for four I will not revoke the punishment;
because they have threshed Gilead with threshing sledges of iron ...

---

3 Barton (2002), p. 66. This section draws on the discussion of natural law in the Old Testament in Barton (2002), chapter 4.

Thus says the Lord:
For three transgressions of Gaza, and for four, I will not revoke the punishment;
because they carried into exile entire communities, to hand them over to Edom ...
Thus says the Lord:
For three transgressions of Israel, and for four, I will not revoke the punishment;
because they sell the righteous for silver, and the needy for a pair of sandals ...

Amos 1.3, 6; 2.6 see also 1.9, 11, 13; 2.1, 4

Amos' words have the effect of placing Israel's moral misdemeanours on a similar footing to those of the other nations: all countries alike will be judged by the same standards when their actions transgress what appear to be commonly agreed moral standards. While nothing is explicitly said in this passage about the origin of such standards, Amos' words seem to assume that the Gentile inhabitants of Israel's neighbouring states should have recognized that justice and care for the helpless were not merely human conventions, but part of the order of nature, even though they have never been given the law of Moses. As Barton comments, 'the logic of the prophet's attack seems to be that all these nations knew or ought to have known that certain practices in time of war, such as enslaving whole populations or torturing conquered enemies are unacceptable'.[4]

A further and more explicit discussion of a similar topic again comes in the opening chapters of the letter to the Romans where Paul weighs the relative merits of Gentiles and Jews. In understanding the will of God, the Jews certainly have many advantages, since they have uniquely been given the divine law, 'entrusted with the oracles of God' (Rom. 3.2). And yet, the Gentiles are not complete strangers to the law since on an instinctive level they have some apprehension of it (Rom. 2.14). Although lacking the written law, 'they show that what the law requires is written in their hearts, to which their own conscience also bears witness' (Rom. 2.15). Thus, Paul can eventually conclude that Jews and Gentiles are in a similar state of moral culpability: all alike are 'under the power of sin' (Rom. 3.9) and ultimately there is 'no distinction, since all have sinned and fall short of the glory of God' (Rom. 3.23).

Classical sources

In addition to such biblical insights, the theologians of the early Church also looked to other ancient sources to ground their embryonic understanding

---

4 Barton (2002), p. 62. See Barton (2002), chapter 4 and Barton (2003), chapter 6.

of natural law. These can be separated into three inter-related strands of reflection.

The first of these concerned what appeared to the philosophers to be the inherent order of the universe. The philosopher Plato (427–347 BC), for example, emphasized the importance of the divine patterning which could be glimpsed in the certainties of mathematics and the regularity of the movements of the planets. By contrast with the relativistic Sophists, whose spokesman Protagoras held the view that 'man is the measure of all things', Plato maintained that if we look beyond the uncertainty and flux of the world as we experience it, we can glimpse a deeper order and regularity, emanating from a single divine intelligence. In the similar outlook of the later Stoic school of philosophy, all reality was pervaded by an intelligent divine force, the Logos or universal reason, which ordered all things. For these and other ancient philosophers, the order, regularity and beauty that exist in the universe correspond to an order that also exists within the human mind and which enables us to apprehend it.

A second strand of reflection, on the nature of the happy life, emphasized the way in which human beings flourish when we not only observe and analyse the inherent order of the world, but actively and consciously participate in it. In a theme that will be discussed in later chapters, ancient philosophers, notably Aristotle (384–322 BC), argued that happiness or flourishing (in Greek, *eudaimonia*) is the aim of all people; the final end towards which each of our individual actions is ultimately directed. Happiness in this sense is 'what we choose always for itself and never for the sake of something else'.[5] In order to achieve this universally desired goal, the philosophers claimed that it is necessary for men and women to live in conformity with the good ordering that we can perceive in the world, attuning our lives to all-powerful, providential wisdom. 'Happiness is a good flow of life', argued the eminent Stoic philosopher Zeno of Citium, in which we align ourselves as closely as possible with the Logos, or universal reason which pervades all things, and makes all things intelligible to us.[6]

A third and final contribution to the natural law tradition comes from classical insights into the nature and demands of justice. In modern discussions of this subject, it is common to hear people invoke a concept of 'natural justice': in other words, a justice which they believe is rooted in deep-seated and universally held principles. Such natural justice would commonly include, for example, the right to a fair trial by an unbiased judge or jury and the right to be heard in defence of oneself. This concept has its roots in reflection on the law in ancient Rome. While the Emperor Justinian (AD 482–565) famously argued that 'what pleases the prince has the force of law',[7] less self-interested commentators argued that the *ius naturale* (that

---

5 Aristotle, *Nicomachean Ethics* 1.7.
6 See Tarnas (1991), p. 76; Mahoney (1987), pp. 37–8.
7 Justinian, *Institute* 1.2.6.

which is just by nature) must be the basis for the *ius gentium* (the law of the people). Thus, the laws of any state should be grounded in fundamental and universally held values. Against Creon, King of Thebes, Sophocles' heroine Antigone argues that a human law cannot 'override the unwritten and unfailing statutes of heaven'. Such eternal laws, she says, are 'not of today or yesterday, but from all time, and no man knows when they were first put forth'. In a more contemporary context, the African-American clergyman and human rights campaigner Martin Luther King (1929–68) makes a similar point when he writes in his *Letter from Birmingham Jail* about the laws of racial segregation in the United States of his day:

> How does one determine whether a law is just or unjust? A just law is a man-made code that squares with the moral law or the law of God. An unjust law is a code that is out of harmony with the moral law ... an unjust law is a human law that is not rooted in eternal and natural law. Any law that uplifts human personality is just. Any law that degrades human personality is unjust.[8]

It was the early Christian Apologists, concerned to establish a tolerant attitude towards Christianity in the Roman Empire, who first gave prominence to the links between the classical concept of natural law and the hints contained in the Hebrew and Christian Scriptures. In an era of intermittent persecution, the Apologists aimed to dispel criticisms that Christianity was barbarous and irrational and, as part of their efforts to do this, sought to reinforce a common set of values with their pagan neighbours. The second-century Apologist, Athenagoras of Athens wrote to his Athenian contemporaries, 'we are in all things always alike and the same, submitting ourselves to reason, and not ruling over it'.[9] His contemporary, Tertullian (AD 160–225) in his *Apology*, argued that the view of ancient philosophy that the universe is ordered and regulated by the Logos corresponds with the Christian understanding of a Trinitarian God who, through his Word and his Wisdom creates and orders all things:

> The object of our worship is the One God, He who by His commanding word, His arranging wisdom, His mighty power, brought forth from nothing this entire mass of our world, with all its array of elements, bodies, spirits, for the glory of His majesty; whence also the Greeks have bestowed on it the name of Κόσμος.[10]

---

8 16 April 1963.
9 Athenagoras, *A Plea for the Christians*, quoted in Mahoney (1987), p. 73.
10 Tertullian, *Apology* 17.

Questions for discussion

The word 'law' can be used in two senses in the following two expressions:

1 'British law'
2 'The laws of gravity'

What is the difference between the two uses of the term?

Can you add further examples to each group?

Would it be right to say that natural law thinking understands the term 'law' in both senses?

Thomas Aquinas and natural law

The classic formulation of natural law in the Christian tradition comes from the Dominican theologian Thomas Aquinas (1225–74), in his *Summa Theologica*. Aquinas's discussion of natural law can be found in a relatively brief section of his massive theological work, but it was nonetheless to become highly significant in subsequent theological ethics.

Eternal and natural law

The starting point for Aquinas's description of natural law is his understanding of God's eternal law, described by Augustine in a passage that Aquinas quotes as 'the supreme exemplar to which we must always conform'.[11] The eternal law is nothing less than God's overarching understanding of all things; the wisdom, 'secret and hidden, which God decreed before the ages for our glory' (1 Cor. 2.7). In the descriptions of two modern commentators, Aquinas's concept of the eternal law is 'how God knows the world to be';[12] 'the divine blueprint existing in the mind of God, according to which all things are as they are'.[13] Indeed, at the deepest level, the eternal law can be identified with God himself: 'things pertaining to the divine nature or essence are not subject to the eternal law, but *are* the eternal law itself'.[14] Thus, the Son of God, the second person of the Trinity, 'is not subject to the divine providence or the eternal law, but rather is Himself the eternal law'.[15]

---

11 Augustine, *On Free Will* 1.6; Aquinas, *Summa Theologica* 1-2. 93.1.
12 Cessario (2001), p. 59.
13 Banner (2008), p. 48.
14 Aquinas, *Summa Theologica* 1-2. 93.4 (my italics).
15 Aquinas, *Summa Theologica* 1-2. 93.4. This point draws on Kerr (2002), p. 107.

Aquinas's understanding of the relationship between the eternal law and the natural law is represented by the diagram below. God's eternal law encompasses everything and includes everything within itself. Because the eternal law is infinite (hence the open-ended nature of the diagram) and human beings are limited creatures, there is a huge amount of the eternal law that we will not know until such time as we attain face to face vision of God: 'no one can know the eternal law as it is in itself except God and the blessed who see God in his essence'.[16] However, because we are also intelligent creatures, we can get some kind of purchase on a small section of the eternal law (this is arbitrarily demarcated by the vertical line), and Aquinas writes that 'this participation of the eternal law in the rational creature is called the natural law'.[17]

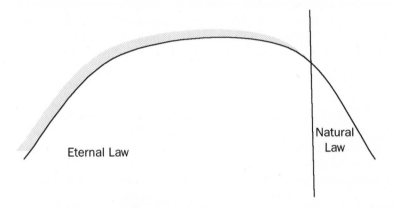

Eternal Law

Natural Law

In one sense, all things are subject to divine law, since nothing can stand outside God's blueprint: 'all things partake in some way in the eternal law, in so far as ... from its being imprinted on them, they derive their respective inclinations to their proper acts and ends'.[18] However, while animals and inanimate objects are subject to the natural law in a simple way because it dictates every aspect of what they are and do, human beings, as God's rational creation, made in the image of God, can participate or share in the eternal law in a further and more sophisticated way. By contrast with other animals, we are able consciously to make this law our own, and allow it to shape our lives and motivate our actions: 'the good are perfectly subject to the eternal law, as always acting according to it'.[19] Aquinas often quotes the Latin translation of Psalm 4.6: 'the light of thy countenance, Lord, is signed

---

16 Aquinas, *Summa Theologica* 1-2. 93.2.
17 Aquinas, *Summa Theologica* 1-2. 91.2
18 Aquinas, *Summa Theologica* 1-2. 91.2.
19 Aquinas, *Summa Theologica* 1-2. 93.6; see Cessario (2001), p. 80.

upon us',[20] inferring that, as intelligent creatures, made in the image of God, human beings share something of God's own knowledge and understanding. As Aquinas glosses the words of the psalmist, 'the light of natural reason, whereby we discern what is good and what is evil, which is the function of natural law, is nothing else than an imprint on us of the divine light'.[21]

Precepts and conclusions

How then do we come to understand the natural law and participate in it? Our starting point is our natural inclination towards the good; that is our intuitive and God-given understanding that such a thing as good exists, and that we want to seek it:

> the first principle in the practical reason is one founded on the nature of good, viz., that good is that which all things seek after. Hence this is the first precept of law: that good is to be done and promoted and evil is to be avoided. All other precepts of the natural law are based on this.[22]

Following on from this initial apprehension that good exists, and that we want to pursue the good because it will indeed be good for us to do so, Aquinas argues that we encounter the good, in its most basic form in the very nature of our creaturely existence and, related to this, in our deepest natural impulses: 'those things to which man has a natural inclination are naturally apprehended by reason as being good'.[23] Aquinas enumerates a variety of these natural inclinations that suggest to us what the basic goods might be. First, in common with all other substances, human beings possess an inclination towards self-preservation. Second, and in common with other animals, we are inclined towards procreating children, and subsequently educating them. Third, as a particular characteristic of human beings, we have an inclination to know the truth (in particular about God), and an inclination to live in society. The goodness of goods such as self-preservation, education of offspring and living in society are, then, so completely woven into the fabric of our lives as these have been created by God, that they appear to be entirely self-evident. It is these self-evident goods, intuitively grasped, that provide us with the underlying principles, or 'primary precepts' that should underlie all of our thinking and acting.

On the solid foundations of our natural human inclinations and the primary precepts that emerge from them, we can start to reason towards some

---

20 See Kerr (2002), p. 106.

21 Aquinas, *Summa Theologica* 1-2. 91.2.

22 Aquinas, *Summa Theologica* 1-2. 94.2. This section draws on May (1991), chapter 2.

23 Aquinas, *Summa Theologica* 1-2. 94.2.

more concrete guidelines for our actions. For example, since human beings are thinking creatures, naturally inclined to want to know the truth, we can conclude that honest communication is to be commended, and likewise that lying or deliberately keeping people in ignorance is wrong. Similarly, understanding that human beings are social creatures, we can commend behaviour that promotes co-operation and harmony with others, and condemn behaviour that is offensive and antisocial.

Such conclusions, drawn from first principles, about moral questions may be divided into different categories. In the first place, the primary precepts give rise to proximate (that is, near) conclusions that flow clearly and naturally from the precepts themselves. Second, as discerning people come to reflect in more detail, they will be able to draw remote conclusions from the primary precepts, that expand on these in more subtle and complex ways, and which the wise can then pass on to those who are less so. Thus, despite the fact that they vary in the extent to which they are self-evident, the primary precepts, proximate conclusions and remote conclusions will all bear a family resemblance to one another: they 'all belong to the law of nature, but not all in the same way'.[24] Finally, and beyond the reach of unaided human reason, there are matters of faith 'of which man cannot judge unless he be helped by divine instruction'.[25]

The role of the Bible

Given that the primary precepts and the conclusions that flow from them are available to reason, what role does this leave for the Bible in conveying moral guidance? Could we do without it, and simply derive our ethics from the natural law? As the table below indicates, Aquinas's answer to this is somewhat complex since the Bible itself contains moral rules and principles that fall into each of the different categories that have been explored. Some of the Bible's moral guidance, Aquinas argues, is on the level of primary precepts that are self-evident to God-given natural reason. Other sections of moral teaching are proximate conclusions that could be quickly and easily deduced from such precepts. Still others are remote conclusions, which do indeed follow from the primary precepts, but in a way that only the very wise could work out for themselves – most will need the Scriptures to instruct them. Still other biblical commandments, less immediately related to ethical matters, cannot simply be derived from reason, but require divine instruction.[26]

---

24 Aquinas, *Summa Theologica* 1-2. 100.1.
25 Aquinas, *Summa Theologica* 1-2. 100.1.
26 Aquinas, *Summa Theologica* 1-2. 100.1, 3.

Type of rule	How grasped	Example
Primary precepts	Self-evident to natural reason; written in the human heart	In everything do to others as you would have them do to you (Matt. 7.12) (the 'golden rule')
Proximate conclusions	Understood after slight reflection on the primary precepts	Honour your father and mother You shall not murder You shall not steal (Exod. 19.12, 13, 15)
Remote conclusions	Understood through the careful reflection of the wise	You shall rise before the aged, and defer to the old (Lev. 19.32)
Matters needing divine instruction	Available only from Christian teaching	You shall not make for yourself an idol You shall not make wrongful use of the name of the Lord your God (Exod. 20.4, 7)

However, although it may be possible in principle for us to work out for ourselves many moral rules, including most of the Ten Commandments, from first principles, in practice things are not so easy. For, as Augustine might remind us, human beings in our current state have a weakened capacity, not only to do, but also to know the good. In the wicked, 'the natural knowledge of good is darkened by the passions and habits of sin'.[27] Although Aquinas, normally characterized as being more optimistic about these matters than Augustine, emphasizes that 'sin does not destroy entirely the good of nature',[28] nevertheless, he argues that the course of human history has seen human reason progressively crippled by sin, to the extent that the scriptural law became necessary to illuminate that which unaided reason could no longer see. Writing in another part of the *Summa*, Aquinas argues that God had to introduce both Scripture and the sacraments as a necessary corrective when sin 'began to take more hold on man, to such an extent that, with his reason darkened ... the precepts of the law of nature were not enough for living rightly, and they had to be determined in the written law'.[29]

So far as Aquinas is concerned, there can be no ultimate conflict between the natural law that is revealed in creation, and the moral law that is revealed in the Bible, since God is the author of both. Thus, if rightly understood,

---

27 Aquinas, *Summa Theologica* 1-2. 93.6.
28 Aquinas, *Summa Theologica* 1-2. 93.6; cf. 85.2.
29 Aquinas, *Summa Theologica* 3. 61.3

they will always complement one another. To return to the example from Augustine's *Confessions* at the start of this chapter, the sinfulness of theft is backed up by the mutually reinforcing witness of the Ten Commandments and the natural law. Aquinas writes that for those who are good, 'besides the natural knowledge of what is good, there is the added knowledge of faith and wisdom'.[30] Characteristic of Aquinas's thought is the insight that God's grace does not obliterate human nature, nor does God's Wisdom invalidate all human knowledge. Rather, God's grace and Wisdom complement, correct, build on, and bring to perfection those things that human beings can achieve and know through their own capacities, which are themselves God-given.

Reason

When it comes to questions of what we actually do to put the natural law into practice, Aquinas is well aware that in any process of reasoning from moral first principles, mistakes can easily be made. As moral agents, the primary precepts may provide us with a starting point as we attempt to work out what exactly we should do in the complex situations that face us in life, but they can never take us the entire way. Aquinas draws a distinction between the speculative reason by which we understand, for example, mathematical questions and the practical reason which we apply when it comes to matters of ethics and morality. In both of these areas, the first principles are fixed and certain, but there is a difference when it comes to the certainty of the conclusions that we are able to draw out of these principles when we are faced with real life situations. In using speculative reason, our conclusions will be as certain as our principles were. For example, because we know in principle that the angles of a triangle come to 180°, whenever we actually come across a triangle, it will be safe to conclude that its angles will always add up to this amount. However, when we apply practical reason to the moral decisions that we face, then we are on less secure ground.

One reason for this is that bad habits can become so ingrained in the life of particular societies that their members become effectively blind even to the basic requirements of natural law. Drawing on Julius Caesar's *Gallic Wars*, Aquinas provides an example of natural law being set aside in this way: 'at one time theft, although it is expressly contrary to the natural law, was not considered wrong among the Germans'.[31] Moreover, even when they do see the natural law clearly, finite and fallen human beings will not always reason correctly from it. Although the primary precepts may be very firm in our minds, the variable and contingent factors about the situations we face in life will mean that the conclusions we draw from those precepts about what we should actually do may be much less certain. As he summarizes it,

30 Aquinas, *Summa Theologica* 1-2. 93.6.
31 Aquinas, *Summa Theologica* 1-2. 94.4.

'the more we descend to matters of detail, the more frequently we encounter defects'.[32] Thus, despite what Aquinas sees as the self-evident nature of natural law precepts, there may be some quite good reasons why people do not always seem to put them into practice or indeed why they sometimes find it difficult to know exactly how to apply their principles in particular cases. Thus, in an example that Aquinas himself offers, we may start from an absolutely self-evident principle that 'goods entrusted to another should be restored to their owner'. However, if we know that the goods somebody has entrusted to us might (if we returned them) be used to fight against our country, then it would be reasonable for us to withhold them.[33] In such a situation, then, we might, for perfectly good reasons, be confused about how our first principles should best be applied in practice. Mahoney comments that, 'On the whole it has been the fate of Aquinas's natural law teaching in moral theology that the logical appeal and coherence of his system has been stressed, while the provisionality and contingency of his conclusions as they come closer to individual situations, features which he himself carefully build into his theory, have been either neglected or ignored.'[34]

Questions for discussion

Can you think of any other places in the Bible which might suggest a theory of natural law?

Do you agree with Aquinas's view that the Bible will always agree with natural law?

Working from Aquinas's first principles, how could natural law reasoning be applied to the following subjects: abortion, capital punishment, child labour or the legalization of drugs?

---

32 Aquinas, *Summa Theologica* 1-2. 94.4.
33 Cf. Aquinas, *Summa Theologica* 1-2. 94.4.
34 Mahoney (1987), 80.

3

Virtue

If anyone loves righteousness,
her labours are virtues;
for she teaches self-control and prudence,
justice and courage;
nothing in life is more profitable for mortals than these.

Wisdom 8.7

The importance of virtue

In ethics, being is as important as doing. It is not only our individual actions
– those things we have done or have failed to do – that are significant in our
moral lives but, more widely, the sort of person we are. Individual actions
do not occur in a vacuum, but come from the backdrop of our wider personality. If, for example, I am a generous person, then when I am confronted
with someone in need, I will tend to give something to them. As the ancient
Greek philosopher Aristotle (384–322 BC), whose writings on this subject
have had a profound influence on the way that we think about virtue, puts
it, 'the generous man will both give and spend the right amounts and on the
right objects, alike in small things and in great, and that with pleasure'.[1] As
Aristotle indicates, if I am a generous person, then no compulsion will be
necessary to make my actions generous. Rather, they will, as one contemporary writer puts it, 'bear the happily radiant seal of spontaneity, of freedom
from constraint and of self-evident inclination'.[2] Human actions are not
random: rooted in basic traits of character, they tend to show consistency.

Thomas Aquinas, who was highly influenced by Aristotle and often uses
the insights of 'the Philosopher', as he often refers to him, to clarify his own
thinking, calls virtue 'a perfect habit by which one only does the good' and
'a habit by which we work well'.[3] The word habit, derived from the Latin
habitus, like several other words that will be discussed in this chapter is
liable to misinterpretation, because we now tend to associate it with minor

---

1 Aristotle, *Nicomachean Ethics* 4.1.
2 Pieper (1988), p. 10.
3 Aquinas, *Summa Theologica* 1-2. 56.3.

33

actions that are repeated in annoying ways by those who, for example, speak with their mouths full or laugh at their own jokes, or we associate it with unthinking and mechanical repetition. However, 'a habit is not a static routine or rut, but a dynamic tendency to act in a certain determinate way'.[4] Almost everything that human beings are able to learn to do depends in some way upon the formation of habits and, as Aristotle and Aquinas argue, this holds true not only in practical matters, like learning to cook, play a musical instrument or be proficient in a craft, but in morality as well: 'the things we have to learn before we can do them, we learn by doing them, e.g., men become builders by building and lyre-players by playing the lyre; so too we become just by doing just acts, temperate by doing temperate acts, brave by doing brave acts'.[5] For Aristotle, then, the acquisition of virtue follows a similar pattern to the acquisition of a craft by a master craftsman.

Aristotle writes that 'the virtues we get by first exercising them':[6] just as good people naturally perform good actions, so also, good actions, habitually performed, make good people. If, over a period of time, I discipline myself to give money to people in need, then eventually this habit will probably become second nature to me. Slowly, and perhaps with some difficulties along the way, my virtuous habit will start to become a settled part of my character, and thus continue to give rise to further virtuous actions. Thus, a virtuous circle is created: a good personality gives rise to good actions, but these good actions, habitually repeated and refined, will in turn form the personality. The reverse also is true: the repeated performance of bad actions will form a bad personality, which will then go on to perform bad actions.

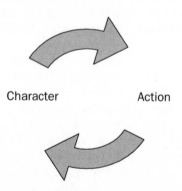

Character   Action

This does not, of course, mean that it is impossible for anyone ever to act out of character, since human beings are not machines which act with absolute consistency. As Aquinas himself notes, even the grammarian who has

---

4 Kreeft (1990), p. 448.
5 Aristotle, *Nicomachean Ethics* 2.1.
6 Aristotle, *Nicomachean Ethics* 2.1.

got into good habits of using language correctly, 'may be guilty of a barbarism or solecism'.[7]

The virtues

Christian moral theology traditionally separates the virtues themselves into two groups. The first of these, the moral or cardinal virtues, are prudence, justice, temperance and fortitude. The word cardinal in this sense means 'hinge', since the moral life is believed to hinge upon them. The moral virtues were initially derived from classical sources, such as Plato, Aristotle and Cicero, but they were the subject of much Christian reflection and effectively 'baptized' at the hands of theologians such as Ambrose of Milan (337–97), Gregory the Great (540–604), Augustine of Hippo and supremely Thomas Aquinas.[8] Despite their primarily classical provenance, the moral virtues are mentioned in the (deuterocanonical) book of Wisdom (see Wisd. 8.7, quoted at the beginning of this chapter) and, as the comments below seek to demonstrate, relate to some important scriptural themes. The second group of virtues are described as the theological virtues. These are, as their name implies, God-focused virtues. Aquinas writes that 'the very idea of a theological virtue is one that has God for its object'.[9] The theological virtues are faith, hope and charity (love), and these derive most directly from Saint Paul in 1 Corinthians 13.

Moral virtues

At the summit of the moral virtues is *prudence*, whose name derives from the Latin term *prudentia*. The virtue of prudence has been given a bad name, perhaps because it sounds similar to prudery and prurience, negative terms which denote excessively modest or morbidly curious attitudes about sexual matters. The former British Prime Minister Gordon Brown (1951–) was notorious for using 'prudence' to describe what one commentator called 'a sort of cosmic chastity belt on fiscal profligacy'.[10] Originally, however, *prudentia*, the Latin translation of Aristotle's term *phronesis*, means practical wisdom. Aristotle writes that 'it is the mark of a man of practical wisdom to be able to deliberate well about what is good and expedient for himself ... about what sort of things conduce to the good life in general'.[11] Prudence, defined by Thomas Aquinas as 'right reason of things to be done',[12]

---

7 Aquinas, *Summa Theologica* 1-2. 56.3.

8 This discussion of the virtues draws on Pieper (1966, 1986 and 1988), Mattison (2008) and the *Catechism of the Catholic Church*.

9 Aquinas, *Summa Theologica* 2-2. 17.5.

10 Faisal Islam.

11 Aristotle, *Nicomachean Ethics* 6.5.

12 Aquinas, *Summa Theologica* 1-2. 56.3.

traditionally holds a prime place among the moral virtues because, if we are to act well in almost any situation, then we must have the capacity to recognize what is good, and then actively to pursue it. The prudent person has the ability to see clearly the complex choices and decisions that confront each of us in life; and then the flexibility, good sense and moral resources to respond appropriately.

Reflecting on the virtue of prudence, the Catholic theologian and philosopher Josef Pieper (1904–97) argues that the essential reason why prudence is so important is that, in a theme that was covered in the previous chapter on natural law, morality must be grounded in reality, and in the truth of things as they are: 'the virtue of prudence resides in this: that the objective cognition of reality shall determine action; that the truth of real things shall become determinative'.[13] Ethical reflection must try to understand the world as it really is – as, Christians would say, God has made it, and not as our own fallen and partial wills, and our self-interested perspectives on life would have it be: 'a man is wise when all things taste to him as they really are'.[14] Having perceived how the world really is, we are then able to respond to it: to 'transform the knowledge of reality into the accomplishment of the good',[15] and this is precisely what the prudent person is able to do.

Writers such as Pieper and others in the tradition of Thomas Aquinas would argue that we acquire prudence in a variety of ways. For example, we can cultivate it by paying attention to the lessons that our experience of life teaches us. We can cultivate it by acquiring habits of stillness and silence that will enable us better to contemplate reality.[16] In the specifically Christian understanding of prudence, we can cultivate prudence by paying attention to Scripture and Christian teaching, since these will give us the most direct insight into God's own wisdom, and the way in which we should act in the light of it.

A second moral virtue is that of *justice*, defined by Aquinas as 'the constant and firm will to give their due to God and neighbour'.[17] For Aristotle, justice enjoys a certain pre-eminence among the virtues: 'neither evening nor morning star is so wonderful.[18] This is because justice is inherently neighbour-oriented: not only about our own self-development, but also about how we treat our neighbour: 'justice alone of all the virtues is thought to be "another's good"'.[19] This, of course, also corresponds with Jesus' own emphasis on the importance of loving our neighbour (cf. Matt. 22.37–40; Mark 12.29–31; Luke 10.26–8).

13 Pieper (1966), p. 15.
14 Pieper (1988), p. 21.
15 Pieper (1988), p. 15.
16 See Pieper (1966), pp. 10–17.
17 *Catechism of the Catholic Church* 1806.
18 Aristotle, *Nicomachean Ethics* 5.2.
19 Aristotle, *Nicomachean Ethics* 5.2. Aristotle quotes Plato, *Republic* 343c.

As in the case of prudence, we may be misled by the connotations that the term justice normally carries – of judges, juries and court rooms. The virtue of justice is certainly a key one for political leaders and others who have the particular task of making laws that promote the common good, and for lawyers, judges and the police, who have the responsibility for enforcing them. However, far from being restricted to people in such positions, justice is an important virtue for everyone, since, pre-eminently among the moral virtues, justice concerns the way in which we deal with other people, and come to understand our responsibilities towards them. Everyone lives within a network of relationships, with obligations, for example, towards friends, family members, employers, work colleagues, or college authorities. The just person will be able to balance these competing loyalties, giving to each person what is truly due to them. Pieper writes that:

> To be just means to recognize the other as other; it means to give acknowledgment even where one cannot love. Justice says: That is another person, who is other than I, and who nevertheless has his own particular due. A just man is just, therefore, because he sanctions another person in his very separateness and helps him to receive his due.[20]

It is certainly possible to imagine somebody fulfilling their duties to other people in a grim and mechanical way, purely out of a sense of obligation but, as with the other virtues, justice entails something more than this: a more open-hearted willingness not only to give others those things that, objectively speaking, are due to them, but also to do this in a generous and joyful spirit; with inner assent as well as external conformity.[21]

Prudence, justice and charitable giving

To give a simple example of both prudence and justice at work, most people are regularly asked for money by a variety of charities, each claiming the importance of their particular cause. Some will be working for the relief of poverty overseas, others will be supporting local projects and initiatives; some will be supporting research into human illness, others will be supporting the care of animals. The choice that we make about which charities we support is a profoundly moral one but, as often in moral decision making, there can be no simply right or wrong answer. The prudent person will be able to weigh up the competing claims of each charity with wisdom and careful discernment. The just person will have the determination to give to each one what is appropriately due to them.

---

20 Pieper (1966), p. 54.
21 See Pieper (1966), pp. 62–3.

Fortitude is 'the moral virtue that ensures firmness in difficulties and constancy in pursuit of the good'.[22] Once again, it is a term that can be misleading, because words such as 'fortitude', 'bravery' or 'courage' may suggest an attitude to life that is free from fear. In fact, Aquinas argues that true fortitude actually moderates daring.[23] He further argues that we can only truly be courageous if we have experienced what it is to be afraid, but are nonetheless willing to face up to and conquer our fears in the interest of a greater good. As Pieper writes, 'fortitude presumes vulnerability; without vulnerability there is no possibility of fortitude. An angel cannot be courageous because it is not vulnerable. To be brave means to be ready to sustain a wound. Since he is substantially vulnerable, man can be courageous.'[24]

The virtue of fortitude is often separated into two parts: determination and endurance. However prudently we may have chosen our course of action, and however just our choice might be, we need determination or, as it is often described, 'aggression' to see it through.[25] The virtue of fortitude should make us not belligerent or inflexible in pursuit of our aims but, equally, we must not be so averse to conflict that we are unable to face it when it is necessary to do so. Fortitude also includes endurance: the ability to withstand hardships and difficulties in life, and to live with the insecurity that is always a feature of contingent human existence. Aquinas describes endurance as 'the chief act of fortitude',[26] because, by contrast with aggression/determination (which will often relate to our own decisions and projects, launched at the time of our own choosing), we typically need to practice endurance in situations that last for a prolonged period, and over which we have little control.

Endurance, far from being a doormat-like acceptance of suffering, is described by Aquinas as the 'deliberate facing of dangers and bearing of toils'.[27] This deliberate aspect of the virtue prevents us from thinking that it is about tolerating a state of passive victimhood. As Pieper points out, a key Christian text on endurance: Jesus' teaching that 'if anyone strikes you on the right cheek, turn the other also' (Matt. 5.39) should not be understood as simply advocating complete passivity in the face of suffering. For Jesus himself models the virtue of fortitude in being ready to accept suffering and death when it is necessary that he should do so. And yet, when in John's Gospel a servant of the high priest Caiaphas strikes Jesus himself on the cheek, he does not simply submit to this attack, but challenges his aggressor, asking him, 'if I have spoken rightly why do you strike me?' (John 18.23).

22 *Catechism of the Catholic Church* 1808.
23 Aquinas, *Summa Theologica* 2-2. 123.6.
24 Pieper (1988), pp. 24–5.
25 See Aquinas, *Summa Theologica* 2-2. 123.2.
26 Aquinas, *Summa Theologica* 2-2. 123.6.
27 Aquinas, *Summa Theologica* 2-2. 123.2.

The final moral virtue of *temperance* has, once again, a name that is potentially misleading, partly because it has an old-fashioned ring to it, reminiscent of the abstinence movements of the nineteenth century. However, although those who have this particular virtue will indeed be moderate in their intake of food and drink, as well as being able to keep their temper and sexual drives under control, temperance is not restricted to these matters. Temperance describes the ability to order our lives so that our pleasures and bodily drives are integrated with our rational faculties, and are not constantly blowing our wider projects and plans off course. Pieper writes that 'without [temperance] the stream of the innermost essential human will could overflow its banks, lose its direction, and never reach the sea of fulfilment ... through its firmness the stream is endowed with an unhindered course, momentum, slope and velocity'.[28] This insight is reminiscent of the passage from Shakespeare's *King John* that was quoted in chapter 1 and suggests that, contrary to what Hedonists might claim, if we are to be truly free, we also need to be able to practise self-restraint.

Uniquely among the moral virtues, temperance is about self-care. If prudence primarily concerns our relationship with the reality of the world outside us and justice our relationship with other people, temperance directs us primarily to our relationship with ourselves.[29] It reminds us that there is a proper and legitimate form of self-love – one that preachers and other commentators have often understood to be implied in Jesus' command to 'love your neighbour as yourself' (Matt. 22.39; Mark 12.31; Luke 10.27). Temperance has been described as 'selfless self-preservation'.[30]

The virtue of temperance as the Christian tradition has understood it, needs to be distinguished from patterns of thought, both ancient and modern, which elevate the spiritual side of existence, but downplay and even denigrate the physical. In a theme that was explored in chapter 1, influential groups in the ancient world, such as the Gnostics and the Manichees, tended to view the body and all that was associated with it with contempt and hatred. Some commentators would argue that Augustine's teaching in particular imported such views into the Christian tradition. 'Blindness only can deny,' writes Pieper, 'that this Manichean undervaluation of the sensual reality of creation ... tinges and surreptitiously qualifies the current Christian notion of the virtue of temperance, and more especially of chastity.'[31] However, seen in a truly Christian perspective, the virtue of temperance acknowledges the original goodness of all that God has made (see Gen. 1.4, 10, etc.), together with the value and potential of the body as a temple of the Holy Spirit (1 Cor. 6.19). However, while 'pleasures of meat and drink

---

28 Pieper (1988), p. 34.
29 See Pieper (1966), p. 147.
30 See Pieper (1966), pp. 147–52.
31 See Pieper (1966), p. 169.

and sexual pleasures'[32] are, in themselves, gifts of God, to be valued and respected, the reality of life in a fallen world is that desire for them can all too easily exert a hold over people, so that they lose their overall grasp of what is good and true and their ability to pursue it.

Finally, as with the other virtues, temperance is only really a virtue when it has become a stable characteristic of a person, so that he or she acts naturally and willingly in a temperate way. Continence – the ability simply to curb our desires through self-discipline – is thus only the first part of temperance. The virtue is fully developed when our desires and emotions are themselves re-trained so as to be in unity with our reason. For example, the so-called 'dry drunk', who has managed by a supreme effort of the will to stop him or herself from actually drinking, and yet continues to exhibit signs of unresolved alcohol dependency, has only got part of the way towards the virtue of temperance. By contrast, the truly temperate person will not only be able to prevent him or herself from drinking immoderately, but will not actually wish to do so.[33]

One final comment on the moral virtues is that, in Aquinas's view, 'the virtues are connected and linked together, so that whoever has one is seen to have several'.[34] Following theologians such as Ambrose, Augustine and Gregory, Aquinas insists that the moral virtues are indeed deeply connected with one another. In Gregory's words, 'there can be no true prudence without temperance, justice and fortitude'.[35] We might feel that this is somewhat counter-intuitive if, for example, we know a person who is kind to his friends and family, but also addicted to cigarettes, and therefore would seem to have the virtue of justice, but not that of temperance. However, if we look more closely, the connections may appear. In fostering the cigarette addiction, he will be spending money on himself, when he might instead spend it on other people. Moreover, by engaging in a habit that may take him prematurely away from his family and friends, he is hardly being just towards them.

Case study: alcohol and American college life

The American Catholic ethicist W. C. Mattison in his book, *Introducing Moral Theology* explores the way that the cardinal virtues are manifested, or fail to be, in the use of alcohol in American universities.[36]

Temperance enables us to desire and use alcohol well, and to develop habits that enable us to enjoy drinking without being governed by it.

---

32 Aquinas, *Summa Theologica* 2-2. 141.4.
33 This point draws on Mattison (2008), pp. 85–93.
34 Aquinas, *Summa Theologica* 1-2. 65.1, following Ambrose.
35 Aquinas, *Summa Theologica* 1-2. 65.1.

Prudence enables us to see this activity rightly; to understand, for example, the positive effects of alcohol, such as 'lightening the heart' and facilitating conversation, while also seeing the negative effects that it can bring. Prudence will also help us understand how some prohibitions concerning alcohol (such as 'Don't drink and drive') are necessary and not just arbitrary impositions.

Justice enables us to consider other people, and think about the many ways in which our own drinking habits may have an impact on them and, if necessary, adjust our behaviour accordingly.

Fortitude enables us to face difficulties well; resisting temptations in our own lives and also perhaps making us able to help others confront the consequences of their habits.

In this example, Mattison aims to show not just how each of the four cardinal virtues is important, but also how the virtues form a unity: in practice, each relies on the others to back it up.

Theological virtues

Faith is 'the assurance of things hoped for, the conviction of things not seen' (Heb. 11.1). Such a virtue may seem anathema to the rational, empirical mindset of many modern Western people, inclined to reject as superstitious any approach to truth that cannot be verified by the evidence of the senses. However, human beings need in a basic way to have faith in order to be able to function. When, for example, we turn the light on in the morning, run the bath or switch on the kettle, we exercise faith that the results we expect from these actions will take place. Moreover, many of the most important questions of our lives, such as whether somebody loves us, whether our moral values are important, or whether a particular course of action will make us happy cannot be simply answered with hard empirical evidence. In the words of John Paul II, 'there are in the life of a human being many more truths which are simply believed than truths which are acquired by way of personal verification'.[37] In this sense, we all live by faith, because we have no alternative. To understand faith as a virtue does not imply rejecting reason or scientific observation, but it is to acknowledge that these can only get us part of the way towards where we need to go; that we currently only see 'through a glass darkly', and only know 'in part' (cf. 1 Cor. 13.12).[38] In practice, much of our reasoning rests on presuppositions that we believe because people such as our teachers have told us about them, not because we discovered them for ourselves. As Aquinas puts it, 'anyone who learns

36 Mattison (2008), pp. 126–30.
37 John Paul II, *Fides et Ratio* 31.
38 This section draws on Mattison (2008), pp. 213–28.

must believe in order that he may acquire science in a perfect degree'.[39]

The theological virtue of faith builds on these foundations, but also transcends them. Faith in this sense is a gift that is initiated by God, and which is born and comes to fruition in the community of the Church. The word describes both an attitude of trust in God, Father, Son and Holy Spirit, and also an assent that is given to the central truths of revelation (most concisely expressed in the Creeds). Once again, trusting in God and believing these truths complements, but does not conflict with our attempts to understand the world. Expressing this complementarity, John Paul II introduces his encyclical *Fides et Ratio* (*Faith and Reason*) with the statement that 'Faith and reason are like two wings on which the human spirit rises to the contemplation of truth'. Finally, faith points forward to its own fulfilment in face to face vision of God, which will perfect it and bring it to completion: 'in order that a man arrive at the perfect vision of heavenly happiness, he must first of all believe God, as a disciple believes the master who is teaching him'.[40]

The second theological virtue is that of *hope* and this virtue also can be understood to build on natural foundations within human beings. The virtue of hope reflects the essential condition of human beings in this life, as pilgrims and travellers: beings who are on the way, but have not yet arrived, and who press onwards towards a goal that they have not yet made their own (cf. Phil. 3.12–14).[41] Echoing the famous words from Augustine's *Confessions*, 'you have made us for yourself and our hearts are restless until they find their rest in you',[42] Mattison writes that 'human persons never do sit back in this life and say, "there is nothing more to do, nothing further I could enjoy"'.[43] Human beings are restless, hopeful, desiring, journeying creatures, who experience incompleteness in many aspects of our lives, even as we try to satisfy our restlessness with short-term solutions such as spending money or taking drugs. As Mattison puts it, 'we long to be closer to others, to work on important life projects, to continue to improve ourselves, to understand more. Furthermore, we yearn for a world without the brokenness found all around us: poverty, injustice, sickness, suffering, and sin.'[44]

The theological virtue of hope places our natural restlessness and longing within the framework of Christian eschatology, which provides us with an understanding of our ultimate destiny. The petitions in the Lord's Prayer 'thy Kingdom come, thy will be done on earth as it is in heaven' express the New Testament hope for the establishment of God's reign. Such a vision of the new future that God has started to inaugurate in the resurrection of

39 Aquinas, *Summa Theologica* 2-2. 2.3.
40 Aquinas, *Summa Theologica* 2-2. 2.3.
41 See Pieper (1986), pp. 91–2.
42 Augustine, *Confessions* 1.1.1.
43 Mattison (2008), p. 252.
44 Mattison (2008), p. 253.

Jesus and the sending of the Holy Spirit, gives the Christian hope its particular substance and context. In Aquinas's view, it is only God and union with God that will ultimately satisfy our human longings. For him, the virtue of hope points us forward, taking our natural restlessness, and directing it towards the supernatural good in which it will find its fulfilment. That good is everlasting life, and the enjoyment of God for ever: 'the proper and principal object of hope is eternal happiness'.[45]

The final theological virtue is *charity* or *love*, 'the mother and the root of all the virtues'.[46] Again, the term can be misleading. Charity is often assumed simply to mean benevolent giving, often with a patronizing edge to it. Bobbie, the heroine of E. Nesbit's *The Railway Children*, fears that the station master, Perks, will interpret her collecting birthday presents for him as 'trying to be grand or charitable or something horrid'.[47] Similarly, in a theme that will be discussed in chapter 10, 'love' is often assumed to be primarily a feeling or an emotion, rather than a settled trait of character. However, in the sense in which it is used in the Bible and the moral tradition, love is the theological virtue that enables us to will the good of another person and truly seek what is best for them. Love is central to the New Testament, as we can see in, for example, Paul's hymn of praise to love in 1 Corinthians 13, as well as in Jesus' own teaching about the love of God and neighbour (cf. Mark 12.28–34; Luke 10.25–28; Matt. 22.34–40).

As with the other theological virtues, charity builds on the foundation of natural human capacities, in this case, our capacity for friendship. Drawing on Aristotle, for whom friendship is essential to the happy life, Aquinas writes that we are friends with somebody when 'we love someone so as to wish good to him'.[48] Just as the love of friends unites us to them, so the theological virtue of charity brings us into unity with God. It is 'a kind of friendship of man for God'.[49] Aquinas quotes with approval Augustine's definition of charity as 'a virtue which, when our affections are perfectly ordered, unites us to God, for by it we love Him'.[50]

Charity has a strongly eschatological dimension, because it is through charity that we are able here and now to share God's life. In one sense, all of the theological virtues continue for ever. As Paul puts it, 'faith, hope, and love abide, these three' (1 Cor. 13.13). However, by contrast with charity, the virtues of faith and hope become redundant when they find their fulfilment in, respectively, the vision of God, and the enjoyment of God. But 'love never ends' (1 Cor. 13.8). As Augustine puts it, 'faith gives way to sight, which we shall see, and hope gives way to bliss itself, which we are

---

45 Aquinas, *Summa Theologica* 2-2. 17.2.
46 Aquinas, *Summa Theologica* 1-2. 62.4.
47 E. Nesbit, *The Railway Children*.
48 Aquinas, *Summa Theologica* 2-2. 23.1.
49 Aquinas, *Summa Theologica* 2-2. 23.5.
50 Aquinas, *Summa Theologica* 2-2. 23.3.

going to arrive at, while charity will actually grow when these other two fade out'.[51] While faith and hope fade out, charity will not be displaced, but remains, 'more vigorous and certain than ever'.[52] Thus, through charity, we can *already* participate in God's life of love, *already* know what it is to participate in the Kingdom of heaven and partake in the divine nature (2 Peter 1.4):

> Faith will vanish into sight;
> Hope be emptied in delight;
> Love in heaven will shine more bright;
> Therefore give us love.[53]

Aquinas describes charity as the 'form' of all of the other virtues because it 'directs the acts of all other virtues to the last end'.[54] As Mattison puts it, charity 'perfects acts of all the virtues by directing them, or whisking them along, toward a person's ultimate happiness in God'.[55] The theological virtues of faith and hope are not complete in themselves: 'both faith and hope are quickened by charity, and receive from charity their full complement as virtues'.[56] Charity also shapes, colours and ultimately transforms the moral virtues. Indeed, without charity, traits of character that might appear to correspond with one or other of the virtues may not be virtuous at all. Attila the Hun, for example, was probably endowed with something like fortitude, and Dickens's Ebenezer Scrooge with something similar to prudence and yet, lacking charity to accompany and transform these characteristics, they appear far more like vices than virtues. Thus, while in his affirmation of the importance of the moral virtues, Aquinas sounds a characteristically more optimistic note than Augustine, for whom the virtues of pagans 'are really themselves vices and not virtues at all',[57] he nonetheless argues that, lacking charity, what may appear to be moral virtues are in fact only *simulacra* of the real things, since, in the words of the apostle Paul: '[if I] have not love, I am nothing' (1 Cor. 13.2).[58]

---

51 Augustine, *De Doctrina Christiana* 1.38.42.

52 Augustine, *De Doctrina Christiana* 1.38.42.

53 From the hymn 'Gracious Spirit, Holy Ghost', by Christopher Wordsworth (1807–85).

54 Aquinas, *Summa Theologica* 2-2. 23.8.

55 Mattison (2008), p. 303.

56 Aquinas, *Summa Theologica* 1-2. 62.4.

57 Augustine, *City of God* 19.25.

58 Aquinas, *Summa Theologica* 2-2. 23.7.

Comparisons and contrasts

The doctrine of the 'mean'

Aristotle famously argues that virtue lies in the mean, or average, between two extremes. Thus, the beauty of a piece of furniture, for example, would be spoiled if anything were added to it, or subtracted from it: 'a master of art avoids excess and defect, but seeks the intermediate and chooses this'.[59] Similarly, when it comes to virtue, the mean will lie somewhere in between the two extremes of excess and deficiency. For example, the virtue of temperance is a mean between the excess of gluttony and the deficiency of extreme self-denial, and the virtue of justice is a mean between the excess of over-generosity and the deficiency of miserliness. To return to a theme that has already been discussed, the virtue of fortitude is not about being absolutely fearless in the face of all dangers. Aristotle acknowledges that almost everyone (with the exception of the foolhardy Celts)[60] approaches life with some mixture of both fear and confidence, but 'to feel (these emotions) at the right times, with reference to the right objects, towards the right people, with the right motive, and in the right way, is what is both intermediate and best, and this is characteristic of virtue'.[61] Thus, the mean is not a simple formula that can be applied crudely or mechanistically. Finding the true mean always requires flexibility and attention to context. Moreover, the doctrine of the mean cannot be applied to every aspect of human action. We do not look for a virtuous mean in acts of, for example, spite, shamelessness or envy since these are, by definition, vices. A man cannot, for example, become virtuous 'by committing adultery with the right woman, at the right time and in the right way'.[62]

While acknowledging the importance of the mean in understanding the moral virtues, Aquinas points out the limitations of this idea when it comes to the theological virtues of faith, hope and charity. He concedes that it might be possible to envisage hope as a mean between presumption and despair, or faith as a mean between opposing heresies, and yet the measured and carefully proportioned concept of the virtuous mean cannot be applied to the theological virtues which, by their nature, are abundant and overflowing: 'never can we love God as much as He ought to be loved, nor believe and hope in Him as much as we should'.[63] Thus Aquinas concludes that 'the good of such virtues does not consist in a mean, but increases the

59 Aristotle, *Nicomachean Ethics* 2.6; cf. Shields (2007), p. 325.
60 See Aristotle, *Nicomachean Ethics* 3.7.
61 Aristotle, *Nicomachean Ethics* 2.6.
62 Aristotle, *Nicomachean Ethics* 2.6.
63 Aquinas, *Summa Theologica* 2-2. 64.4.

more we approach to the summit'.[64] Kreeft comments that in his teaching on this subject, 'St Thomas bursts out of the Greek, classical, finite mould to a Christian "extremism" or Romanticism'.[65]

The ends of the virtues

A further distinction between the two sets of virtues concerns the different ends to which they lead. The ethics of Aristotle and Aquinas are often described as *teleological*, a word that derives from the Greek term *telos*, meaning 'end'. Human beings are purposive creatures, seeking, as Aristotle sees it, all the time to fulfil our potential. Thus, whenever we act, we do so in order to achieve an end. In a theme that was discussed in the previous chapter, for Aristotle, as for other ancient philosophers, the final end of all our actions is *eudaimonia*: happiness in its wider sense of human flourishing and fulfilment, and for Aristotle, 'happiness ... comes as a result of virtue and some process of learning or training'.[66] When we possess and exercise the virtues, then we will be made happy by so doing. For example, if we possess the virtue of prudence, the fact that our moral choices tend to lead to the good outcomes that we intend they should will make for our flourishing and overall welfare. If we possess the virtue of temperance, we will be happy because our good intentions and plans will not have been derailed by excessive desires.

Following on from Aristotle, Aquinas acknowledges that the moral virtues can bring happiness and flourishing in a limited human sense, but this will never be an eternal and God-sized happiness, but a happiness that is only 'proportionate to human nature'.[67] Beyond *eudaimonia*, however, Aquinas claims, there is a still greater happiness that, through the grace of God and the work of Christ, we can hope for, but towards which only the theological virtues (and not the moral ones alone) can bring us. *Beatitudo*, in English 'blessedness', is a happiness 'surpassing man's nature ... which man can obtain by the power of God alone, by a kind of participation of the Godhead, about which it is written that by Christ we are made partakers of the Divine nature (2 Peter 1.4)'.[68] Ultimately, it is only the grace of God, and in particular, Christ's sharing in and redeeming the life of humanity that enable sinful men and women to participate in his divine life:

With regard to the full participation of the Divinity, which is the true bliss of man and end of human life ... this is bestowed upon us by Christ's

---

64 Aquinas, *Summa Theologica* 2-2. 64.4.
65 Kreeft (1990), p. 473.
66 Aristotle, *Nicomachean Ethics* 1.9.
67 Aquinas, *Summa Theologica* 1-2. 62.3.
68 Aquinas, *Summa Theologica* 1-2. 62.3.

humanity; for Augustine says in a sermon: 'God was made man, that man might be made God'.[69]

How we become virtuous

This last point also relates to the distinction Aquinas draws between the ways in which human beings come to possess the moral and theological virtues. While, following Aristotle's emphasis on training and habituation, Aquinas acknowledges that the moral virtues can be acquired through our own efforts; the theological virtues must always be understood first and foremost to be works of God's grace. Thus, just as in the previous chapter, we saw that, in order fully *to know the good*, human beings need divine revelation in addition to natural law, so also when we try to *do the good*, we need God's grace in addition to any efforts that we might make. Thus, a truly virtuous life requires not only those achievements that human beings can generate out of their own resources, but also 'some additional principles, by which ... [they] may be directed to supernatural happiness'.[70] The theological virtues of faith, hope and charity are not simply habits that we ourselves can acquire. Rather, for Aquinas, as for Paul himself, they have the essential quality of a gift, since they are a work of God's grace within us. They are not so much acquired as '*infused* in us by God alone'.[71] Pinckaers comments that:

> Paul obviously did not construct an organized moral system like that of St Thomas Aquinas. However, it is clear that for him the organism of charisms and virtues possessed an entirely Christian head, formed by three virtues of which the philosophers were ignorant. Faith, hope, and charity guaranteed a direct bond with the source of Christian life, Christ and his Spirit. These virtues were unique in their dependence on the initiative of divine grace. They governed all of Christian action and gave to the other virtues, working in harmony with them, an incomparable value, measure, dynamism, and finality.[72]

---

69 Aquinas, *Summa Theologica* 3.1.2.
70 Aquinas, *Summa Theologica* 1-2. 62.1.
71 Aquinas, *Summa Theologica* 1-2. 62.1 (my italics).
72 Pinckaers (1995), p. 127.

Summary

Classification	Virtue	Source	How obtained?	Leads us to	Analogous with	Order of
Theological	Charity	Biblical	Infused	*Beatitudo*	Divine law	Grace
	Hope					
	Faith					
Moral/	Prudence	Classical	Acquired	*Eudaimonia*	Natural law	Nature
	Justice					
Cardinal	Fortitude					
	Temperance					

The table above summarizes the distinctions between the sets of virtues that have been discussed so far in this chapter, but it is necessary to emphasize that these distinctions are less neat and less rigid than they appear to be. For example, although the theological virtues are works of grace, infused by God, rather than acquired by our own efforts, nonetheless they still need to be honed and practised. The formation of good habits remains important. C. S. Lewis, for example, advises those who find it difficult to love their neighbour not to 'waste time bothering whether you "love" (in the sense of affectionate feelings) your neighbour; act as if you did'.[73] Even more important, the moral virtues, although acquired by our efforts, must nonetheless be understood as a work of God's grace. It is only because God has created us in the first place, giving us gifts of reason and will, and orienting us towards himself that we possess the natural endowments that enable us to acquire any virtues whatsoever.[74]

Moreover, in Aquinas's scheme, the gifts of the Holy Spirit, traditionally prayed for in the Christian liturgy of Confirmation, are poured out on the Church at Pentecost (see Acts 2), and these gifts complement, complete and crown the virtues. Their role is to make us open and receptive to the work of God in our lives, as Aquinas expresses it, to 'dispose all the powers of the soul to be amenable to the Divine motion'.[75] Following Isaiah 11.1–3, the gifts of the Spirit are traditionally enumerated as wisdom, understanding, counsel, fortitude, knowledge, piety and fear of the Lord. Aquinas, more or less smoothly, coordinates them with the virtues as in the table below.

---

73 C.S. Lewis (2002), *Mere Christianity* (London: HarperCollins), p. 131, see also Mattison (2008), p. 298.

74 See Aquinas, *Summa Theologica* 1-2. 62.1.

75 Aquinas, *Summa Theologica* 1-2. 68.8.

Virtue	Corresponding Gift
Charity	Wisdom
Hope	Fear of the Lord
Faith	Knowledge, Understanding
Prudence	Counsel
Justice	Piety
Fortitude	Fortitude
Temperance	Fear of the Lord

There is not the space here to discuss the gifts in detail and, indeed, theologians have disagreed about how helpful it is to multiply entities, such as the theological virtues and the gifts, that are infused into the soul. However, it is worth noting that the gifts again point to the importance of grace in Aquinas's theology, since our ability to receive the gifts depends entirely upon divine initiative. The seventeenth-century theologian John of Saint Thomas compares the relationship between the virtues and the gifts with a boat, moved both by the rowing of oarsmen (the virtues) and by the force of the wind (the gifts).[76]

Questions for discussion

Which virtue(s) do you think would be particularly needed by the following and why?

A parent bringing up a child
The owner of a business
A church pastor
A police officer
A teacher

Is reflection on virtue compatible with a belief in the importance of grace?

---

76 John of St Thomas, *Cursus Theologicus*, Disp XVIII, a.2, n.29, quoted in Cessario (2001), pp. 207–8.

4

Conscience

The conscience is the focal point of an absolute perspective in a finite being, the means by which this perspective is anchored in that being's emotional structure. It is because of this presence of the universal, the objective, the absolute, in the individual person, that we talk of human dignity; there is no other reason.[1]

Defining conscience

Despite its importance in ethical thought, the term 'conscience' is a notoriously slippery one, and has been used to mean a variety of different things. The diagram below summarizes the distinctions between the different uses of conscience that will be discussed in this chapter.[2]

	Type of conscience	Description
Syneidesis	Particular	Judgement made about particular actions, based on reasoned and thoughtful evaluation
Synderesis	General	Awareness of law of God written in the human heart; of basic principles of morality
	Transcendental	Awareness of ourselves as moral beings, calling us to full humanity
Superego	Psychological	Prolongation of parental (and other) influences from childhood

---

1 Spaemann (1989), p. 58.

2 This chapter draws in particular on Macquarrie (1970), pp. 111–19; May (1991), pp. 30–40.

Syneidesis

The English word 'conscience', derived from the Latin *conscientia*, is the usual translation of the New Testament term *syneidesis* which appears some 20 times in the New Testament, and means literally 'knowing-with'.[3] *Syneidesis* has a background in classical philosophy, in particular Stoic thought, in which it refers to the 'experience of self-awareness in the forming of moral judgments'.[4] It is not a concept easily to be found in the Old Testament, where the human faculties of moral discernment are less important than obedience to the will of God as revealed in the Torah. However, conscience is sometimes used to translate the Hebrew term *lēb*, meaning *heart*, to be understood not so much in the modern sense as the seat of the emotions, but as the centre of self-consciousness devoted to making decisions. In the New Testament, *syneidesis* comes to particular prominence in two particular passages from the letters of Saint Paul.

Romans 2.14–16

> When Gentiles, who do not possess the law, do instinctively what the law requires, these, though not having the law, are a law to themselves. They show that what the law requires is written on their hearts, to which their own consciences [*syneidēseōs*] also bear witness; and their conflicting thoughts will accuse or perhaps excuse them on the day when, according to my gospel, God, through Jesus Christ, will judge the secret thoughts of all.

In a passage from the letter to the Romans that was considered in chapter 2 in relation to natural law, Paul argues that, even without the benefit of the revealed law, the Gentiles still have some instinctive awareness of morality. Such an awareness is, as Wright puts it, 'part of the universal human makeup'.[5] The Gentiles, as Paul characterizes them, debate internally the rightness or otherwise of their actions: they have 'conflicting thoughts' about their actions, similar perhaps to what we might understand as 'pangs of conscience'. Paul's words indicate that the Gentiles' consciences are morally significant, and indeed that their salvation depends on them; but that the role of their conscience is an ancillary one. It is not, in itself, the source of moral rules, but rather bears witness to God's law as this is written in their hearts.

---

3 This section draws on Freedman (1992) (ed.), vol. 1, pp. 1128–30; Mahoney (1987), pp. 184–93; Wright (2010), pp. 138–43; Ziesler (1989), p. 88.

4 Mahoney (1987), p. 185.

5 Wright (2010), p. 142.

1 Corinthians 8

The first letter to the Corinthians provides an important case study of conscience in action over the question of whether it is permissible for Christians to eat food that has been sacrificed to idols. The context for Paul's comments in this passage is a disagreement between the so-called 'strong' and 'weak' members of the Corinthian church. The 'strong' members of the church understand that, according to monotheistic faith, there is only one God, and so eating idol food does not present a problem to them. However, the 'weak' members of the church, probably Gentile converts, not yet entirely assimilated to monotheism, find that their consciences are wounded by what appears to them to be an idolatrous act. Eating such food might even be the start of a slippery slope that eventually leads them back to full-blown worship of idols. In these circumstances, Paul encourages the 'strong' members of the community to bear with the failings of the 'weak', as their brothers and sisters in Christ (verse 12; cf. Rom. 15.1). The conscience, then, is not seen here as an infallible guide to action. Objectively speaking, the consciences of those who object to eating idol meat are wrong (verse 8), and need to be educated by further reflection on monotheism and Christian identity (cf. verses 4–6). However, stressing the importance of relationships and mutual forbearance within the body of Christ, Paul argues that the strong should bear with the consciences of the weak, and not create stumbling blocks for them (verse 9). As Wright explains this, 'Paul will not ride roughshod over another's scruples, presumably because once you do so, you crush the moral compass altogether.'[6]

Although the reflection on conscience in these passages is still at an embryonic stage, some crucial and enduring points have already emerged:

1. Conscience bears witness to, but does not generate the moral law.
2. Conscience must be formed and educated.
3. Respect is due to conscience even when, objectively, it is perceived to be in error.

A final point relating to the understanding of conscience in the New Testament relates to the timescale on which it is believed to operate. Conscience as we understand it today can be understood in two senses:

- *Antecedent conscience* is conscience understood as a guide to future action. 'Always let your conscience be your guide' is Jiminy Cricket's advice to his young friend in Disney's film *Pinocchio* about how to face the challenges that lie ahead of him.

---

6 Wright (2010), p. 141.

- *Consequent* conscience refers to the retrospective judgement that we make upon actions that we have already taken. 'How smart a lash that speech doth give my conscience'[7] remarks King Claudius in Shakespeare's *Hamlet*, as a remark of Polonius causes him to feel guilty about having murdered his brother.

In the New Testament, as in the classical sources that inform its writers' use of *syneidesis*, the term is normally used in this latter, consequent and generally negative sense. Conscience manifests itself 'in the pain felt by someone who is aware of having done wrong'.[8] Indeed, some New Testament scholars, especially those from the Reformed tradition such as C. A. Pierce in his influential study *Conscience in the New Testament*, argue that the New Testament writers understand the concept of conscience only in this limited sense. However, it is perhaps a mistake to understand this distinction too rigidly. In the controversy about food sacrificed to idols, for example, Paul himself appears to use the concept of *syneidesis* in an antecedent sense when he instructs the Corinthians to 'eat whatever is sold in the meat market without raising any question on the ground of conscience' (1 Cor. 10.25). And indeed, we might question whether the antecedent and consequent senses *can* be completely separated from one another. I may well decide in advance not to perform a particular action if I know that afterwards I will suffer a guilty conscience because of it.

Synderesis

This somewhat obscure term refers to human beings' innate understanding of moral principles: our 'habitual, intuitive grasp of the first principles for action, the precepts of the law of nature, which prompts us to good and complains at what is bad'.[9] The word is first used in the way that later moral theology would come to understand it by Saint Jerome (347–420) who, in his commentary on Ezekiel's vision of the four animals (Ezek. 1), compares *synderesis* with 'the eagle that corrects from above when knowledge and sensitivity err'.[10] In a memorable image, Jerome describes *synderesis* as the *scintilla*, the tiny spark of pure flame that continues to flicker in human beings after the Fall.

Making use of the further precision that the term *synderesis* was able to supply, writers, such as Aquinas, distinguish between two aspects of conscience as this term is understood in its widest sense:

---

7 *Hamlet* Act 3, Scene 1, 49–50.
8 Ziesler (1989), p. 88.
9 Mahoney (1987), pp. 187–8.
10 Pinckaers (2005), p. 351.

- *synderesis*: our intuitive grasp of moral first principles
- *syneidesis* (= *conscientia* in its more restricted sense): our application of these principles in particular situations.[11]

Commentators who make this distinction have typically argued that while our awareness of moral principles (*synderesis*) is certain, because fixed by God, our ability to apply these in concrete situations (*syneidesis*) is much more uncertain. As Aquinas puts it, in a phrase that was discussed in chapter 2, 'the more we descend to matters of detail, the more frequently we encounter defects'.[12]

In his work *Ductor Dubitantium* or *The Rule of Conscience*,[13] the Anglican theologian Jeremy Taylor (1613–67) provides an account of *synderesis*, which draws on Aquinas and further clarifies the distinction between *synderesis* and *syneidesis*. Taylor compares *synderesis* with a phylactery: the black leather box carrying scriptural verses that Jewish men wear at certain times of the day on their foreheads and left arms, so as to remind them of the basic precepts of the Torah. Like the phylactery, *synderesis* provides a perpetual reminder of the moral first principles that God, naturally and through revelation, has given to human beings: 'all that law by which God governs us is written in our hearts, put there by God immediately, that is antecedently to all our actions, because it is that by which all our actions are to be guided'.[14] Although such innate moral knowledge is vital, in and of itself it is inactive, and waits on *syneidesis* to apply its insights to the situations that we actually face. Conscience in its fullest sense, then, as Taylor describes it, is not one simple entity or activity, but rather an integrated movement, a 'complication of acts'; 'a conjunction of universal practical law (*synderesis*) with the particular moral action (*syneidesis/conscientia*)', and a consequent judgement that arises from these. Thus, what Taylor calls the 'full process of conscience' or the 'full proceeding of the court' consists in three stages:

1. The *synderesis* or first, general act of conscience, described, as above, by Jerome as the *scintilla conscientiae*: a 'spark or fire put into the heart of man'.
2. The *syneidesis*: the understanding of the action that may be taken: 'the bringing fuel to this fire'.
3. The *judgement* that ensues when these two actions of conscience are combined: 'when they (the spark and the fuel) are thus laid together, they will either shine or burn, acquit or condemn' (cf. Rom. 2.15).

---

11 Aquinas, *Summa Theologica*. See, 1. 79.12–13.
12 Aquinas, *Summa Theologica* 1-2. 94.4.
13 Taylor (1660/1885), pp. 12–21.
14 Taylor (1660/1885), p. 17.

An obvious criticism of the concept of *synderesis* as Taylor and others explain it, is that, unlike *syneidesis*, it does not appear in the Bible. In answer to this, Taylor argues that conscience is a composite idea, understood in the New Testament in a variety of different ways, as a faculty, a habit, an act, etc., so that *synderesis* as he has described it, accurately describes part of what the New Testament writers understand conscience to be.[15] Moreover, Taylor seeks to demonstrate that, although we may not find the actual word *synderesis* in the New Testament, nonetheless, when we come to paradigm cases of biblical individuals who are examining their consciences, the concept is taken for granted. Taylor uses the accounts of David's adultery with Bathsheba (2 Sam. 11) and Peter's denial of Jesus (Mark 14.66–72) to demonstrate that *synderesis* is an integral part of what he calls the 'full process of conscience' as we encounter it in the Bible.[16] As can be seen from the table below, Taylor describes the workings of conscience in the form of a syllogism: an argument with a major premise (P1), a minor premise (P2) and a conclusion (C). In each case, *synderesis* provides the major premise, without which it would be impossible for the argument as a whole to work, and thus for the judgement of conscience to be made.

		David committing adultery	Peter betraying Jesus
P1	*Synderesis*	'Adultery ought not to be done'	'He knew he ought not to have done it'
P2	*Syneidesis*	'This action I go about, or which I have done is adultery'	'He also knew that he had done it'
C	Final judgement of conscience	'Therefore it ought not to be done, or to have been done'	'There followed a remorse, a biting or gnawing of his spirit, grief and shame, and a consequent weeping'

Protestant moral commentators have characteristically argued that not only is the biblical provenance of *synderesis* dubious, but also that if we emphasize the concept too strongly we will underestimate the extent to which the moral vision of men and women is clouded by original sin. Taylor himself was suspected throughout his life of having Catholic leanings, and fell out of favour during the Puritan protectorate of Oliver Cromwell. In response, Taylor might have argued that the origins of the concept of *synderesis* and of the imagery that he uses to describe it come from the writings of Jerome, a friend of Augustine's, and staunch opponent of Pelagius, entirely convinced

---

15 Taylor (1660/1885), p. 15.
16 Taylor (1660/1885), pp. 14–15.

of the seriousness of humanity's fallen condition. Indeed, Augustine himself says that 'there is no soul however perverted ... in whose conscience God does not speak'.[17]

Most importantly, *synderesis* should surely be seen in a dynamic rather than static way. As was argued in chapter 2, there are good grounds, both biblical and philosophical, to believe that a basic awareness of moral first principles exists in embryonic form in all human beings. However, it would be absurd to think that this basic awareness sits passively inside us unchanged throughout our lives. Rather, like our other faculties, our underlying sense of moral first principles is capable of being educated by exposure to Scripture and Church teaching, drawn out by experience of Christian life, and transformed by the working of God's grace. As Pinckaers writes:

> The action of the Holy Spirit ... will be engrafted precisely upon this moral source in our depths, the *synderesis*, by infusing within our spirit new principles of action through the theological virtues, which will effect our conformation to Christ by making us children of the Father through grace.[18]

Transcendental conscience

The 'transcendental conscience' takes the concept to an even deeper level of human identity. Conscience in this sense means 'a special and very fundamental mode of self-awareness – the awareness of "how it is with oneself"':[19] a dynamic quality, that calls us not only to understand ourselves as we are, but to live up to the fullness of what God has created us to be. Macquarrie writes that:

> The basic function of conscience is to disclose us to ourselves. Specifically, conscience discloses the gap between our actual selves and that image of ourselves that we already have in virtue of the 'natural inclination' toward the fulfillment of man's end. Thus, conscience is not merely a disclosure; it is also ... a call or summons. It is a call to that full humanity of which we already have some idea or image because of the very fact that we are human at all, and that our nature is to exist, to go out beyond where we are at any given moment.[20]

Examples of conscience viewed in this way are the stock in trade of many Victorian novels. One of these, *The Warden*, by Anthony Trollope (1815–82) may be used to illustrate some central points about this subject. The

17 Augustine, *On the Sermon on the Mount*, quoted in Mahoney (1987), p. 187.
18 Pinckaers (2005), p. 331.
19 See Macquarrie (1970), pp. 114–15; May (1991), pp. 34–5.
20 Macquarrie (1970), pp. 114–15.

hero of the novel, Mr Harding, is the saintly and other-worldly warden of Hiram's Hospital: a set of almshouses in the fictional cathedral city of Barchester. According to the will of their benefactor, John Hiram, a small fixed daily allowance of one shilling and fourpence per day is paid to the residents of the almshouses, while the remainder of the proceeds from Hiram's estate are to be retained by the warden. By the start of the novel, however, income from the estate has risen steadily over many years, so that Mr Harding receives a very comfortable stipend of 800 pounds per year, as compared with the meagre fixed allowance to which the residents continue to be entitled, albeit that Mr Harding has increased this out of his own pocket. During the novel, a social reformer named John Bold, who is also in love with Mr Harding's daughter, Eleanor, draws attention to this perceived injustice in the columns of the *Jupiter* newspaper. As the novel progresses, Mr Harding becomes increasingly unhappy with his situation. He is assured by his lawyers, Cox and Cumming, and by his son-in-law, the choleric Archdeacon Grantly, that he is entirely within his legal and moral rights to retain his post and his income. And yet Mr Harding becomes increasingly clear in his own mind that, for him, the virtuous path must go beyond what the lawyers and the archdeacon tell him about what is strictly permissible. If he is to keep his integrity – his sense of the person he is, and that he hopes to be – then he must resign the wardenship at Hiram's:

> The names of Cox and Cumming had now no interest in his ears. What had he to do with Cox and Cumming further, having already had his suit finally adjudicated upon in a court of conscience, a judgement without power of appeal fully registered, and the matter settled so that all the lawyers in London could not disturb it.[21]

Mr Harding thus exemplifies Pinckaers's description of conscience operating at this transcendental level: that it 'no longer designates the awareness of a law that obliges and constrains, but rather the knowledge of a law that appeals to the heart and touches it'.[22]

The authority of conscience

One prominent aspect of the situation in which Mr Harding finds himself is that he experiences his conscience on the matter as absolutely binding. It is, in this respect, similar to Kant's 'categorical imperative': a concept that will be explored in chapter 6. Mr Harding tells the attorney-general, Sir Abraham Haphazard, that 'I cannot boast of my conscience when it required the violence of a public newspaper to awaken it; but, now that it is awake, I

---

21 Trollope (1980), *The Warden* (Oxford: Oxford University Press), pp. 249–50.
22 Pinckaers (2005), p. 337.

must obey it'.[23] For Mr Harding to go against what his conscience tells him he must do is unthinkable. It would amount to a loss of integrity, and indeed a destruction of his sense of himself as a moral being.

Such an insistence that conscience should be followed has a central and honoured place in the Christian moral tradition. As was seen in the controversy over food sacrificed to idols, respect continues to be due to conscience even when its judgements are perceived to be in error. This emphasis on conscience's binding nature is articulated by the Fourth Lateran Council of 1215, which famously decreed that 'whatever is done against conscience builds towards hell'. In line with this, moral theologians have traditionally argued that although, objectively speaking, our consciences may be mistaken, we should nonetheless always follow them, since to do otherwise would be to act in a way that we believe to be wrong, and this can never be right.[24] This deep-seated respect for conscience was reiterated in the Second Vatican Council's Pastoral Constitution on the Church in the Modern World, *Gaudium et spes*:

> Deep within their consciences men and women discover a law which they have not laid upon themselves and which they must obey. Its voice, ever calling them to love and to do what is good and to avoid evil, tells them inwardly at the right moment: do this, shun that. For they have in their hearts a law inscribed by God. Their dignity rests in observing this law, and by it they will be judged.[25]

One of the theologians who most influenced the Council's elevated view of conscience was John Henry Newman, whose spiritual autobiography, *Apologia pro Vita Sua*, details his own agonies of conscience in the 1830s and 1840s over his ecclesial allegiance. Like his fictional contemporary, Mr Harding, Newman, a keen reader of Trollope's novels, both before and after he left the Church of England to become a Roman Catholic,[26] experienced his conscience calling him not simply to obey rules, but to transcend his previous way of life. And, like Mr Harding, he senses the call of conscience as one that he cannot resist: 'I feel His hand heavy on me without intermission, who is all Wisdom and Love.'[27]

In a later work, his *Letter to the Duke of Norfolk* Newman writes of conscience in its fullest sense as the law of God 'as apprehended in the minds of individual men', which 'though it may suffer refraction in passing into

---

23 Trollope, *The Warden*, p. 236.
24 See Aquinas, *Summa Theologica* 1-2. 19.5.
25 *Gaudium et Spes* (1965), 16; cf. *Catechism of the Catholic Church* paragraphs 1776–94.
26 See *The Tablet*, 19 June 2010, p. 18.
27 Newman, *Apologia pro Vita Sua* (1864), p. 247.

the medium of each ... is not therefore so affected as to lose its character of being the Divine Law, but still has, as such, the prerogative of commanding obedience'.[28] Because conscience is the divine law written in the human heart, it always draws us back in dutiful obedience to God and to God's law. Thus it can be understood, in Newman's famous description, as 'the aboriginal Vicar of Christ, a prophet in its informations, a monarch in its peremptoriness, a priest in its blessings and anathemas'.[29] Newman contrasts what he sees as this properly theological understanding of conscience as the 'voice of God' with secular misunderstandings which make it little more than the right of self-will and self-determination, as Newman puts it, 'the Englishman's prerogative, for each to be his own master in all things, and to profess what he pleases, asking no one's leave, and accounting priest or preacher, speaker or writer unutterably impertinent, who dares to say a word against his going to perdition, if he like it, in his own way'.[30]

Writing at a time when the doctrine of papal infallibility was becoming more explicitly defined within Roman Catholicism, Newman presents a nuanced but firm assertion of the claims of Christian conscience. On the one hand, in line with the letter to the Romans, conscience does not create the truth, but bears witness to the truth that is already there. The central duty of the Pope's office is to safeguard conscience, because the Pope's role, like that of conscience is to bring people back to the authority of divine truth: 'did the Pope speak against Conscience in the true sense of the word, he would commit a suicidal act'.[31] Moreover, Newman argues, conscience is most unlikely to conflict with the teaching of the Pope, since conscience is concerned primarily with what should be done here and now (matters about which the Pope is not infallible), while papal teaching is engaged with 'general propositions, and in the condemnation of particular and given errors'.[32] However, in those rare cases when conscience and papal teaching do seem to conflict, Newman strongly asserts that the weight of the Catholic tradition holds that conscience must be followed, even where it is misguided. He memorably ends the *Letter to the Duke of Norfolk* by remarking that:

If I am obliged to bring religion into after-dinner toasts (which indeed does not seem quite the thing) I shall drink – to the Pope, if you please, – still to conscience first, and to the Pope afterwards.[33]

---

28 Newman, *Letter to the Duke of Norfolk* (1875), p. 247.
29 Newman, *Letter to the Duke of Norfolk*, pp. 248–9.
30 Newman, *Letter to the Duke of Norfolk*, p. 250.
31 Newman, *Letter to the Duke of Norfolk*, p. 252.
32 Newman, *Letter to the Duke of Norfolk*, p. 256.
33 Newman, *Letter to the Duke of Norfolk*, p. 261.

Discussion point

Can you think of any time when the claims of conscience seem to have been in conflict with church teaching, either on a local level, or more widely?

How was this situation resolved (if it was)?

Conscience and the superego

The Austrian psychologist and founder of psychoanalysis, Sigmund Freud (1856–1939), provides a possible fourth range of meaning for the term 'conscience'. Freud argues that the basic structure of the human personality is composed of three elements which are translated from the original German into English by the Latin terms *ego*, *id* and *superego*. The *ego* approximates to the conscious, rational self. The *id* is the part of the personality responsible for our basic drives, and the *superego* is the part that regulates our sense of right and wrong. The *superego*, which equates most closely with the conscience, is formed by the child's experience of parental discipline, and it is through the *superego*, that we continue throughout our lives to hear the voice of authority figures echoing within us: 'the long period of childhood during which the growing human being lives in dependence on his parents leaves behind a precipitate, which forms within his ego a special agency in which this parental influence is prolonged. It has received the name of "superego".'[34] This is not an entirely negative process: what Iris Murdoch described as the 'fat, relentless ego' does need to be disciplined. If it were not for the influence of parental figures, the human *ego* would be left at a babyish stage of development, unable to free itself from the instinctive drives of the *id*. The *superego* thus enables the *ego* to transcend itself, so as to achieve the so-called *ego-ideal*. However, Freud's contention was that, for many people, the domination of authority figures mediated through the *superego* was the cause of neurotic conditions. With the help of psychoanalysis, patients could be released from the power of the *superego*, their *egos* liberated to live and to act, unimpeded by irrational feelings of guilt and anxiety: 'where the superego was, there shall the ego be'.[35]

---

34 S. Freud (1940), *An Outline of Psychoanalysis*, trans. J. Strachey (London: Hogarth Press, 1949), p. 3.

35 Freud (1973), *New Introductory Lectures in Psychoanalysis*, quoted in Campbell (1981), p. 67. This summary draws on A. Campbell (1981), *Rediscovering Pastoral Care* (London: Darton, Longman and Todd), pp. 66–8; Spaemann (1989), p. 61; Macquarrie (1970), pp. 113–14; May (1991), pp. 30–1.

The work of Freud in this area obviously resembles in some respects the theological understanding of conscience that has been explored in this chapter, but there are also some important points of contrast. The first of these is that the view of conscience influenced by Aquinas stresses its rational side, reflected in the *Catechism of the Catholic Church*'s description of it as a 'judgment of reason'.[36] It is the work of *syneidesis* to bring moral principles to bear in a reasoned way on particular situations that face us. Aquinas calls it 'the application of knowledge to what we do'.[37] This contrasts strongly with the *superego* which, as Freud describes it, is essentially sub-conscious and irrational, tending to create unnecessary anxiety, and needing to make way for the more rational self to emerge. Moreover, in the theological understanding of it, our conscience is entirely at one with the person we are. To go back to Newman's fullest definition of conscience, it may be the voice of God, but it is the voice of God *as we apprehend it*. For example, when Mr Harding resigns from the wardenship at Hiram's Hospital, this conscientious action springs from the very centre of his own personality. He entirely identifies himself with the decision that he has made, even when legal and ecclesiastical authority figures try to dissuade him from it. By contrast, the voice of the *superego* as Freud presents it, is essentially an alien voice, coming from an exterior source such as a parent or authority figure, and 'introjected' into us, from which we must seek to be liberated.

Forming conscience: information, formation, conformation

The Anglican moral theologian Stephen Holmgren (1956–) writes succinctly that 'conscience must be followed, but conscience must also be educated'.[38] In the discussion of writers such as Newman, this chapter has so far stressed our duty to follow our conscience, and that of others to respect it. However, as Mahoney writes, 'as well as being responsible *to* conscience, the individual is also responsible *for* his conscience – for the quality of its judgements, the range and seriousness of its enquiries, and the respect accorded it in other areas of his life'.[39] This final section will outline briefly some aspects of what might be involved in the Christian education or, as it is often described, 'formation' of conscience.

Precisely because in the Christian tradition, the exercise of conscience involves men and women using their critical faculties, true formation of conscience differs from the brainwashing and mind-control practised by some political and indeed religious groups. Brainwashing attempts to by-pass the critical faculties of those who are being indoctrinated or, in the

---

36 *Catechism of the Catholic Church* 1778.
37 Aquinas, *Summa Theologica* 1. 79.13.
38 Holmgren (2000), p. 126.
39 Mahoney (1987), p. 290.

most extreme cases, even to lobotomize parts of their brains. By contrast, Christian formation of conscience seeks to respect and engage the God-given powers of thinking and reasoning, aiming not to stop the mind working, but to renew it (cf. Rom. 12.2).

If we claim a right for our consciences to be respected on account of the fact that we are rational beings who can think for ourselves, then this implies that we also have a duty to exercise our rationality by informing our conscience as far as possible with the best available sources of moral knowledge and teaching. To quote a pastoral letter of the American Catholic bishops, 'common sense requires that conscientious people be open and humble, ready to learn from the experience and insight of others, willing to acknowledge prejudices and even change their judgements in light of better instruction'.[40] In a Christian context, the moral teaching of, for example, parents, teachers and clergy may all inform the consciences of men and women from an early age. Most of all perhaps, regular reflection on Scripture in the context of the Church's worshipping life will profoundly inform those who are exposed to it.

However, the instruction of conscience that comes through exposure to moral teaching, discussion groups, and indeed reading books about ethics can only take anyone so far in the Christian moral life. Gula writes that:

> The aim of forming conscience is not simply to inquire about the right thing to do by gathering information and thinking it over, but it must also include the fuller texture of a person's moral character: one's attitudes, motives, intentions, affections and perspective. The moral life is a matter of who we are as well as what and how we choose.[41]

Making a similar point in an essay on the importance of spirituality for the formation of conscience, Kenneth Himes draws attention to what he regards as an overemphasis on the very rational process of *syneidesis* in the education of conscience. The result is that the human person is essentially regarded as a problem solver; 'the valued traits then become analytic reasoning, rational discourse, disinterested judgment (with the result that) other qualities – imagination, openness, creativity, passion, self-criticism, compassion – may be undervalued in such a framework'.[42] Himes emphasizes that the education of conscience is not just about honing the intellect (although this is an inescapable dimension), but about retraining the affections, so that we come not just to know about the good and the bad, but to desire the good and to shun the bad.

Such insights draw attention to the important link between spiritual discipline, in particular contemplative prayer, and the formation of conscience.

---

40 Quoted in May (1991), p. 38.
41 Hoose (1998), p. 116.
42 Keating (2000), p. 74.

The document of the Second Vatican Council, *Gaudium et Spes*, which was discussed earlier in this chapter, refers to conscience as 'people's most secret core and their sanctuary ... [where] they are alone with God whose voice echoes in their depths'.[43] That sanctuary can hardly be reached nor God's voice heard if the education of conscience is entirely about argumentation, debate and academic study. Thus, for the fuller formation of conscience, deeper dimensions of the human person emphasized by the contemplative tradition must be awakened and engaged.[44] This is a practical, and not just a theoretical, insight. Time given over to contemplation and silence is surely essential if we are to develop conscience in the different dimensions in which it has been described in this chapter. It is necessary if we are to develop our innate capacity to grasp what is good and true (*synderesis*); if we are to bring this knowledge to bear on the situations with which we are confronted in life (*syneidesis*); and if we are to gain an overall awareness of ourselves, and of the direction in which God is drawing us forward (transcendent conscience).

Above and beyond the *in*formation of conscience through moral teaching and its formation by spiritual discipline, is the specifically Christian *con*-formation of conscience to Christ. In one of the earliest parts of the New Testament, Paul urges the Philippians to 'let the same mind be in you that was in Christ Jesus' (Phil. 2.5). For Paul, being 'in Christ Jesus' denotes the way in which our entire self, including our faculties of moral discernment, comes into the risen Christ's sphere of influence. At its deepest level, Christian formation of conscience is about being drawn ever more deeply into Christ.

Questions for discussion

Can you think of further examples of conscience that come from history or fiction?

What do you think are the main ways in which conscience is formed?

---

43 *Gaudium et Spes* 16.

44 See Martin Laird (2006), *Into the Silent Land* (Oxford: Oxford University Press), chapter 2.

PART TWO

Contrasts and Controversies

5

Catholic and Protestant Ethics

Pursuing the good: happiness and commands

Happy the man, and happy he alone,
He, who can call today his own:
He who, secure within, can say,
Tomorrow do thy worst, for I have lived today.

John Dryden, translation of Horace, *Odes*, book 3, no. 29

It would surprise many people to hear that ethics is essentially about being happy. But this is the view of the Greek philosopher Aristotle. In his *Nicomachean Ethics*, Aristotle depicts human beings as purposive creatures, who seek to achieve what we understand to be good in the various endeavours that we undertake during the course of our lives.[1] A person practising a musical instrument is probably doing so with the aim of being able to play more proficiently, or a person going for a walk might be doing so because they want to be fitter. However, these and other short term objectives have, Aristotle argues, a wider and longer-term aim in view. For him, as for other ancient philosophers, the final end and chief good towards which all our actions are dedicated, and which gives each of them their ultimate meaning and purpose, is described by the Greek word *eudaimonia*. This is normally translated 'happiness', for it is happiness, Aristotle argues, that 'we choose always for itself and never for the sake of something else'. Happiness in this sense is wider and deeper than a short-lived feeling of pleasure, and is sometimes described by terms such as 'flourishing' or 'human fulfilment'. It includes, as MacIntyre puts it, 'both the notion of behaving well and the notion of faring well' – the happy person will both do good things and also enjoy life.[2] This type of happiness is, for Aristotle, 'final and self-sufficient, and is the end of action'.[3] Thus, if we are asked why we do any particular thing, although there may be a variety of short-term answers, the ultimate answer, after which we can go no further, will be that we do it because we

---

1 See Aristotle, *Nicomachean Ethics* 1.7.
2 MacIntyre, A. (1998), *A Short History of Christian Ethics* (Abingdon: Routledge), p. 57.
3 Aristotle, *Nicomachean Ethics* 1.7, cf. 1.5.

want to be happy and as Christopher Shields writes, 'the question "Yes, but why do you want to be happy?" is otiose; in the domain of purposive behaviour, why-questions come to an end with happiness'.[4]

Q. Why are you learning to play the violin?
A. Because I want to become better at it.
Q. Why do you want to become better at it?
A. So that I can join an orchestra.
Q. Why do you want to join an orchestra?
A. Because it will give me a hobby and because I like the thrill of playing to an audience.
Q. Why do you want these things?
A. Because they will make me happy.
Q. Why do you want to be happy?
A. I can't answer that. I just do!

Christian thinking on ethics often shares the interest that Aristotle and other ancient writers have in happiness, while also redefining their view of it. The centrality of happiness is evident, for example, in the stress that Jesus lays in his own teaching on his followers enjoying fullness of life: 'I came that they may have life, and have it abundantly' (John 10.10).[5] The Latin word *beatitudo* (blessedness), which has often been used to describe happiness in the sense that Christianity has understood it, is perhaps most familiar from the 'beatitudes': the passages of Jesus' teaching in which he describes certain groups of people, for example, the poor in spirit, those who mourn and the meek as being 'blessed' or 'happy' (see Matt. 5.1–12; Luke 6.20–26). Originally recorded at a time when many Christians were undergoing persecution for their faith, the Beatitudes differ from classical accounts of happiness, such as that of the poet Horace, quoted at the start of this chapter, because they emphasize the eschatological character of the Christian hope. Jesus teaches in the Beatitudes that his followers are happy if they can endure suffering in the present, for the sake of the coming Kingdom of God. He encourages men and women to develop personal characteristics (otherwise known as virtues), such as meekness, peacefulness and purity of heart, that will witness to the blessed life of the Kingdom, and start to establish it in the present.

Augustine of Hippo provides further Christian reflection on this theme, sharing with other ancient philosophers the belief that happiness is 'our final good ... that for the sake of which other things are to be desired'.[6]

---

4 Shields, C. (2007), *Aristotle* (Abingdon: Routledge), p. 311.
5 See also Mark 10.17; Matt. 19.16; Luke 18.18 and Mattison (2008), pp. 21–7.
6 Augustine, *City of God* 19.1. This section draws on Harrison (2000), pp. 79–82.

Strongly influenced before his conversion to Christianity by Platonic modes of thought, Augustine stresses in some of his early works, such as *De Beata Vita* (*On the Happy Life*), that true happiness comes from seeking that which is eternal and immutable, rather than that which is physical and temporal. In such early works, he holds out some hope that we can attain happiness in this life through the practice of the virtues emphasized by Stoic philosophers, such as moderation and limitation of desire. As Augustine's career continued, his engagement with the Bible, and particularly with the writings of Saint Paul, was to lead him to reassess some aspects of his earlier understanding of happiness. In his later works, and with an increasingly negative view of the human condition, he stresses that human beings often look in all the wrong places for happiness, and use unreliable guides, such as philosophers, to tell them where to find it.[7] In a sermon preached late in his life on Psalm 118 (119 in modern English translations), Augustine points out that this, the longest of all the psalms, 'from its very first verse ... urges us to seek happiness'. However, it is the specifically Christian disciplines of repentance and forgiveness, rather than, for example, the cultivation of classical virtues that will enable them to find it:

> You desire to be happy, but the paths along which you are running are wretched, and lead to wretchedness deeper still. If you want to attain (happiness) ... come this way, travel by this route. You cannot give up your longing for happiness, but you can and must abandon the malice of your twisted ways.[8]

As his thought develops, Augustine increasingly emphasizes that for Christians happiness has an eschatological quality: final happiness cannot be achieved in this life, but we wait for it with hope: 'a man who is happy in hope is not yet happy. He is waiting in patience for the happiness which he does not yet possess.'[9]

Thomas Aquinas also extensively explores this theme, drawing explicitly both on Aristotle and Augustine. In a theme that was discussed in chapter 3, Aquinas's ethics, like those of Aristotle, are often described as 'teleological', since he also emphasizes that 'all actions are done for an end': the end being that of happiness.[10] For Aquinas, beatitude will finally consist in loving union with God, in which we will be with God and enjoy him for ever. For him, as for Aristotle, happiness is ultimately rooted in the contemplation of God: 'final and perfect happiness can consist in nothing else than the vision of the Divine Essence'.[11] Such happiness, Aquinas teaches, is achieved

---

7 See Augustine, *On the Trinity* 13.9–11.
8 Psalm 118 (numbering from the Latin Psalter) Exposition 1.1, trans. M. Boulding.
9 Augustine, *On the Trinity* 13.10.
10 Aquinas, *Summa Theologica* 1-2. 1.1.
11 Aquinas, *Summa Theologica* 1-2. 3.8.

primarily through the work of Christ, who makes us 'participants of the Divine nature' (2 Peter 1.4).[12] However, Aquinas also teaches that human beings have been endowed with a natural orientation towards happiness, goodness, being, truth, and ultimately towards the God who has created us and to whom, by grace, we will eventually return. Because we have been created with such an inclination, although our final happiness depends on the work of Christ, we can to a certain limited extent through our own God-given capacities know what is good and cultivate the virtues that will lead us towards happiness. In an assessment of the human condition that is normally regarded as more positive than that of Augustine, Aquinas teaches that an essential feature of the human make-up is that we have been programmed to seek happiness; that our efforts to strive towards it are not entirely futile, and that we can even enjoy some measure of happiness in this life, despite its unavoidable evils.[13]

Teleological ethics

This term is derived from the Greek *telos*, meaning 'end'. Teleological understandings of ethics therefore emphasize that we act with a particular end or purpose in view.

Catholic ethics

In the aftermath of Aquinas, the Middle Ages witnessed a movement away from the emphasis on the importance of happiness that had previously been so dominant in moral thought.[14] This movement was given impetus by two related currents of philosophical thought: Nominalism and Voluntarism. The most famous early exponents of these were John Duns Scotus (c. 1265–1308) and William of Ockham (c. 1288–c. 1348).

Nominalism regards universal ideas simply as names (in Latin *nomina*) that are used to classify groups of things that would not otherwise be connected. In ethics, this approach rejects abstract talk about long-term goals such as happiness, and patterns of behaviour, such as the virtues, regarding these as essentially convenient fictions. Nominalism instead tends to understand the moral decisions that individual human beings make as unique and unconnected events. As Pinckaers describes it, Nominalism sees human con-

---

12 Aquinas, *Summa Theologica* 1-2. 62.3.

13 Aquinas, *Summa Theologica* 1-2. 5.3; Pinckaers (1995), pp. 221–9.

14 See Pinckaers (1995), chapters 10–11; Mahoney (1987), pp. 180–4; O'Donovan (1986), pp. 131–9.

duct as 'a succession of individual actions, drawn as it were with perforated lines, the dots being the unrelated moral atoms'.[15]

The related mindset of Voluntarism (derived from the Latin *voluntas*, meaning 'will') stresses the sovereign will of God above all other things, and God's freedom to command whatever he wills. For William of Ockham, 'what God willed was necessarily just and good precisely because he willed it'.[16] Accordingly, ethical thought influenced by Voluntarism stresses obligation and obedience to the will of God, rather than the long-term aim of achieving loving enjoyment of God. Taking this to its extreme conclusion, Ockham famously argues that God could command a person to hate him and that, if he were to do so, this action would become good:

> Every will can conform to the divine precepts; but God can command the created will to hate him, and the created will can do this (thereby refusing its own happiness and ultimate end). Furthermore, any act that is righteous in this world can also be righteous in the next, the fatherland; just as hatred of God can be a good act in this world, so can it be in the next.[17]

As Ockham's words in this passage indicate, for Voluntarist thinkers, acting morally is not primarily about following any human orientation towards happiness and towards God, but about the importance of bending our own wills to obey God's sovereign will.

Euthyphro's dilemma and its two 'horns' or options

In Plato's dialogue Euthyphro, *Socrates asks Euthyphro,*
'Is the pious loved by the gods because it is pious (horn 1), or is it pious because it is loved by the gods (horn 2)?'

In monotheistic terms, this can be stated:
'Does God command a particular action because it is right (horn 1), or is it right because God commands it (horn 2)?'

The ethics of happiness emphasizes horn 1: God commands us not to steal, for example, because stealing is wrong. If we steal, we will not flourish or be happy.
Voluntarism emphasizes horn 2: actions are good because God decrees that they are so. If God decreed that stealing was right, it would be right.[18]

---

15 Pinckaers (1995), p. 243.
16 Pinckaers (1995), p. 246.
17 Ockham, *Sentences*, quoted in Pinckaers (1995), p. 247.
18 See Wells and Quash (2010), p. 116.

Influenced by Nominalism and Voluntarism, Catholic moral thinking in the period between the late Middle Ages and the early twentieth century often downplayed Aquinas's teaching on happiness, and indeed on grace, emphasizing instead themes such as obligation, duty and law. For the same reasons, moral theology throughout this period tended to replace Aquinas's stress on the importance of the virtues – long-term characteristics of human beings that lead them to a happy life – with a stress on the absolute freedom of the human will either to obey or disobey God at any moment. In recent years, a variety of Catholic theologians, both 'conservative' and 'liberal', have advocated a shift in moral theology away from Nominalist and Voluntarist thinking, and back towards what they regard as the more authentic moral tradition, with its emphasis on happiness, often described in terms such as 'integral human fulfilment'. Two representative examples of this can be briefly considered.

The first is found in the teaching of Pope John Paul II (1920–2005) in his encyclical letter, *Veritatis Splendor* (*The Splendour of Truth*) a work that will be discussed in more detail later in this chapter. John Paul starts his encyclical with the question of the rich young man in Matthew's Gospel, 'master, what shall I do to inherit eternal life?' (Matt. 19.16). The young man wants to know how he can receive the fullness of life, in other words how he can be happy. This is, John Paul writes, 'an essential and unavoidable question for the life of every man'. Drawing on Aristotle and Aquinas, John Paul affirms that God's command is not an arbitrary divine diktat. Rather, because the young man, like all human beings, has been created by God, he has an orientation towards God, and his happiness comes in pursuing his true end:

> He is the source of man's happiness. Jesus brings the question about morally good action back to its religious foundations, to the acknowledgment of God, who alone is goodness, fullness of life, the final end of human activity, and perfect happiness.[19]

A further example of this renewed emphasis on happiness may be found in a statement of the Catholic Bishops' Conference of England and Wales entitled *Choosing the Common Good*, published prior to the British General Election in 2010. The bishops write that the concept of human happiness forms the basis of the common good of society, which it is the duty of those in political life to pursue. Concern for the common good – a central theme in Catholic social thought – should lead politicians to try and create the circumstances in which all members of society (including the poor, the elderly, migrants and indeed the unborn) can attempt to be happy:

> The common good is about how to live well together. It is the whole network of social conditions which enable human individuals and groups to

---

19 John Paul II, *Veritatis Splendor* 9.3.

flourish and live a full, genuinely human life ... The fulfilment which the common good seeks to serve is the flourishing of humanity, expressed in the phrase 'integral human development'.[20]

Protestant ethics

Nominalism and Voluntarism have perhaps had an even greater influence in Protestant moral thinking than they have in the Catholic tradition. In his book *Fear and Trembling*, the Danish Protestant philosopher and theologian Søren Kierkegaard (1813–55) presents some of their more dramatic implications. Written under the pseudonym Johannes de Silentio, indicating perhaps that the views expressed may not exactly represent Kierkegaard's own attitude to the subject, *Fear and Trembling* offers an extended meditation on Abraham's (almost-) sacrifice of Isaac in Genesis 22. Kierkegaard emphasizes that Abraham is the archetypal biblical example of a human being who lives purely by faith (see Heb. 11), and throughout his life enjoys a direct relationship with God. Through faith, Abraham goes out from his homeland in Egypt, trusting only in the promise of God (see Gen. 12–13): 'he left behind his worldly understanding and took with him his faith'.[21] Through faith also Abraham believes God's promise that, through his descendants, 'all the Gentiles shall be blessed in you' (Gal. 3.8; cf. Gen. 17.1–8), even when he and his wife Sarah had come to a childless old age. The final test of Abraham's faith comes in God's command that he should sacrifice his son (Gen. 22.2). Here again, Abraham has faith enough immediately to follow God's command and, in an apparently absurd way, to carry on believing God's earlier promise that the earth would be blessed through his descendants: he 'believed on the strength of the absurd, for all human calculation had long since been suspended'.[22]

Abraham does not expect that answering God's call to sacrifice Isaac will make him happy, either in the short or the long term. On the contrary, the loss of his son would cause him and Sarah unutterable grief and anguish. Moreover, to any outside observer, Abraham's actions would appear to be the opposite of virtuous: completely irrational and cruel. There is no way that the action of killing your son could lead to a good or happy *telos* for any of the people involved, nor could such a gruesome action ever be fitted into any sane ethical system. And yet this is God's command to Abraham at this precise moment in his life, a command to which he must respond in faith, putting aside thoughts of happiness or reason: 'faith begins precisely where thinking leaves off'.[23] In terms of any system of ethics, Abraham

---

20 *Choosing the Common Good* 8–9.
21 Kierkegaard (1843), p. 50.
22 Kierkegaard (1843), p. 65.
23 Kierkegaard (1843), p. 82.

is a murderer, but from a religious point of view, he is a man of faith.[24]

Kierkegaard's analysis of this story pushes some of the insights of Nominalism and Voluntarism to their limits. It reflects the Voluntarist emphasis on the absolute will and commandment of God, which must be obeyed, even when God's will and command seem by any objective standards to be actively immoral. Even murdering a son can be good if God commands that this should be done. Kierkegaard's exposition of Abraham's predicament further reflects a Nominalist stress on the drama of the decision that confronts the person of faith at each moment. It is this decision that is truly significant, rather than overarching systems of ethics, or long-term patterns of behaviour aimed at securing happiness. Finally, and again reflecting both Voluntarist and Nominalist developments, Kierkegaard's analysis of the story of Abraham is marked by extreme individualism: 'the single individual is higher than the universal'.[25] Nothing, including religious authorities, ethical systems, or a sense of accountability should come between God and the single individual to whom God addresses his command: 'in this tie of obligation the individual relates himself absolutely, as the single individual to the absolute'.[26]

In line with Kierkegaard's analysis, although generally in a moderated form, Protestant ethicists have often sought to preserve the freedom of God, and the freshness of his command to individuals in the particular circumstances of their lives. In the words of Dietrich Bonhoeffer, 'the will of God is not a system of rules which is established from the outset; it is something new and different in each different situation in life, and for this reason a man must ever anew examine what the will of God may be'.[27] As a result, while Catholic moral thought systematically builds up and draws upon established bodies of teaching on subjects such as the common good, the just war, or the ethics of 'life', Protestant ethics tends to be more occasional, seeking to address particular moral questions as and when these arise.

However, despite the strong influence of Nominalist and Voluntarist ideas on Reformed theologians, evidence can be seen of an increasing interest in the ancient theme of happiness among them. An example is the Evangelical Anglican theologian Tom Wright, the title of whose book *Virtue Reborn* (2010) indicates a debt to the virtue-oriented ethics of Aristotle and Aquinas, but also to the Protestant, and indeed New Testament, insistence on the importance of believers being 'born again'. While Wright questions what he sees as the self-preoccupation of Aristotle's vision of virtuous living, he nonetheless argues that it is important to retain the teleological shape of his ethics, and his emphasis upon the importance of seeking true happiness

---

24 See Kierkegaard (1843), p. 85.
25 Kierkegaard (1843), pp. 84, 97.
26 Kierkegaard (1843), p. 98.
27 Bonhoeffer (1949), p. 22.

through virtuous living.[28] Wright argues that the Kingdom of God, which Jesus announces and inaugurates, is the true *telos* of the Christian life, and that the Church's life should be oriented towards it at every level. This overall vision of our true end requires Christians, aided by God's grace, to cultivate certain key 'strengths of character' – the virtues – that point towards the kingdom, and help to establish it. As Wright summarizes his arguments,

1. The goal is the new heaven and new earth, with human beings raised from the dead to be the renewed world's rulers and priests.
2. This goal is achieved through the kingdom-establishing work of Jesus and the Spirit, which we grasp by faith, participate in by baptism, and live out in love.
3. Christian living in the present consists of anticipating this ultimate reality through the Spirit-led, habit-forming, truly human practice of faith, hope, and love, sustaining Christians in their calling to worship God and reflect his glory into the world.[29]

Doing the good: faith and works

My true-love hath my heart, and I have his,
By just exchange, one for the other giv'n.
I hold his dear, and mine he cannot miss;
There never was a better bargain driv'n.

Sir Philip Sidney, *Arcadia*, book 3

According to the ethics of happiness as described by theologians such as Thomas Aquinas, God has created men and women to be creatures who have an inbuilt orientation towards happiness, and are able to some extent to cultivate the virtues that will lead to it through self-discipline and the formation of good habits. This approach to virtue, which is discussed in chapter 3, came into conflict with the strong emphasis laid by many of the Reformers on the importance of justification by faith in Christ, and their consequent downgrading of the importance of human effort and good works.

Protestant ethics

The most notorious exponent of the priority of faith over works is the German Reformer, formerly an Augustinian friar, Martin Luther (1483–1546), who succinctly articulates his approach to the subject in his *Treatise on Christian Liberty* of 1520. For Luther, theology comes before ethics, so

---

28 See Wright (2010), pp. 30–1.
29 Wright (2010), p. 60.

that in order for us to understand the Christian moral life, we must first have a clear theological picture of the overall relationship between God and human beings. This relationship is determined by Christ's saving work and, in his description of this in *Christian Liberty* and elsewhere, Luther draws on his two theological heroes: Paul and Augustine.

In many of his sermons and other writings, Augustine reflects on Paul's depiction of the unity of Christ with the Church, drawing attention both to marital metaphors in the Bible, in which Christ is understood as the Church's bridegroom, and also to physical metaphors in which Christ is understood as the head and the Church as his body (for example Eph. 5.25–33; 1 Cor. 12). For Augustine, this unity is central to the Christian gospel: 'Christ and his vine ... the head and the body, the King and his people, shepherd and flock: in short Christ and his Church [are] that total mystery with which all the scriptures are concerned.'[30] And Luther also takes up this theme, although significantly while Paul and Augustine emphasize the unity between Christ and the Church as a corporate body, Luther tends to stress the unity between Christ and the individual soul: 'faith unites the soul with Christ as a bride is united with her bridegroom. By this mystery, as the Apostle teaches, Christ and the soul become one flesh.'[31] So close is this unity between bridegroom and bride that both Augustine and Luther find in the erotic imagery of the Song of Songs an appropriate language in which to describe it: 'my beloved is mine and I am his' (S. of Sol. 2.16).[32] Drawing once again on Paul and Augustine, Luther emphasizes the way in which the unity between Christ and the believer causes an exchange between them, in which each takes on the characteristics of the other: 'he must take upon himself the things which are his bride's and bestow upon her the things that are his'.[33] When an individual has faith, then the sins, death and damnation that rightly belong to him or her are taken on by Christ and, similarly, the grace, life and salvation that belonged to Christ are now transferred to the believing individual: 'by the wedding ring of faith [Christ] shares in the sins, death and pains of hell which are his bride's' and, similarly, 'she [the soul] has the righteousness in Christ of her husband'.[34]

The context of any Christian life is then the grace of God in Jesus Christ, and the faith of the individual believer. The intense unity that characterizes the relationship between Christ and the believer, and the dramatic exchange that this unity effects, completely overshadow any attempts that human beings make to do the right thing in our daily moral lives, and their efforts to try and make themselves into better people. God's grace is given to us free

---

30 Augustine, *Exposition of Psalm* 79.1, trans. M. Boulding.
31 Luther (1520), p. 14.
32 Luther (1520), p. 15; see Augustine, *City of God* 17.20.
33 Luther (1520), p. 14.
34 Luther (1520), p. 15.

and unmerited by grace, through faith in Jesus Christ, and it is 'faith alone, without works [that] justifies, frees and saves'.[35] Here again, Luther echoes Paul's insistence, particularly in the letters to the Romans and the Galatians, that 'a person is justified not by the works of the law but through faith in Jesus Christ' (Gal. 2.16), and also that of the anti-Pelagian Augustine (highly influenced by Paul) that by grace alone men and women 'are delivered from evil, and without [it] ... they do absolutely no good thing'.[36] Thus, while Luther's particular criticisms of the medieval Church were sparked by the practice of selling of indulgences (full or partial remissions of the penances granted after absolution), underlying them was a wider attack on an entire mindset, shared, as Luther (controversially) believed, by Pharisees, Pelagians and medieval Catholics: a mindset that believes it possible for justification to come through good works and human effort. By contrast, Luther argues that 'it ought to be the first concern of every Christian to lay aside all confidence in works and increasingly to strengthen faith alone and through faith to grow in the knowledge ... of Christ Jesus, who suffered and rose for him'.[37]

Luther's condemnation of justification by works is highly influenced by the Nominalist insistence that human actions, like other entities in the world, are essentially one-off events, and not intrinsically linked together. It is impossible to make a moral judgement that a particular action is good or otherwise based on its similarity to other actions, since everything depends upon the context in which it is performed. For Luther, an action can be said to be truly good only, as Pinckaers puts it, 'when [it is] lifted up for justification by faith and accepted by the grace of God'.[38] Even the 'corporal works of mercy' such as feeding the hungry, clothing the naked and visiting the sick cannot be judged good in themselves, but will only be so if they are done in the context of faith. For, Luther writes, however commendable an individual's acts of kindness or charity might seem, 'if he were not first a believer and a Christian, all his works would amount to nothing and would be truly wicked and damnable sins'.[39]

Given the overriding importance of grace and faith, and the impossibility of our becoming righteous through our own efforts, it might then be asked what is the point of having any moral rules at all such as, for example, the Ten Commandments? Luther argues that the commandments show us what we ought to do, but do not give us the power to do it. Through knowing the commandments, we come to understand how far we fall short of the expected standard; that we are incapable of doing God's will through our own

---

35 Luther (1520), p. 11.
36 Augustine, *On Rebuke and Grace* 3.
37 Luther (1520), p. 10.
38 Pinckaers (1995), p. 282.
39 Luther (1520), pp. 23–4.

efforts, and thus that we must rely totally on grace. A particularly strong example of this is the commandment 'you shall not covet' (Exod. 20.17). Since it is virtually unthinkable that anyone could obey this commandment, it thus proves us all to be sinners. By this commandment, 'a man is compelled to despair of himself, to seek the help which he does not find in himself elsewhere and from someone else'.[40] Paradoxically, this despair in our own abilities takes us back to precisely where we need to be: to the awareness of our need for grace and incorporation into Christ's life through faith.

A further question, and one which also troubled Paul and Augustine,[41] is whether, given the overriding importance of grace, any efforts and struggles that men and women might make to live a good life are pointless. Luther argues trenchantly, however, that while in the life of a justified sinner, such works will arise naturally from faith and grace, as a good tree gives rise to good fruit (Matt. 7.18): 'we do not ... reject good works; on the contrary, we cherish and teach them as much as possible. We do not condemn them for their own sake but ... the perverse idea that righteousness is to be sought through them.'[42]

The emphasis laid by Luther and other Reformers on justification by faith, and their suspicion of anything that resembled 'works righteousness' has come to epitomize Protestant approaches to ethics. However, in the modern period, the German theologian and martyr Dietrich Bonhoeffer (1906–45) was to criticize the way in which the German Lutheran Church of his day had interpreted Luther's teaching. In *The Cost of Discipleship*, which Bonhoeffer wrote shortly before the start of the Second World War, he argues that the authentic Lutheran teaching that grace is *free* had been misunderstood by Protestant (and in particular, Lutheran) Christians to support an apparently similar but in fact quite different belief that grace is *cheap*. Bonhoeffer contends that the Protestant insistence that grace is given to us unmerited and free of charge had led many people to believe that it could be obtained without the costly discipleship to which the title of his book refers:

> Cheap grace is the preaching of forgiveness without requiring repentance, baptism without church discipline, Communion without confession, absolution without personal confession. Cheap grace is grace without discipleship, grace without the cross, grace without Jesus Christ, living and incarnate.[43]

In Luther's own life, Bonhoeffer argues, grace had been anything but cheap. Twice he had to leave everything he had to follow Christ: the first time

---

40 Luther (1520), p. 11.
41 See Romans 6.1.
42 Luther (1520), p. 26.
43 Bonhoeffer (1937), p. 36.

when he became a monk and 'the call to the cloister demanded of [him] the complete surrender of his life', and the second time when he had, as he saw it, obeyed Christ's call to re-enter the world and preach the gospel of pure grace in what he believed to be a corrupt Church. In the life of subsequent Lutheran Christians, the preaching of cheap grace had been a disaster, more damaging by far than the doctrine of justification by works, which it had been intended to supersede.[44]

Do we ... realise that this cheap grace has turned back upon us like a boomerang? The price we are having to pay today in the shape of the collapse of the organised church is only the inevitable consequence of our policy of making grace available to all at too low a cost. We gave away the word and sacraments wholesale, we baptised, confirmed, and absolved a whole nation unasked and without condition. Our humanitarian sentiment made us give that which was holy to the scornful and unbelieving. We poured forth unending streams of grace. But the call to follow Jesus in the narrow way was hardly ever heard.[45]

In Bonhoeffer's view, a clear connection could be drawn between the preaching of cheap grace and the political events unfolding in 1930s' Germany. The assurance of free and abounding grace to the whole nation, with the resultant loss of the costly spiritual disciplines necessary to follow Jesus Christ, had made the mainstream Evangelical Church in Germany so accommodated to its society, and so spiritually flaccid that it lacked the muscle to resist the rise of the real evil of National Socialism under Adolf Hitler. Thus, in the opinion of Bonhoeffer, as of his fellow leaders of the breakaway Confessing Church, such as Martin Niemöller and Marga Neusel, real resistance to National Socialism would require both a revision of Luther's teaching about the absolute rights of secular authority, and also a correction of the way that his teaching about grace had been understood. In order to stand against Hitler, Christian men and women would have to be renewed in the costly disciplines of following Jesus.

Catholic ethics

While Bonhoeffer's words in *The Cost of Discipleship* call into question some aspects of the way in which Protestants have understood the doctrine of justification by faith, in a parallel movement, some more recent Catholic commentators have expressed dissatisfaction with the way in which their own tradition has sometimes presented the Christian moral life primarily as a matter of unflinching obedience to a rigid set of rules. Recent Catholic

---

44 See Bonhoeffer (1937), p. 46.
45 Bonhoeffer (1937), p. 45.

moral theology has sought to redress this balance by emphasizing more strongly the importance of the work of Christ, and of the key role played by grace and faith.

An example of this may be found in a work that has already been discussed in this chapter: Pope John Paul II's encyclical *Veritatis Splendor*. It was noted above that this encyclical on ethics begins not with the philosophical abstractions about human nature that have sometimes characterized Catholic moral theology, but with the very human story from the gospels: that of Jesus' encounter with the rich young man (Matt. 19.16–22 and parallels) – a story that incidentally is also central to Bonhoeffer's *The Cost of Discipleship*. Commenting on Mark's version of Jesus' response to the rich young man's initial question, 'why do you call me good? No one is good but God alone' (Mark 10.18), John Paul notes how Jesus insists that ethical questions are primarily theological questions. 'Jesus', he writes, 'shows that the young man's question is really a religious question, and that the goodness that attracts and at the same time obliges man has its source in God, and indeed is God himself. God alone is worthy of being loved "with all one's heart, and with all one's soul, and with all one's mind" (Matt. 22.37).'[46] Thus, John Paul shares Luther's concern that theology should come before ethics; that moral thought must be framed within an overall understanding of who God is, and of the nature of our relationship with God. Indeed, he affirms that the second 'table' of the Ten Commandments (commandments 5–10), which give rules for specifically ethical behaviour about matters such as stealing, murder and adultery, only make sense when it is seen within the context of the first table of the Decalogue (commandments 1–4) 'which calls us to acknowledge God as the one Lord of all and to worship him alone for his infinite holiness'.[47]

Further to this, John Paul is also, like Luther, concerned that Christian ethics should be Christological. Commenting on Jesus' words, 'Come follow me' (Matt. 19.21), he emphasizes that the Christian moral life, far from being legalistic obedience to a set of static precepts, is about a relationship with Jesus, following in his way and, through the work of the Holy Spirit, ultimately becoming conformed to him and sharing in his life.[48] The moral life is 'not a matter only of disposing oneself to hear a teaching and obediently accepting a commandment [but] ... it involves holding fast to the very person of Jesus, partaking of his life and his destiny, sharing in his free and loving obedience to the will of the Father'.[49] John Paul adds to this a characteristically Catholic insistence that following Jesus is not just an individual matter, but entails life within the Church, since it is through baptism and

---

46 John Paul II, *Veritatis Splendor* 9.3.
47 John Paul II, *Veritatis Splendor* 11.1; cf. Exodus 20.1–11.
48 See John Paul II, *Veritatis Splendor* 21.1.
49 John Paul II, *Veritatis Splendor* 19.1.

the Eucharist that men and women are assimilated into Christ and become not just his followers but members of his body. As Augustine can even go so far as to say to newly baptized Christians in Hippo, 'Marvel and rejoice: we have become Christ!'[50]

The encyclical further emphasizes the importance of grace: human beings cannot respond to Christ's call to perfection through their own unaided efforts. Commenting on Jesus' words at the end of the narrative, 'For God all things are possible' (Matt. 19.26), John Paul affirms the absolute importance of grace in the Christian moral life: 'the moral life presents itself as the response due to the many gratuitous initiatives taken by God out of love for man'.[51] He emphasizes that 'no human effort, not even the most rigorous observance of the commandments, succeeds in "fulfilling" the law'.[52] For John Paul, as for Luther, the law has a 'pedagogic' function because its commandments teach sinful man 'to take stock of his own powerlessness and by stripping him of the presumption of his self-sufficiency, leads him to ask for and to receive "life in the Spirit"'.[53] It is only in the new life of grace that human beings have any hope of fulfilling the commandments in their fullness. In Augustine's words, 'the law was given that grace might be sought; and grace was given, that the law might be fulfilled'.[54]

Thus, in some key aspects of its overall approach to these questions, *Veritatis Splendor* illustrates a shift in Catholic moral theology away from a legalistic emphasis upon duties and laws that is more reminiscent of Kant (see next chapter) than of Christianity. For, while John Paul II in *Veritatis Splendor* is very clear about the rules that he expects Catholics to obey, he nonetheless locates the centre of Christian moral life not in obeying rules, but in God's freely given gift of grace, through which, animated by the Holy Spirit, men and women can live in union with Christ, and do the will of the Father: 'the New Law is the grace of the Holy Spirit given through faith in Christ'.[55]

---

50 Augustine, *Tractates on the Gospel of John* 21.8, quoted in John Paul II, *Veritatis Splendor* 21.2.

51 John Paul II, *Veritatis Splendor* 10.3.

52 John Paul II, *Veritatis Splendor* 11.2.

53 John Paul II, *Veritatis Splendor* 23.1.

54 Augustine, *Tractates on the Gospel of John* 21.8, quoted in John Paul II, *Veritatis Splendor* 23.1.

55 Aquinas, *Summa Theologica* 1-2. 106, quoted in John Paul II, *Veritatis Splendor* 24.4.

Knowing the good: reason and revelation

Nature with open volume stands
To spread her Maker's praise abroad,
And every labour of his hands
Shows something worthy of a God.

Isaac Watts (1674–1748)

Aquinas's generally positive assessment of human beings as oriented towards happiness and towards God as their origin and ultimate end has further repercussions for his assessment of our capacity for moral knowledge. Exercising our God-given intellectual faculties in reasoned reflection on ourselves and on all God has created through his Word and his Spirit, human beings can understand in some measure what are God's good purposes for them. Such an approach underlies much reflection on natural law. Natural law thinking, in a theme that was discussed in chapter 2, assumes a basic confidence that our observation (of ourselves, of other people, and of the world around us) is capable of teaching us some important lessons about ethics. The Protestant tradition however has characteristically questioned whether such confidence can be justified.

In the natural law tradition, since God is the author both of what later theologians would describe as 'the book of nature' and 'the book of scripture', we may confidently expect that both of these will teach the same moral lessons. Human reason used rightly will reinforce biblical teaching and, indeed, show how sensible and true-to-life that teaching truly is. For many of the Reformers, however, assigning anything like this role to human reason was problematic. Highly influenced by Augustine's assessment of human potentialities after the Fall, Protestant ethics characteristically emphasizes the intellectual limitations of fallen human beings, whose vision is clouded by original sin, when they try to perceive God's ways in the created world. Rather, to use the best-known motto of the Reformers, knowledge of God's will may be gained *sola scriptura*: 'by Scripture alone'. As Luther writes in *Christian Liberty*, 'let us consider it certain and firmly established that the soul can do without anything except the Word of God and that where the Word of God is missing there is no help at all for the soul'.[56]

Thus a rift emerged between Catholic ethics, reliant upon natural law, as understood by human reason, and Protestant ethics, looking instead to the scriptural revelation. Although this debate was to become very polarized, it is important to note that the original divisions were not as sharp as we might expect. The Reformers would have been aware that Augustine himself believed that, even after original sin, human beings retained an inner sense of God's law: 'the law written in the hearts of men which not even iniquity

---

56 Luther (1520), p. 8.

itself destroys'.[57] Similarly, many of the Reformers including John Calvin (1509–64) and Luther himself retained some sense that knowledge of God as creator, if not of God as redeemer, could be discerned from 'the things he has made' (cf. Rom. 1.20). Anglican writers in particular, among those of the reformed churches, often retained a strong sense of the importance of natural law. Richard Hooker (1554–1600), for example, argued that 'the benefit of nature's light [should] be not thought excluded as unnecessary, because the necessity of a diviner light [that of Scripture] is magnified'.[58] In more modern times also, although we can still see this rift between revelation and reason, it is important to note a degree of convergence that makes this polarization less extreme than it might appear.

Protestant ethics

This is partly apparent in the stress that many Protestant ethicists lay on the role that reason must play when we are attempting to understand the moral teaching of Scripture. An example of such an approach may be found in the work of the Anglican ethicist Andrew Goddard on the implications of Calvin's interpretation of the biblical condemnation of lending out money at interest (see Exod. 22.25). Analysing the manner of Calvin's appeal to the Bible on this question Goddard asserts, in typically Protestant style, the priority of the Bible for ethics as for other matters of doctrine, over and above other sources. As Calvin himself writes, 'we shall have to turn back to the Word of the Lord, in which we have a sure rule for understanding. For Scripture is the school of the Holy Spirit.'[59] However, while asserting the primacy of Scripture for ethics, Goddard also emphasizes the crucial role that reason has to play if the rules and norms of Scripture are to be successfully applied to contemporary moral questions.

The form that such reasoned reflection on Scripture should take goes, in the first place, beyond subjecting relevant biblical passages to closer and closer exegesis. Careful exegesis of Scripture is of course necessary for Christian ethical reflection, but it is 'certainly not *sufficient* for good Christian moral reasoning'.[60] Goddard quotes with approval O'Donovan's observation that 'interpreters who think they can determine the proper ethical application of the Bible solely through more sophisticated exegesis are like people who believe that they can fly if only they flap their arms hard enough'.[61] The inadequacy of such an approach is particularly obvious when the Bible does

---

57 Augustine, *Confessions* 2.4.9.

58 Hooker, *Laws of Ecclesiastical Polity* 1.14.4.

59 Calvin, *Institutes of the Christian Religion* III.xxi.3, quoted by A. Goddard in S. W. Chung (2003) (ed.), *Alister E. McGrath & Evangelical Theology: A Dynamic Engagement* (Carlisle: Paternoster Press), p. 258.

60 Goddard in Chung (ed.) (2003), p. 251, my italics.

61 Goddard in Chung (ed.) (2003), p. 251.

not even address particular issues that are being considered, for example fox-hunting or genetic engineering. However, even when a moral question under scrutiny *does* appear to answer directly to a piece of moral guidance provided by the Bible, it is nonetheless necessary to reason from biblically derived moral and theological principles, rather than simply assembling a series of apparently relevant individual texts.

Goddard cites with approval the work of the Baptist ethicist and biblical scholar, C. H. Cosgrove who argues in his book *Appealing to Scripture in Moral Debate* that 'analogical reasoning is an appropriate and necessary method for applying scripture to contemporary moral issues'.[62] Thus, every time we move from some biblical paradigm case to a contemporary moral question, we must be aware that we are crossing a wide cultural gap. We reason, Cosgrove argues, 'from like to like, not from identical to identical'.[63] Inevitably, there will be occasions when we find that the meaning and context of a particular biblical text is so different to our own that we cannot reasonably draw an analogy between them and, in some cases, this discrepancy between the different contexts may be so extreme that even some clearly defined rules in the biblical context must be reframed or even abandoned altogether in a different context. On this subject, Goddard cites Calvin's reflection that the enormous differences between Jewish society in the Old Testament and the realities of financial life in sixteenth-century Europe mean that the categorical condemnation of usury in the Old Testament may justifiably be relaxed. However, whether or not we ultimately are able to draw analogies between the biblical situation and our own, the exercise of reason will always have a vital, if ancillary, role if we are to bring such teaching to bear on contemporary issues.

Case study: the exodus[64]

An inter-denominational group of university students decide to set up a club to campaign on social issues. The leader of the group Stacey launches the club with a stirring speech. She talks about the foundational story of the exodus in the Old Testament and its message for the liberation of all people here and now. Stacey concludes her speech with the following words: 'brothers and sisters, the story of Moses leading the people of Israel out of slavery in Egypt inspires us, in fact commands us to do something about oppression wherever we encounter it. This group needs to stand up not

---

62 Cosgrove (2002), p. 51.
63 Cosgrove (2002), p. 53.
64 This case study is suggested by Cosgrove (2002), pp. 72–89, and draws on his analysis.

only for people who live in circumstances of extreme economic poverty in today's world, but also for all other oppressed groups in our society whose humanity is denied them. These include the poor, women, ethnic minorities, gay and transgender people, animals and indeed the whole environment.' After her speech, Stacey is approached by two of her fellow students who want to question different aspects of what she has said.

The first of these, Gavin, a postgraduate Old Testament student, says, 'Stacey, I enjoyed your speech and felt inspired by it, but I'm uncomfortable with some of the things you said at the end. My main problem with it was that I think the Old Testament authors really thought that it was wrong to treat the Israelites like slaves because the Israelites were God's chosen people. If they'd been any other people, it wouldn't have mattered so much. Also, you've got a rather modern view of what's wrong with slavery: what the Israelites probably resented the most wasn't that their humanity was denied, but just that they were made to work unreasonably hard.

A second student, Anne, is the head of the Christian Union. She says, 'Stacey, I was quite frankly appalled by what you said at the end of your speech. You can't possibly read all that into Exodus. Yes, God does want us to stand up for people who are economically disadvantaged, but that doesn't have anything to do with gay and transgender people – that's more of an issue about personal morality. And it certainly doesn't have anything to do with animals, because Genesis tells us that we've got dominion over them. I think you went way too far, and I'm resigning from the group.'

Questions for discussion

What do you think about the analogies that Stacey draws in her speech?

How strong do you find the objections to them put forward by Gavin and Anne?

Catholic ethics

If the writing of ethicists such as Goddard and Cosgrove within the Reformed tradition indicate an enhanced, if secondary, valuation of the role of reason in ethics, it is also evident that much Catholic moral thought has tended to show a fuller engagement with revelation. This is related to wider developments within Catholic theology, which were given impetus by the Second Vatican Council in the 1960s, and which have resulted in the flowering of Catholic biblical scholarship since that time. This fuller engagement with the Bible has had profound effects on the way in which ethical questions are approached: a development reflected in the Council's decree on the training of priests, *Optatam Totius*:

> Special care is to be taken for the improvement of moral theology. Its scientific presentation, drawing more fully on the teaching of holy scripture, should highlight the lofty vocation of the Christian faithful and their obligation to bring forth fruit in charity for the life of the world.[65]

Evidence of this shift towards a more biblically based approach to moral theology may be found in many places, including, again, John Paul II's encyclical *Veritatis Splendor*. As has already been noted, John Paul uses a passage from the Bible, the rich young man's question to Jesus, as the basis for the entire encyclical's subsequent ethical teaching. Similarly, the 1994 *Catechism of the Catholic Church* places the Beatitudes from Matthew's Gospel under the corresponding title *Our Vocation to Beatitude* at the start of its section on the Christian moral life.[66]

In an essay entitled *Scripture and the Renewal of Moral Theology*,[67] Pinckaers reflects on this development. He criticizes much Catholic ethics from the end of the Middle Ages until the modern period for having been primarily based on a somewhat static conception of natural law. Reflection on the Bible tended to concentrate narrowly on the few parts of it that were seen to be in obvious conformity with natural law, in particular the Ten Commandments. The renewed attention given to Scripture by Catholic ethicists in more recent years has demonstrated that a variety of key biblical themes are in fact central to the Christian moral (and not just spiritual) life. These include some themes that have already been discussed in this chapter, such as the Christian hope for eternal beatitude, the importance of faith and the 'new law' of grace. In line with the *Catechism of the Catholic Church*, Pinckaers emphasizes the moral teaching of the Sermon on the Mount (Matthew 5–7), which he argues is particularly important precisely because it cannot be reduced to the strict commands and minimum requirements that have often characterized Catholic moral teaching in recent centuries. Rather, Pinckaers writes that the Sermon on the Mount 'is animated by a continuous tendency towards exceeding and surpassing, a tendency toward the progress and perfection of love in imitation of the Father's goodness'.[68]

---

65 *Optatam Totius* 16.
66 *Catechism of the Catholic Church* 1716.
67 See Pinckaers (2005), chapter 3.
68 Pinckaers (2005), p. 52.

Describing the good (and the bad): sin and sins

Sins oft committed now we lay before thee:
With true contrition, now no more we veil them:
Grant us, Redeemer, loving absolution.

Lent Prose, *New English Hymnal*

A final distinction between Catholic and Protestant ethics lies in the emphasis of the former on sins (in the plural) and the latter on sin (in the singular). This distinction is connected to the importance of auricular confession (confessing sins to a priest), described by Mahoney as 'the single most influential factor in the development of the practice and of the discipline of moral theology'.[69]

The early Christians interpreted Jesus' conferral of power on the apostles to bind and loose (see John 20.22–23; Matt. 16.19; 18.18) as giving the Church authority publicly to excommunicate sinners from, and reconcile them to, the Christian community. Some rigorist groups were reluctant to acknowledge that there could be any way back to communion for those who had committed the three most serious sins of idolatry, adultery and murder. However, by the fourth century, in most parts of the Church, a system had developed whereby those who had committed serious sins would do penance over a long period of time before being readmitted to communion. This system's extreme rigour led many converts to Christianity in this period, notoriously the Emperor Constantine (272–337), to delay baptism until they were close to death.

A means of addressing this unsatisfactory situation came from within the monastic communities that, by the fourth century, were emerging in various countries, particularly Ireland and Wales. In such communities, it was necessary to develop mechanisms for the forgiveness of small sins, and as monasticism became increasingly influential, its internal system of penitence was exported to the wider Church. This spawned an extensive literature of handbooks for confessors, often described as *Penitentials*, 'practical and indispensable ready reckoners',[70] which enabled confessors to adjudicate the seriousness of particular sins, and to assign appropriate penances. Through the emerging practice of confession and absolution, the Church acquired a way to extend the forgiving and healing power of Christ to repentant sinners. However, the Penitentials reveal a rigidly systematized and often lurid understanding of morality and human sin. In one particularly significant development for later disputes within the Church, in some places penitents

---

69 Mahoney (1987), p. 1. This section draws on Mahoney (1987), chapter 1; Pinckaers (1995), chapter 12.
70 Mahoney (1987), p. 15.

unable to discharge their penance could 'redeem' it by giving money to good causes, or even pay others to share the penance, or assume it altogether.[71]

Confession terminology

Confessor	the priest hearing the confession
Confessional	the place (traditionally an enclosed box) in which confessions are made to a priest
Penitent	the person making the confession
Penance	the task assigned to the penitent to be done before (in earlier practice) or after (in later practice) absolution
Absolution	the priest's declaration of God's forgiveness
Contrition	the penitent's sorrow for his or her sins
Seal	the rule that strictly forbids confessors to reveal the content of confessions

---

Catholic ethics

By 1215, the importance of confession had become so embedded in the Church that the Second Lateran Council, convoked by the powerful reforming Pope Innocent III, decreed that 'all the faithful of both sexes, after they have reached the age of discernment, should individually confess all their sins in a faithful manner to their own priest at least once a year'.[72] This decree inevitably led to an increased demand for the clergy to hear confessions, which itself gave rise to the publication of numerous *Summas* or compendiums for confessors during the course of the Middle Ages. The importance of confession was further emphasized at the Council of Trent which took place through the 1550s and 1560s, and aimed to consolidate and reform Roman Catholic teaching in response to the Reformation. This led to a renewed emphasis on the training of clergy for ministry as confessors, a particular work of the newly founded Jesuit and Redemptorist orders. A notable member of the latter order was Alphonsus de Liguori (1696–1787), whom Pope Pius XII declared patron saint of confessors and moral theologians, thus reinforcing the link between these two professions.[73]

---

71 See Mahoney (1987), pp. 10–11.

72 This was the Council's twenty-first decree.

73 See Mahoney (1987), p. 36.

Moral theology in the Catholic tradition has thus largely been at the service of confessional practice: equipping priests for their work in the confessional. As James Gustafson summarizes it:

> Writings in moral theology are used not only to teach persons what principles ought to guide their conduct and what actions are judged morally illicit; they also provide the priest whose vocation is to administer the sacrament of penance with criteria by which he can enumerate and judge the seriousness of various sinful acts in order to assign the appropriate penance.[74]

The importance of developing literature that would guide priests in their hearing of confessions gave rise to systematic and precise analysis of sinful actions of all kinds, and of the intentions that lead to them. Among the many distinctions that were drawn between different types of sin, two that were particularly important were those between mortal and venial sins (see below), or between formal and material sin (see chapter 8).

Mortal and venial sins

Mortal sin destroys charity in the heart of man by a grave violation of God's law; it turns a man away from God, who is his ultimate end and his beatitude, by preferring an inferior good to him.

Venial sin allows charity to subsist, even though it offends and wounds it.

Catechism of the Catholic Church, paragraph 1855.

The practice of confession in the Catholic tradition extended the assurance of God's forgiveness to countless people. It was said, for example, of John Henry Newman's confessional work in Birmingham that 'the chapel where he sat for hours in a bug-ridden confessional seems above all to have represented a source of help, warmth and meaning for factory girls who had lost contact with any other'.[75] However, modern commentators have criticized some of aspects of confessional practice and the moral theology to which it gave rise. Among such criticisms is that many confessors and moralists were so busy adjudicating the seriousness of sins that they tended to ignore the importance of virtue in the Christian moral life. Moreover, the concentration on individual moral laws and their infringement – on *sins* as opposed to *sin* – tended to reinforce the Nominalist view of the moral life as a series

---

74 Gustafson (1978), p. 2.
75 J. Bossy, quoted in Mahoney (1987), p. 28.

of isolated decisions, and thus to lose the wider picture of an individual's longer-term orientation towards, or away from, God, the good and human happiness. As Mahoney writes, 'it led ... to an approach to the moral life as discontinuous; "freezing" the film in a jerky succession of individual "stills" to be analysed and ignoring the plot'.[76] More recently, Catholic moral theologians have sought to redress this by arguing that, in addition to enumerating specific sins, it is also necessary for men and women to look more widely at people's so-called 'fundamental option', in other words, at the overall orientation of their lives. The importance of the fundamental option is addressed by John Paul II in *Veritatis Splendor*, who affirms that:

> The morality of the New Covenant is ... dominated by the fundamental call of Jesus to follow him – thus he also says to the young man: 'If you wish to be perfect ... then come, follow me' (Matt. 19.21); to this call the disciple must respond with a radical decision and choice.[77]

Protestant ethics

Although the practice of confession has continued in some of the Reformed churches, it is far more usual for congregations to confess their sins together, as they do for example when making the 'General Confession' in the Anglican Book of Common Prayer. Moreover, in such general confessions, whatever the denomination, congregations are normally encouraged to own up to a more general state of separation from God and need for grace, rather than to enumerate specific sins.[78] Emphasizing Paul's insistence that 'all have sinned and fall short of the glory of God' (Rom. 3.23), Protestant moral teaching has tended to have little use for the precise distinctions developed by Catholic moral theology between different types of sin, with their varying levels of seriousness. As the evangelical preacher and writer Nicky Gumbel puts it:

> The New Testament says that if we break any part of the Law we are guilty of breaking all of it (James 2.10). It is not possible, for example, to have a 'reasonably clean' driving licence. Either it is clean or it is not. One driving offence stops it from being a clean licence. So it is with us. One offence makes our lives unclean.[79]

---

76 Mahoney (1987), p. 31.

77 John Paul II, *Veritatis Splendor* 66.1. It should be noted, however, that while affirming the importance of the fundamental option, the encyclical nonetheless also affirms traditional confessional practice and criticizes the way in which some Catholic ethicists have, as he sees it, come to 'separate the fundamental option from concrete kinds of behaviour'. See John Paul II, *Veritatis Splendor* 67.2.

78 See Gustafson (1978), p. 3.

79 N. Gumbel (2001), *Questions of Life* (London: Kingsway Publications), p. 43.

One small but significant indication of this difference between the two traditions may be found by comparing the wording of the *Agnus Dei* (the prayer at the breaking of the bread) in the English translation of the 1962 Roman Missal to that in the Church of England's *Common Worship*. While in the former, the congregation says or sings, 'Lamb of God, you take away the *sins* of the world', the words of the latter are 'Lamb of God, you take away the *sin* of the world'.

A result of the Protestant emphasis on sin in the singular has been a weakness in the area of casuistry. Casuistry, a key term in theological ethics, is the activity of applying general moral rules and principles to particular cases, which historically has been the task not only of Catholic confessors and moral theologians, but also of Jewish rabbis. (The *halakha* – literally the 'way of walking' – is a form of casuistry, since it enables Jewish men and women to apply the principles enshrined in the law to the daily conduct of their lives.) For a variety of historical and theological reasons, however, casuistry has long had a pejorative sense: associated with finding ingenious ways to keep the letter of the law, while ignoring its spirit. The Catholic tradition has often been criticized, not least by some Catholic moral theologians, for placing an excessive emphasis on casuistry, in the belief that it is possible to remove all moral ambiguity from life by settling difficult cases once and for all. Such an emphasis can ignore the provisional nature of human moral judgements, and downplay the key virtue of prudence: the ability to react appropriately to the complex and unpredictable moral situations that life inevitably throws at us (see chapter 3). Echoing such criticisms, Michael Banner comments that 'a moral theology which busies itself only with identifying and categorizing sins will be prone to legalism, individualism, and moralism'.[80]

However, casuistry remains an important activity: careful thought about the particular forms that sin might take, and the principles that might be applied to particular situations in order to avoid it, must surely always be an essential part of ethical reflection. The tendency of ethics in the Reformed traditions to emphasize sin as an overall condition, and to be uninterested in analysing specific forms of sinful behaviour can lead to vagueness about what men and women are actually supposed to do, or not to do. As Banner writes:

There is ... nothing wrong in thinking clearly and carefully about our moral obligations in particular and difficult cases, and thus about what constitutes wrongdoing or sin ... Indeed, if one looks at the best examples from the tradition, the value of careful and rigorous examination of an issue is evident – thus the sixteenth-century Spanish Dominican, Vitoria, in his work *De Indiis* (On the American Indians), provides a careful and

---

80 Banner (2009), p. 54.

thorough demolition of the motley collection of claims which were being advanced to justify the king of Spain's conquest of the Americas. Since 'casuistry' means careful examination of a cause or issue or problem, there is no good reason for casuistry as such to have a bad name.[81]

Questions for discussion

What do you think are the most significant differences that this chapter has covered between Catholic and Protestant ethics?

How fundamental do you think these differences are?

---

81 Banner (2009), p. 54.

6

Modern Approaches to Ethics

Theological ethics do not take place in a vacuum, but relate to and interact with wider developments and controversies. The following somewhat whimsical case study, suggested by the philosopher R. M. Hare (1919–2002), can be used to highlight some of the different approaches that are discussed in this chapter.[1]

Case study

A fat man leading a group of people out of a cave on a coast is stuck in the mouth of that cave. In a short time high tide will be upon them, and unless he is unstuck, they will all be drowned except the fat man, whose head is out of the cave. But, fortunately, or unfortunately, someone has with him a stick of dynamite. There seems no way to get the fat man loose without using that dynamite which will inevitably kill him; but if they do not use it everyone will drown. What should they do?[1]

Consider what should be the proper response and why.

Deontological ethics

Deontological ethics emphasize the importance of duty (in Greek: *deon*) and obligation. Immanuel Kant (1724–1804), the classic expositor of such ethics in the modern period lays out his approach to the subject in his short book, *Groundwork of the Metaphysic of Morals*. Kant's starting point is the will of the individual human subject. The good will is the only thing that is good in itself, irrespective of any effects that it may or may not accomplish.[2] Although we would certainly hope that our good will would bring to fruition the good purposes that we intend, its goodness does not depend

---

1 This version of a story well-known to philosophers is from www.friesian.com/valley/dilemmas.htm

2 Kant (1785), p. 3; see Wells and Quash (2010), pp. 121–4.

upon our ability to do this. Thus, even if we are completely inept at bringing our plans to fruition, our good will would nevertheless 'still shine like
a jewel for its own sake as something which has its full value in itself'.[3] In
life as we normally experience it, with its many complications and difficulties, we cannot always simply will what is good, and so need the concept of
duty which indicates to us how a good will would direct us to act. As Kant's
translator, H. J. Paton puts it, *'under human conditions*, where we have to
struggle against unruly impulses and desires, a good will is manifested in
acting *for the sake of duty'*.[4] A truly moral action is one that we take from
the motive of duty, and not out of self-interest. A human agent acting well is
one who consciously and consistently acts from the motive of duty.

Where do we gain moral guidance?

For Kant, the mainspring of morality is to be found in human reason. While
animals follow their instinct, human beings are guided by reason, and the
true function of reason is to show us where our duty lies, and thus where
our will should be directed. If I, as an autonomous agent, choose a particular action for its own sake, because I am convinced on rational grounds
that it is my duty, rather than because I am influenced by other, what Kant
terms *heteronomous*, considerations, then this action is truly my own, and
I am truly free. Kant's emphasis on the importance of reason, and of deriving moral rules from human rationality alone accompanies his view that
we should *not* look for moral guidance in three places where we might be
tempted to try and find it.

First, we should not look for moral guidance from the outside world that
we can experience through our senses. Kant writes that moral concepts
'cannot be abstracted from any empirical, and therefore merely contingent,
knowledge',[5] but are available to us through reason alone. Things that we
might see, touch, hear or otherwise experience are subject to flux and alter-
ation, and thus cannot dictate to us our moral duty. Neither can we derive
our ethics from any supposed facts about human nature (as a natural law
approach might seek to do), since these also derive from empirical observation.[6] Rather, as Roger Scruton puts it, morality 'finds the ends of action by
abstracting from everything but the fact of rational agency'.[7]

A second place in which we should not look for ethical guidance is our
own inclinations, however worthy or otherwise these may be, for these too,
as most of us know only too well, are also subject to change. We must

---

3 Kant (1785), p. 3.
4 Kant (1785), p. 10.
5 Kant (1785), p. 34.
6 Cf. Kant (1948), p. 59.
7 Scruton, R. (2001), *Kant, a Very Short Introduction* (Oxford: Oxford University
Press), p. 86.

choose instead 'only that which reason *independently of inclination* rec-ognises ... to be good'.[8] Rationally derived morality dictates its own terms and plays according to its own rules. Thus, Kant diverges from the ethics of Aristotle and Aquinas that were discussed in the previous chapter by insist-ing that the purpose of acting morally is not primarily to be happy. Rather, we should act well simply because it is our duty to do so, whether this makes us happy or not: 'let justice be done, though the heavens fall'. Kant affirms that happiness is sought by all, and rightly so: 'to assure one's own happiness is a duty'.[9] However, he rejects the belief that happiness can be fundamental to ethics: 'making a man happy is quite different from making him good and making him prudent or astute in seeking his advantage quite different from making him virtuous'.[10]

A third and final place where we should not look for moral guidance is in religious codes of right and wrong. In a way that is characteristic of the Enlightenment, Kant advocates that morality must make its own rules and stand on its own terms. Ethics should be rooted in the rational powers of the human subject, independent of theology or Church teaching. Thus, his stated aim in the *Groundwork* is to develop 'a completely isolated meta-physic of morals, mixed with no anthropology, no theology, no physics or hyper-physics, still less with occult qualities'.[11] Indeed, far from deriving moral duties from religious codes, things almost work the other way round. It is not so much that God reveals to us our moral duties, but rather that our awareness of moral duties is so strong that they themselves seem to imply that God exists. 'The moral life,' writes Scruton, 'imposes an intimation of transcendental reality; we feel compelled towards the belief in God, in immortality, and in a divine ordinance in nature.'[12]

By rigorously excluding these possible different sources of moral know-ledge, Kant demonstrates that, for him, true ethics are pure ethics, somewhat similar to pure mathematics or pure logic: 'to behold virtue in her true shape is nothing other than to show morality stripped of all admixture with the sensuous and of all the spurious adornments of reward and self-love'.[13] Kant argues that this very abstract and formal starting point should not mean that his ethics is completely impractical. In the same way that, once we have a sure grasp of pure mathematics or logic, we are well equipped to apply these disciplines in particular situations so, once we have a sure grasp of ethical theory, this too can be applied in real-life situations.

---

8 Kant (1785), pp. 36–7 (my italics).
9 Kant (1785), p. 11.
10 Kant (1785), p. 32.
11 Kant (1785), pp. 32–3.
12 Scruton (2001), p. 95.
13 Kant (1785), p. 61, n. 1.

What is the moral guidance that we gain?

In the *Groundwork of the Metaphysic of Morals*, Kant develops a contrast between what he calls the hypothetical and categorical imperatives. The former of these tells us what we must do if we want to achieve a particular aim. Hypothetical imperatives 'declare a possible action to be practically necessary *as a means to the attainment of* something else that one wills',[14] such as 'if you want to become fit, take exercise'. Hypothetical imperatives are thus not absolute, because they only bind us under certain circumstances: the particular precept or command depends upon the purpose that we are ultimately pursuing. If we no longer have the purpose of becoming fit, then we could abandon the precept of taking exercise, and so 'we can always escape from the precept if we abandon the purpose'.[15]

The categorical imperative, however, does not contain an 'if', but rather, makes a particular action 'objectively necessary in itself apart from its relation to a final end'.[16] Categorical imperatives are precepts that always bind us, whatever our particular purposes and plans may be. The categorical imperative delivers a command to us that is absolute, objective and unconditional: it is what it is our duty to do, irrespective of our particular circumstances, at all times and in all places. Jesus' statement in the Gospels of the so-called 'golden rule': 'Do to others as you would have them do to you' (Matt. 7.12; Luke 6.31), provides an obvious example.

In order to know exactly which actions are required of us in this categorical way, we must use our reason to reflect upon the 'maxim' or principle that lies behind an action that we intend to take. We will know whether our projected action is right if we find that the maxim that lies behind it could be 'universalized' or, in other words, applied across the board in every conceivable situation. If our projected action can be seen to be based upon a universalizable maxim, then we will know that it is right to take it, but if it cannot be, then we should refrain from carrying it out, whatever the consequences. Thus, the first form of Kant's categorical imperative is:

Act as if the maxim of your action were to become through your will a universal law of nature[17]

Kant provides some examples of what such universalizing might mean in practice by applying this procedure to some particular ethical questions. In one, a man contemplates suicide because he despairs of his life. The maxim, or principle, of his action in doing so would be 'from self-love I make it my principle to shorten my life if its continuance threatens more evil than it

---

14 Kant (1785), p. 39 (my italics).
15 Kant (1785), p. 50.
16 Kant (1785), p. 39.
17 Kant (1785), p. 52.

promises pleasure'.[18] But this, Kant argues cannot be willed as a universal maxim because it is self-contradictory: self-love and self-destruction cannot be compatible with one another. Another example concerns a man who borrows money in the knowledge that he will not be able to pay it back. His maxim is that 'whenever I believe myself short of money, I will borrow money and promise to pay it back, though I know that this will never be done'.[19] However, this also could never become a universal law since to promise something that you know you cannot deliver contradicts the very purpose of promising.

The second form of the categorical imperative, which Kant believes to be very directly related to the first form, is:

> Act in such a way that you always treat humanity, whether in your own person or in the person of any other, never simply as a means, but always at the same time as an end[20]

As Kant recognizes, there is nothing wrong with treating other people partially as means: all of us in different ways profit from the capacities and achievements of others and modern society, built as it is on the division of labour, would not be able to function if we did not.[21] But other people are never *simply* means, since all human beings are independent rational creatures who must be revered, respected and even loved for what they are. Thus, when, for example, we are dealing with colleagues in a college or in the work place, or when we are trying to convince other people of our point of view, the categorical imperative requires us to respect their rational powers, and not try to manipulate or coerce them to fit in with our own requirements.[22]

Kant explores again his earlier examples, aided by this second form of the categorical imperative, and finds that it reinforces his previous conclusions. Those involved in these situations would not only be unable to universalize their maxims, but they would also discover that they were treating human beings as means towards an end. Thus, the man contemplating suicide would be treating a person (himself) as the means to his desired end of escaping from a painful situation. Similarly, the man who borrows money never to repay it would not be respecting others as rational beings.[23]

Kant brings the first and second forms of the categorical imperative together in a third and final form:

---

18 Kant (1785), p. 53.
19 Kant (1785), p. 54.
20 Kant (1785), p. 66.
21 See Spaemann (1989), pp. 55, 73.
22 See MacIntyre (1984), p. 46.
23 Cf. Kant (1785), pp. 67–8.

So act as if you were through your maxims a law-making member of a kingdom of ends.

Human beings are law-makers because the moral law binds us not by rules that somebody else has imposed on us, but rather by a law that emerges out of our own powers of thinking and reasoning. The rational subject 'obeys no law other than that which he at the same time enacts himself'.[24] And we always go about our moral self-legislation conscious of the fact that we belong to a kingdom of ends: a 'union of different rational beings under common laws',[25] all of whom grant each other the respect that they deserve.

Discussion point

Consider how Kant's categorical imperatives might be applied to the following issues:

Fraud
Torture
Prostitution
Slavery

Reason

As Wells and Quash comment, the enormous influence of Kant's ethics is evident in the way that the first two forms of the categorical imperative are often invoked by people who would not normally describe themselves as philosophers:

> Whenever a parent says to a child 'What if everybody scribbled on the walls of other people's houses?' or a union member says to an employer, 'You can't treat people like that,' they are, whether they know it or not, deeply in debt to Immanuel Kant.[26]

Although Kant's ethics are explicitly non-theological, his emphasis on the importance of rationality is one that, broadly speaking, Christians have been able to welcome. For theological ethics, as much as any other type, require a reasoned and disciplined approach to moral questions. Moreover, it is surely part of prudent moral thinking to consider as rationally as we can the principles (or maxims) that lie behind any course of action that we might

---

24 Kant (1785), pp. 54, 77.
25 Kant (1785), pp. 54, 75.
26 Wells and Quash (2010), p. 124.

be intending to take. However, while accepting the importance of the use of reason, we might want to question the precise way in which Kant presents the role of reason in moral decision making.

For Kant, men and women are autonomous legislators in the kingdom of ends, making the laws to which they themselves are subject, in splendid isolation, and on purely rational grounds, uninfluenced by their religious beliefs or the communities from which they have come. However, writers such as MacIntyre and Stanley Hauerwas argue that it is in and through particular communities, with their distinctive narratives and commitments, and not in spite of these, that human beings actually learn how to see the world and to think about how best to act within it. Thus, it is from within the contingent and often precarious lives of, for example, families, schools, churches, community groups and so on, and not from some supposedly neutral vantage point provided by reason, that moral training actually occurs:

> Confronted by the fragmented character of our world, philosophers have undoubtedly tried to secure a high ground that can provide for security, certainty, and peace. It is a worthy effort, but one doomed to fail, for such ground lacks the ability to train our desires and direct our attention; to make us into moral people.[27]

Indeed, MacIntyre argues that the moral rules that appear to Kant to be self-evident and entirely derived from reason, such as the importance of the 'golden rule', of not lying and not committing suicide, can in fact clearly be seen to derive from his own Pietist upbringing in Königsberg: 'the maxims which he had learnt from his own virtuous parents were those which had to be vindicated by a rational test'.[28]

Moreover, as MacIntyre points out, there are many different maxims that could be consistently universalized, and these include not only trivial ones such as 'always eat mussels on Mondays in March' but also ones that are positively oppressive, such as 'persecute all those who hold false religious beliefs'. For sure, the latter of these would conflict with Kant's second form of the categorical imperative, because it would not be respecting human beings as ends in themselves, but this perhaps only highlights the fact that these two forms of the categorical imperative do not go quite so naturally together as Kant assumes they do.

And even when we do universalize in the way that Kant suggests, it is possible to imagine situations in which the rigidity and inflexibility of the categorical imperative causes things to go off track. A famous example of this came when the liberal French-Swiss philosopher Benjamin Constant (1767–1830) took issue with Kant for having reportedly said that it would be a crime to tell a lie to a murderer about whether a friend, whom the murderer

---

27 Hauerwas (1983), p. 11.
28 MacIntyre (1984), p. 44.

is pursuing, is taking refuge in our house. Constant argued that under these circumstances, the murderer would not have the right to the truth, and so we would be justified in withholding it from him. In an article entitled 'On a Supposed Right to Lie because of Philanthropic Concerns', however, Kant replied uncompromisingly to Constant that 'to be truthful in all declarations is ... a sacred and unconditionally commanding law of reason that admits of no expediency whatsoever'.[29] For Kant, the duty of truthfulness underlies all understanding that human beings can have of one another, and this is 'an unconditional duty which holds in all circumstances'. Without truthfulness, laws would break down and language would become meaningless, and therefore a maxim to lie under certain circumstances could never be universalized. Moreover, when we lie to anyone, even a would-be murderer, we fail to respect the dignity that is due to them as rational beings, treating them as a means rather than an end. Although it is possible to follow, and even admire, Kant's reasoning about this question, many would see it as an example of how adherence to his concept of rationally-derived rules might lead us, ironically, into absurd and apparently irrational courses of action.

Happiness

In many ways, Kant, with his insistence that morality should not be based on religious claims, may seem to be a very non-theological figure and yet his approach to ethics bears comparison with that of some moral theologians. Many people outside the Church might indeed assume that, for religious people, ethics is primarily about attending to moral duties and obeying moral rules. Indeed, some contemporary Catholic moral theologians such as Servais Pinckaers have criticized their predecessors in recent centuries for emphasizing duties, rules and obligations in a way that seems to owe more to Kant than to Christianity. Pinckaers comments that traditional manuals of moral theology were characteristically divided into two sections, the first dealing with moral obligations, laws, commandments and norms, and the second with the application of these to specific actions and particular hard cases.[30] Thus, the study of rules and of the obligations that derived from them was presented as the sum total of moral teaching. Renewed attention to Scripture in the Catholic tradition has, Pinckaers argues, confirmed the view that ethical teaching is not only found in 'strictly imperative texts', such as the Ten Commandments which prescribe moral rules, but that we also need to look beyond these at the far greater number of texts that describe and illustrate the way in which human beings flourish and grow when they live the life of faith.

---

29 A summary of the disagreement between Kant and Constant and a translation of Kant's article may be found at http://philosophyfaculty.ucsd.edu/faculty/rarneson/Courses/KANTSupposedRightToLie.pdf

30 Pinckaers (1995), p. 15.

This brings us back to the key concept from the previous chapter of happiness and human flourishing. It has been noted that Deontological ethics relegates happiness to a secondary and subordinate position behind moral rules, duties and obligations, and this also is a key part of Pinckaers's critique of previous generations of Catholic moral writers. This mistaken emphasis can, Pinckaers argues, be rectified by closer attention to the writings of Saint Paul and to the Beatitudes as sources of moral guidance. Paul's emphasis on themes such as the grace of God, union with Christ and life according to the Spirit indicate that, for him, 'the leitmotif of morality was happiness and salvation'.[31] Similarly, Jesus' own teaching in the Sermon on the Mount is highly significant because the Beatitudes, as their name suggests, also emphasize the theme of happiness in its fullest and most long-term sense. Pinckaers argues that, contrary to what the theologians he discusses might have intended, the disconnection between morality and happiness has led, both in secular and religious circles, to ethics being seen as a rather grim affair in which people reluctantly do their duty, and follow rules that they would rather did not exist. This is not to say that duties are unimportant, or even that doing them is necessarily arduous and unpleasant, but duties exist in order to enable people to live virtuous and happy lives and those living such lives will go beyond a sense of duty. As Jesus himself says, 'Woe to you Pharisees! For you tithe mint and rue and herbs of all kinds, and neglect justice and the love of God; it is these you ought to have practised, without neglecting the others' (Luke 11.42).

Consequentialism

In contrast to the deontological emphasis on the duties and obligations that men and women must fulfil, consequentialist ethics, as its name implies, holds that actions can be judged by their consequences. The Utilitarian version of Consequentialism – an approach to ethics that continues to be enormously influential, not least in politics and education, is articulated by Jeremy Bentham (1748–1842) in his classic work, *An Introduction to the Principles and Morals of Legislation*, which begins with these stirring words:

Nature has placed mankind under the governance of two sovereign masters, pain and pleasure. It is for them alone to point out what we ought to do, as well as to determine what we shall do. On the one hand the standard of right and wrong, on the other the chain of causes and effects, are fastened to their throne. They govern us in all we do, in all we say, in all we think: every effort we can make to throw off our subjection,

---

31 Pinckaers (1995), p. 107.

will serve but to demonstrate and confirm it. In words a man may pretend to abjure their empire: but in reality he will remain subject to it all the while.[32]

Given the importance of pain and pleasure, Bentham invokes what he describes as the 'principle of utility' to decide between courses of action. When an individual reflects on an action they might take, or a legislator, for example, a Member of Parliament, reflects on laws that they might seek to enact, this principle can be used to adjudicate 'according to the tendency which it appears to have to augment or diminish the happiness of the party whose interest is in question'.[33] Thus, the utility principle aims to maximize pleasure and to minimize pain for those concerned. Actions or laws will be good if their consequence is to produce pleasure and bad if they result in pain.

In real life, of course, situations are almost always complex and tend to give rise not only to one result, but to a number. So, Bentham acknowledges that our actions will often produce *both* pleasures and pains, sometimes termed *hedons* and *dolors*, in some measure for those involved. If we want to maximize the former and minimize the latter so as to realize the classic Utilitarian goal of 'the greatest happiness of the greatest number', we will need to work out more precisely what is the exact 'force' or 'value' of the pleasure or pain that our actions are likely to generate. In order to do this, Bentham outlines a process similar to the cost/benefit analysis that, for example, a business might undertake when debating whether to embark upon a new project. We must calculate both pleasures and pains in terms of their intensity, duration, certainty or uncertainty (to result from a particular action), propinquity or remoteness, fecundity (the likelihood that it will be followed by similar pleasures or pains), purity and extent (the number of people affected). Bentham's protégé, John Stuart Mill (1806–73) was to go further, differentiating between higher (intellectual) and lower (bodily) pleasures. Once we have made this assessment, we will be in a position to weigh the pleasures and pains against one another. This computation of competing pleasures and pains, often referred to as the *hedonic* or *felicific* (that is happiness inducing) *calculus*, will thus yield an almost mathematically precise indication of whether we should go ahead with a particular action:

Take an account of the *number* of persons whose interests appear to be concerned; and repeat the above process with respect to each. *Sum up* the numbers expressive of the degrees of *good* tendency, which the act has, with respect to each individual, in regard to whom the tendency of it is *good* upon the whole: do this again with respect to each individ-

32 Bentham (1780), p. 1.
33 Bentham (1780), p. 2.

ual, in regard to whom the tendency of it is *bad* upon the whole. Take the *balance*; which if on the side of *pleasure*, will give the general *good tendency* of the act, with respect to the total number or community of individuals concerned; if on the side of pain, the general *evil tendency*, with respect to the same community.[34]

Consequentialism has the advantage of appearing to provide a pragmatic way to resolve difficult dilemmas, and decide upon what is sometimes inelegantly described as the 'least worst' course of action. Historically, the explicitly non-religious basis of consequentialism made it attractive to people living in the aftermath of the Thirty Years' War in Europe in which the continent had been torn apart by religious divisions. And the fact that consequential-ism is 'non-transcendental, non-religious and makes no appeal to anything outside human life'[35] continues to commend it to many people who live in modern-day Western, pluralist contexts. Because of its commitment to happy outcomes, consequentialism sits light to the idea that certain actions are intrinsically right or wrong for us to do, whatever the consequences of them might be. To Saint Paul's rhetorical question, 'Should we continue in sin in order that grace may abound?' the consequentialist answer, in sharp distinction to Paul's 'by no means!', is 'under certain circumstances, yes' (cf. Rom. 6.1; 3.8).

Although part of consequentialism's attraction to many people is pre-cisely its apparently pragmatic and non-religious nature, it does not need to be seen as entirely inimical to theological ethics. It is surely part of prudent decision making that, when we are contemplating a possible future action, we should try to predict what the likely consequences of it will be, and allow this prediction to influence whether to take the action or not. If we did not do this, we would quite literally be insane. However, consequentialist theo-ries take the importance of consequences a few stages further than this. They assert not just that consequences are important, and that we need to think about them, but that among all the ways in which we might think about the ethics of a particular action, assessing its consequences are really the only important ones. Thus, to the aggressive consequentialism that can be evident in modern moral discourse, Banner argues that non-consequential-ists 'don't need to reply with a countervailing dogmatism that consequences don't matter one iota; it is enough for them to agree that consequences really do matter, and to say quietly, but firmly, that they are not the only things that matter'.[36] Related to this point, some further questions might be raised about consequentialism.

---

34 Bentham (1780), p. 31.
35 McCoy (2004), p. 100.
36 Banner (2009), p. 124.

Unpredictability of outcomes

> Our wills and fates do so contrary run
> That our devices still are overthrown;
> Our thoughts are ours, their ends none of our own.[37]

The Player King in Shakespeare's *Hamlet* draws our attention to the gap that exists between, on the one hand, our intentions and plans and, on the other, our ability to put these into practice. The 'law of unintended consequences' dictates that it is not always possible for us to predict with any accuracy what the outcome of our actions will be, or to control their wider repercussions. An example of this problem with consequentialism, as well as some others, may be found in John's Gospel where, shortly before Jesus' crucifixion, the high priest Caiaphas makes what is often regarded as a classic Utilitarian statement: 'it is better for you to have one man die for the people than to have the whole nation destroyed' (John 11.50; cf. 18.14). Caiaphas's advice can perhaps be read on three levels which, in the manner of the Church Fathers, we might label spiritual, moral and literal.

On a spiritual level, Caiaphas, perhaps despite himself, utters what can be seen as a high priestly prophecy 'that Jesus was about to die for the nation, and not for the nation only, but to gather into one the dispersed children of God' (John 11.51–52). In this sense, Christians affirm that Caiaphas's prophetic words are fulfilled by what subsequently happens: Jesus' death does indeed lead to the chain of events in which the new Israel starts to be constituted and the Gentiles gathered in.

However, on a moral level, the Gospel seems to invite us to be far more critical of Caiaphas. His judgement that it will be expedient to sacrifice innocent life in the hope that this will reduce the suffering that the rest of the Jewish people will have to endure at the hands of the Romans seems a shabby and unjust application of the hedonic calculus, in which deeper principles of right and wrong are sacrificed to what is expected to be a better outcome for the majority. It is a good example of the maxim often associated with consequentialism: 'the ends justify the means'.

Finally, if we consider Caiaphas's statement on a literal level, there is a further problem with his advice. Early readers of John's Gospel would have understood that Caiaphas got his prediction disastrously wrong. The death of Jesus did *not*, as it turned out, stop the Romans sacking Jerusalem and destroying the temple in AD 70. Thus, Caiaphas's prediction that the sacrifice of an innocent man would secure a safer future for the rest of the Jewish people in Jerusalem proved to be wrong, foundering not just because it was morally questionable, but also because, like the rest of us, Caiaphas

---

37 Shakespeare, *Hamlet*, Act 3, Scene 2.

was unable to predict the long-term outcome of his actions with any degree of accuracy.

Further and more modern examples of the difficulty of predicting outcomes include the ethical issues that surround some recent developments in modern science, such as the attempt to clone animals or to make food from genetically modified organisms. Clearly those involved in making ethical judgements about such issues need to try their hardest to understand precisely what the consequences of such developments might and might not be, and use these to inform their decisions. However, if the moral analysis of such issues rests entirely on predicted outcomes, then the analysis will be called into question if such outcomes fail to take place.

Discussion point

Consider how the law of unintended consequences is relevant to ethics in the following areas:

The ethics of war
Sexual ethics

Incommensurability of goods

Further questions surround Bentham's optimistic claim that we can measure pleasures and pains in an almost mathematical way, and weigh these up against one another so as to secure maximal happiness for all concerned. It is difficult to know how, according to Bentham's formula, we would decide about a course of action that would cause a great deal of pleasure or pain, but for only one person or a small group, against another that would produce a smaller amount of pleasure or pain, but spread around a larger number? In practice, consequentialist reasoning would probably tend to favour the latter course of action, thus maximizing the pleasure and minimizing the pain of the majority, since this would probably be thought to bring about the greatest happiness of the greatest number. However, as the example of Caiaphas shows, this can easily lead to a tyranny of the majority and the resulting oppression of minorities or individuals. Christopher McAllister asks 'if, within a certain jurisdiction or geographical area, racial intolerance maximizes the satisfactions of the majority ... does a Consequentialist approve of that intolerance and if not why not?'[38] Moreover, people experience not just different degrees of pleasure and pain, which could theoretically

---

38 C. McAllister, *Towards the Bright Horizon*, chapter 4, accessed at http://christophermcallister.org.

be balanced against each other, but also different types of pleasure and pain, which elude precise comparison. As Alasdair MacIntyre puts it:

> The pleasure-of-drinking-Guinness is not the pleasure of swimming-at-Crane's-Beach, and the swimming and the drinking are not two different means for providing the same end-state. The happiness which belongs peculiarly to the way of life of the cloister is not the same happiness as that which belongs peculiarly to the military life. For different pleasures and different happinesses are to a large degree incommensurable: there are no scales of quality or quantity on which to weigh them. Consequently appeal to the criteria of pleasure will not tell me whether to drink or swim and appeal to those of happiness cannot decide for me between the life of a monk and that of a soldier.[39]

Case study

Andrea is a 15-year-old girl. She has recently split up with her boyfriend and, after having done so, discovered that she was pregnant. She is considering having an abortion, and trying to weigh up what would be the best course of action both for herself and for her unborn child. On the one hand, she realizes that, if she were to go ahead with the pregnancy, she would find it difficult to finish her schooling, possibly go to university or get a good job. Moreover, her child would be brought up in an unstable home, without a father, and with a mother who is not yet ready to be a good parent. On the other hand, she expects that if she aborts the child, this decision will stay with her for the rest of her life. She also thinks, in a rather speculative way, that her child will be unhappy if he or she is not even given the chance to be born in the first place.

Questions for discussion

What are the different types of pleasures and pains that Andrea is weighing up?

Does the language of 'pleasures' and 'pains' seem appropriate in this context?

Is it possible to weigh the possible outcomes in this situation against one another?

---

39 MacIntyre (1984), p. 64.

Impracticality of process

A further question may be raised about some practical issues surrounding Bentham's suggested process for weighing up outcomes. Although he acknowledges that 'it is not expected that this process should be strictly pursued previously to every moral judgment or to every judgment, or to every legislative or judicial operation',[40] he appears to believe that we will generally have not only the information we need to make a reasonably accurate prediction of the likely consequences of our actions, but also the time at our disposal to undertake the process of weighing up the pleasures and pains that it might generate. Recognizing some of the difficulties of this, John Stuart Mill proposed what is often called 'rule utilitarianism', by contrast with 'act utilitarianism' espoused by Bentham. Rule utilitarianism seeks to provide happiness-maximizing rules, so that it is not necessary for everything to be resolved on a case-by-case basis. However, to reduce a system of ethics based on the importance of outcomes to a system based on the importance of following rules risks becoming incoherent. As Banner asks, 'if observing the rule ... looks likely in a particular instance to result in poorer consequences than breaking the rule, why wouldn't the consequentialist break it?'[41]

In practice then, deontologists need time and leisure to assess whether their maxims can be universalized and consequentialists need time to assess which course of action will lead to the most pleasurable outcome. But, although it is surely necessary to take time to make important decisions when we can, time is not always available. Many decisions in life come upon us fairly suddenly.

In order to illustrate this and some other related points, we might look at a paradigmatic story about good moral action: Jesus' parable of the Good Samaritan in Luke's Gospel. In this story, a man who has been attacked by robbers, stripped and beaten on the road from Jerusalem to Jericho has his plight ignored by a priest and a Levite who pass by him, but a third person is more sympathetic:

> a Samaritan while travelling came near him; and when he saw him, he was moved with pity. He went to him and bandaged his wounds, having poured oil and wine on them. Then he put him on his own animal, brought him to an inn, and took care of him. (Luke 10.33–34)

Jesus' parable provides an archetypal account of good, benevolent action but some features of it appear to contrast sharply with the account of good actions provided both by deontological and consequentialist ethics. First, when the Samaritan comes upon the injured man, he is 'travelling'. In other

---

40 Bentham (1781), p. 31.
41 Banner (2009), p. 122.

words, he is going about his business when his moment for action comes, and does not have the opportunity to engage in leisured decision making. In real life, it is often the case that, as Bonhoeffer puts it, 'we have literally no time to sit down and ask ourselves whether so-and-so is our neighbour or not'.[42] Moreover, the Samaritan acts as he does because he is 'moved with pity'. In other words, and again by contrast with both deontological and consequentialist ethics, his emotions motivate him as well as his reason. And indeed, when the Samaritan does act, it appears that he does so almost as a reflex. He instinctively knows what he has to do and how to help the injured man. His good habits are, as it were, hard-wired into him, and not the result of a protracted process of rational calculation. He is, in other words, a virtuous person.

Unclarity of goals

A final question about consequentialist ethics again concerns the all-important theme of the role of happiness in the moral life. By contrast with deontological ethics, in which, as we have seen, happiness is relegated to a secondary position, for consequentialists, seeking the greatest happiness for the greatest number, it is clearly at the forefront of their aims. However, what kind of happiness is this? Given the non-religious nature of conse-quentialism, this type of happiness is clearly less than the everlasting life with God which, for example, Thomas Aquinas means by happiness. But it also falls short of Aristotle's understanding of happiness as a fulfilled and flourishing human life. Happiness for Bentham and Mill is essentially pleasure: a short term and much reduced version of the fuller happiness that, in the view of much theology and philosophy, all things ultimately long for. Aristotle himself says that mistaking happiness for pleasure is a mistake made by men of the most vulgar type.[43] In a well-known thought experiment, Robert Spaemann demonstrates that pleasure is not in fact what human beings actually most desire:

> Let us imagine a man strapped to a table in an operating theatre. He is under anaesthetic and there are electrodes attached to his scalp. Pre-cisely measured electrical impulses are transmitted through these wires to certain brain-centres which induce a permanent state of euphoria. The person's beatific expression reflects his state. The doctor who is carrying out the experiment explains to us that the man will remain in this condi-tion for at least another ten years. When at last it is no longer possible to prolong it, the machine will be switched off and he will immediately die without feeling any pain. The doctor offers the same to us. The ques-

---

42 Bonhoeffer (1937), p. 67.
43 Aristotle, *Nicomachean Ethics* 1.5.

tion is, who amongst us would be prepared to allow him- or herself to be transported into this kind of bliss?[44]

Spaemann's conclusion is that almost all of us would actually prefer our everyday lives, with all their pains, tensions, difficulties and ambiguities to such an artificial situation, however much pleasure it would give us. Neither human beings, nor indeed other animals, see pleasure as the ultimate goal to strive for, and thus we need a richer account of what it means to be happy than consequentialism is able to provide.

Questions for discussion

Look back at the case study at the start of this chapter.
In view of what you have now read in this chapter, what would be the likely deontological and consequentialist approaches to this situation?

Has your initial reaction to the case changed in any way?

Relativism

Cultural relativism

Relativism – the idea that no point of view has absolute validity – is not a new phenomenon. It can be traced back to the Skepticism of ancient Greek thinkers such as Pyrrho of Elis and Sextus Empiricus, who argued that we cannot be certain about anything that we take for truth, and that consequently, the most rational course of action is to suspend judgement about everything. In the words of Arcesilaus, a philosopher of this kind, 'nothing is certain, not even that'.

The more specific term cultural relativism describes the widely held view that there are no ethical standards that transcend culture, and thus that all standards of right and wrong are based on the norms of the society in which we happen to live.[45] Cultural relativism has been given further impetus in recent times by philosophical trends associated with 'Postmodernity', which have caused people to turn away from Kant's understanding of the self as autonomous and rational, and drawn attention to the role that culture and language play in the construction of human identity, often claiming that no stable 'self' exists outside these. The far greater opportunities to be exposed to other cultures in an increasingly globalized world have led many people

---

44 Spaemann (1989), p. 19.
45 The section below draws in particular on McCoy (2004), pp. 69–77.

to an acute awareness of the deep differences that exist between societies and ethnic groups. Christians have particular reasons to remember and indeed celebrate the importance of such differences, since the Church herself is a multicultural society, whose members are not a homogeneous group, but 'a great multitude ... from every nation, from all tribes and peoples and languages, standing before the throne and before the Lamb' (Rev. 7.9; cf. 13.7; 14.6).

Awareness of cultural differences is not a peculiarly modern phenomenon, and indeed, ethical reflection in the form that we know it probably began when Greek philosophers began to reflect on the shared standards and concepts of the good that might underlie the varied customs that they heard about in contemporary travel stories. In a theme that was discussed in relation to natural law, reflection upon these led philosophers to draw a distinction between *nomos* and *phusis*: the former of these terms referred to the humanly constructed conventions that underlie the rules of different societies, while the latter term denoted the deeper law of nature that gave certain customs and moral rules a deeper and more certain grounding. Thus, the existence of varying codes of ethics in different cultures does not necessarily mean that we should give up any hope of being able to find common ground between them. Indeed, the existence of such variations might instead spur us on to try and gain deeper understanding of the moral standards and understandings of the human good that underlie the varied customs of different cultures.[46]

While it would certainly be wrong to ignore or minimize such variations, there are also good reasons not to exaggerate the importance of them either. As Spaemann writes:

> We often fall victim to a kind of optical illusion. We see differences more clearly because common features are self-evident. In all cultures, parents have duties to their children, children have duties to their parents, everywhere gratitude is regarded as 'good', so too everywhere the miser is despised and the man of generous spirit held in high esteem; almost everywhere impartiality is regarded as the principal virtue of the judge and courage is regarded as the principal virtue of the warrior.[47]

The widely held assumption that anthropological research into different societies always reveals how much societies and civilizations differ from one another is echoed by Wells and Quash, who, in an apparently unsupported generalization, write that 'anthropologists observing a wide variety of cultures came to the conclusion that while there are particular customs, there is no general morality'.[48] By contrast, however, in a passage from his

---

46 See Spaemann (1989), pp. 4–6.
47 Spaemann (1989), p. 5.
48 Wells and Quash (2010), p. 128.

book *Natural Law and Natural Rights*, which will be quoted in chapter 7, John Finnis outlines the ways in which anthropological studies in fact reveal that quite a large number of basic values appear to underlie the moral codes of different human societies, thus undermining the factual basis for extreme forms of cultural relativism. All societies, Finnis argues, have some sense of the value of human life, of stability in sexual relations, the importance of truth, the common good, friendship, property and respect for the dead.

Moreover just as cultural relativism can overestimate the differences between cultures, so it can underestimate the differences within cultures. For if codes of behaviour are purely culturally determined, then this implies that everyone who belongs to a particular culture should logically share a similar ethical code. In fact, however, modern societies tend to be pluralistic, with different viewpoints coexisting and competing within them. Moreover, within almost every culture particular individuals stand out strongly against the prevailing moral norms. If extreme cultural relativism is justified, 'what sense would we then make,' McCoy asks, 'of individuals who have spurned or rejected the morality of their group? Are we to regard them as ill?'[49] If all morality were entirely a matter of cultural conditioning, then it would be impossible for anyone to find a perspective from which to criticize the morals of their own society, and yet clearly some people, such as the Old Testament prophets, do precisely this.

Finally, if the morality of all societies is entirely relative, this must imply that it is impossible for any society to develop over time. For the concept of progress becomes meaningless if no society can, on principle, ever be judged to be better than any other. However, most people living in the West, and in particular many ardent cultural relativists, would in practice affirm that on certain issues, such as the role of women in society and the eradication of slavery, their societies have indeed progressed and developed.[50]

Subjectivism and emotivism

> In those days there was no king in Israel; all the people did what was right in their own eyes.
>
> Judg. 21.25; cf. 18.1; 19.1; Deut. 12.8

These final words of the book of Judges describe a period of Israel's history before the institution of the monarchy, and epitomize the belief that moral values are primarily decided by the individual who holds them. Such an approach contrasts, of course, with any idea that morality is universal (such as advocated, for example, by religious traditions and by Kant), or even that morality is largely culture-dependent (as in cultural relativism).

---

49 McCoy (2004), p. 73.
50 See McCoy (2004), pp. 74–6.

Among such individualistic approaches, subjectivism claims that all ethical viewpoints can be said to be true for those who hold them, while emotivism, which will be the main focus of this section, questions more fundamentally whether terms such as 'true' or 'false' actually have any meaning in ethics at all. In emotivist thinking, terms such as 'right' or 'wrong' have no real content: they do not say anything objective, but rather are simply used 'to express feeling about certain objects'.[51] The term emotivism denotes both a philosophical understanding of the way in which language works, one that is particularly associated with philosophers such as C. L. Stevenson (1908–79) and A. J. Ayer (1910–89), and also a more popular set of assumptions about ethics.

One of the most notorious philosophical expositions of emotivism is made by Ayer in his book *Language, Truth and Logic* (1936), which he wrote at a precociously young age – although he was later to rethink various parts of it. Ayer's exposition of ethics, which is influenced by the philosophical movement known as Logical Positivism, is based on a grammatical distinction within descriptive sentences between the subject and the predicate. In such sentences, the predicate tells us something about the nature of the subject. So, in the statement 'the cat is furry', the cat would be the subject of the sentence and 'furry' the predicate. Similarly, in the statement 'the car is blue', the car is the subject and blue the predicate. Drawing on a distinction drawn by Kant and other philosophers, Ayer divides statements that we might make into two categories: analytic and synthetic.

In analytic statements, the predicate can be seen to be implied or contained in the subject: 'an analytic judgement is one in which the predicate B belonged to the subject A as something which was covertly contained in the concept of A'.[52] Thus, examples of analytic statements would be 'all cats are feline', 'all bodies are extended' (Kant's example), or 'all bachelors are unmarried men'. In each of these cases, the predicate is contained within the subject, and is therefore necessarily true. Such statements may not be as otiose as they might appear, because they can help us to clarify what we mean by a certain term by breaking it up 'into those constituent concepts that have all along been thought in it'. However, they are essentially tautologies, because they do not strictly tell us anything new about the subject.

By contrast, in synthetic statements, the predicate *does* tell us something new about the subject, which it would be impossible to deduce for ourselves. Thus, examples of synthetic statements might be that 'all cats like to eat mice' or that 'all bodies float in water' or 'bachelors like to get drunk every evening'. We can investigate each of these statements in order to determine its truthfulness or otherwise. Reflecting the Logical Positivist view that true knowledge can be gained only through observation, Ayer writes that 'a

51 Ayer (1936), p. 111.
52 Ayer (1936), p. 71.

synthetic proposition is significant only if it is empirically verifiable'.[53] Any synthetic statement that cannot be verified is insignificant or meaningless.

For Ayer, ethical statements cannot count as synthetic, because they cannot be verified. Thus, they are literally meaningless. Any ethical statement that we might make expresses our feelings about a particular action, but it does not and cannot convey any factual information. In this respect, ethical judgements are, as Ayer sees it, similar to aesthetic ones. He understands both ethics and aesthetics to be simply matters of taste, about which there cannot be any real dispute since in both fields 'beauty is in the eye of the beholder'. In a well-known passage, he applies this insight to the question of stealing:

> The presence of an ethical symbol in a proposition adds nothing to its factual content. Thus if I say to someone, 'You acted wrongly in stealing that money,' I am not stating anything more than if I had simply said, 'You stole that money.' In adding that this action is wrong I am not making any further statement about it. I am simply evincing my moral disapproval of it. It is as if I had said, 'You stole that money,' in a peculiar tone of horror, or written it with the addition of special exclamation marks ... If now I say ... 'Stealing money is wrong,' I produce a sentence which has no factual meaning – that is, expresses no proposition which can be either true or false. It is as if I had written 'Stealing money!!' – where the shape and thickness of the exclamation marks show, by a suitable convention, that a special sort of moral disapproval is the feeling which is being expressed.[54]

Some comments may be made about Ayer's analysis that take us in a somewhat different direction from the one that he indicates. For, viewed as a synthetic statement, 'stealing money is wrong' can be understood as a shorthand way of summing up a number of things that we might say about stealing, including some that can be empirically verified. These might include 'stealing breaks down society'; 'people who habitually steal are unlikely to flourish as human beings'; or 'almost all societies think that people shouldn't be allowed to steal'. When we make the moral statement 'stealing is wrong' we, as it were, bundle together these and a great many other similar statements. Thus, while no simple empirical test can confirm that 'stealing is wrong', we do not need to conclude from this that moral language exists on some rarefied plain, completely removed from anything that can be tested or verified.

Finally, we can also note that 'stealing money is wrong' also holds true as an analytic statement, since in this sentence the subject (stealing) implies the

---

53 Ayer (1936), p. 109.
54 Ayer (1936), p. 110.

predicate (wrongness). The term 'stealing', like 'fraud' and 'abortion' is not neutral, but ethically loaded. Once we describe a particular action as 'stealing', we are implicitly making a moral judgement about it: that it is wrong. Another way of putting this would be to say that it is self-evidently true that stealing money is wrong.

Ayer's arguments show why emotivism has been described as a moral 'non-theory': it evacuates any meaning out of moral discussion, with the result that, as Peter Vardy puts it, 'all moral debate becomes, at the end of the day, just so much hot air and nothing else'.[55] But while Ayer's theory may seem to be a rather abstract theoretical one about the way in which language is used, many people in modern Western society, including many members of religious groups are instinctively in tune with it. In my own experience of Christian ministry, I have often encountered the attitude that morality is essentially a matter of individual preference, based on feelings, and thus not really susceptible to reasoned discussion and debate. As a member of my congregation once said to me, explaining why she had taken a particular action, 'those are just my values, Father'.

As with the other theories discussed in this chapter, Christians can affirm some good things about emotivism, among them the importance of emotion and passion in morality. Far from being guided by austere Kantian rationalism, the Christian tradition generally finds feelings and emotions to have an important role in directing our actions and decisions. Jesus, after all, is recorded in the Gospels as having been deeply moved over the death of his friend Lazarus (John 11.33–35), and having wept also over the city of Jerusalem (Luke 19.41). In the *City of God*, Augustine adduces examples from both the Old and New Testaments to prove that the passions can have a positive role to play in the Christian life: a point that particularly holds true for compassion: 'a kind of fellow-feeling in our hearts for the misery of another which compels us to help him if we can'.[56] Thus, he argues that the goal of wise people should not simply be to free themselves from emotion, rather, 'what is important ... is the quality of a man's will ... If the will is perverse, the emotions will be perverse; but if it is righteous, the emotions will be not only blameless, but praiseworthy'.[57]

However, if moral standards are only a matter of feeling and preference, and if they do not rest on any objective and rational grounds, then this opens up a terrifying world in which all sorts of actions can only be thought to be wrong on the flimsy basis that particular individuals happen to feel strongly about them. These might include, for example, incest, paedophilia, human sacrifice, genocide and all the other ways in which, over the course of history, people have used other human beings as means rather than ends. By the same token, actions that we might be used to regarding as good, such

---

55 Vardy (1994), p. 90.
56 Augustine, *City of God* 9.5.
57 Augustine, *City of God* 19.6.

as living peaceably and co-operatively with our neighbours, educating our children, and seeking to protect the vulnerable would turn out not to be really good at all, but rather to be based on arbitrary personal preference.

In a moral climate strongly influenced by subjectivism and emotivism, there are two criteria that can still be used to assess the seriousness or otherwise of people's moral values: sincerity and consistency.[58] In the absence of agreed and objective standards, both of these criteria can be very prominent in current discussion of moral questions. So far as sincerity is concerned, even if there is no way of knowing whether a particular moral view is correct or not, we can still admire people who advance their opinions wholeheartedly, with feeling and conviction. However, although it is surely good to be sincere rather than disingenuous, the amount of sincerity with which somebody holds their views does not help us to judge whether the content of these views is right or not. In all probability, for example, Hitler was a very sincere person.

So far as consistency is concerned, once an individual or a group has espoused a particular set of moral values, then, even if there are no objective tests to indicate whether or not these are correct, we can still perhaps judge whether or not they live up to them. A notorious campaign led by the British Prime Minister John Major entitled 'Back to Basics' in the early 1990s fell foul of this criterion, when it was discovered that members of his government were involved in financial and sexual irregularities. The moral pronouncements of Church leaders have also been subjected to similar criticism. Such a criticism is directed not so much at the views that are espoused, but at the hypocrisy of those who say one thing, and then do another.

In a slightly different way, extreme forms of relativism fail the test of consistency also. For, it is contradictory to assert as an absolute truth that there are no such things as absolute truths. As McCoy comments:

> subjectivism cannot hold consistently, on the one hand, that each person is free to choose his or her own moral principles or that no group has the right to impose its moral view on any other group and yet hold, on the other hand, that tolerance is obligatory or even just preferable.[59]

If all morality is entirely relative, then it must be equally right to be tolerant as it is to be intolerant. In fact, therefore, the belief that we should bear with others, even when we do not like them or do not agree with them, must be grounded in a firmer and more absolute set of values than relativism is able to provide:

> 'You have heard that it was said, "You shall love your neighbour and hate your enemy." But I say to you, Love your enemies and pray for those

---

58 See McCoy (2004), p. 58.
59 McCoy (2004), p. 60.

who persecute you, so that you may be children of your Father in heaven; for he makes his sun rise on the evil and on the good, and sends rain on the righteous and on the unrighteous.'

Matthew 5.43–45

Case study

In the following extract from a national newspaper the screenwriter and novelist Ronan Bennett discusses the evidence given by former British Prime Minister Tony Blair to the Chilcot Inquiry into the Iraq war.

"I only know what I believe." Sincerity has always been Tony Blair's first and last line of defence. When his back is against the wall, when the evidence of miscalculation or worse is incontrovertible, he will acknowledge common human fallibility with the British public school version of an "Aw, shucks" shrug ...

When Sir Lawrence Freedman asked if he believed that Saddam Hussein had weapons of mass destruction, Blair answered: "I did believe it. And I did believe it beyond doubt." He reiterated his belief in 45 minutes, that sanctions were not working, that a second UN resolution was possible, that war was legal, that Iraq posed a threat, shamelessly conflating 9/11, al-Qaida and Iraq.

So much sincerity, so much belief. "His evidence has been that of a man who believed he was doing the right thing," BBC correspondent Nicholas Witchell said. We can all think of other leaders who have, in their time, believed they were doing the right thing – quite a few of them were monsters.

The only point of what the elected leader of the country believed is whether it corresponded with the facts. Because when what we believe becomes what is true, the road is open to take any action that suits our purpose.

Ronan Bennett, *Guardian*, 29 January 2010

Questions for discussion

Is Bennett right to dismiss the importance of Blair's apparent sincerity?

How does this article (which it should be noted is one-sided and polemical) relate to the topics discussed in this chapter?

PART THREE

Further Perspectives

7

Further Perspectives on Natural Law

Natural law was discussed in chapter 2, which explored its origins in the Bible and in the early Christian apologists, and the way in which Thomas Aquinas deepened and systematized these early insights. In the aftermath of Aquinas, different versions of natural law have been evident not only in the work of Catholic moral theologians, but also of Anglicans such as Richard Hooker (1554–1600), and Protestants such as Hugo Grotius (1583–1645). Other theologians, for reasons that will be discussed below, have reacted strongly against the entire concept. This chapter will explore a range of approaches to natural law that are evident in the work of some modern theologians and philosophers, and assess some of the responses that this controversial subject has inspired.

Modern natural law theories

Physicalist approaches

'Physicalist' approaches to natural law concentrate primarily on the observable physical structures of the world and of human beings, and attempt to discern God's creative purposes within these structures. Such an approach is often found in, among other places, the manuals of Catholic moral theology of the seventeenth to the twentieth centuries. Physicalist reflection on natural law is often presented in terms of legal obligations to conform to nature and, in particular, prohibitions of behaviour that appears to be *un*natural.

Pope Paul VI's encyclical of 1968, *Humanae Vitae* (*Of Human Life*) has often been described as physicalist, because it includes reflection on the moral lessons that can be learned from the structure and apparent purposes of the human body. Although this description is controversial, *Humanae Vitae* provides a noteworthy example of this type of natural law approach. Reflecting the general thrust of natural law ethics, embryonically present in Romans 1.20, the encyclical understands marriage and sexuality to be part of God's good creation, carrying God's purposes within their very structure. In them, Paul VI writes, we see 'the wise and provident institution of God the Creator, whose purpose was to effect in man his loving design'.[1] Human beings, he argues, do not invent the purposes of marriage and sex: the individual is 'not the *master* of the sources of life but rather the *minister* of the design established by the Creator'.[2] The encyclical teaches that it is possible to observe two purposes which seem to be written into God's creative design of human sexuality. In the first place, there is a *unitive* purpose, by which husband and wife are brought together in the closest possible union with one another and, in addition, there is a *procreative* purpose in which sexual intercourse is inherently ordered to the transmission of new life – albeit that not every act of sex between married partners will result in procreation. Men and women are called to honour both the unitive and procreative purposes in their sexual lives. Masturbation in which sex takes place as a solitary activity, or rape, in which one party forces sex on the other, thwart the unitive purpose of sexuality, because these actions by their very nature do not bring two people together. Similarly, masturbation (again), homosexual practice and contraception contravene the procreative purpose of sex because they do not have an 'intrinsic relationship to the procreation of human life'. Hence also Paul VI controversially concludes that sexual intercourse which is 'deliberately contraceptive' is 'intrinsically wrong' because this too is inherently non-procreative.[3] He writes that 'an act of mutual love which impairs the capacity to transmit life which God the Creator, through specific laws, has built into it, frustrates His design which constitutes the norm of marriage, and contradicts the will of the Author of life'.[4]

Varieties of natural law thinking	
Physicalist	Focus on the structures of the human body
Personalist	Focus on the goods and behaviour of persons

In a somewhat developed form, Paul VI's teaching is taken on by a variety of predominantly Catholic theologians who develop the central teachings of *Humanae Vitae* in a somewhat different direction, albeit a direction that they would argue the encyclical itself suggests. Such writers characteristically focus not so much on the functions of different parts of the human body, as on the way in which physical actions act as a means of communi-

---

1 Paul VI, *Humanae Vitae* 8.
2 Paul VI, *Humanae Vitae* 13 (my italics).
3 Paul VI, *Humanae Vitae* 14.
4 Paul VI, *Humanae Vitae* 13.

cation between persons, and carry messages like words in a language.[5] It is not only, of course, in a sexual context that bodies speak a language. For example, we use a handshake to greet somebody, or a wave to attract attention. Humpty Dumpty famously claims that 'when I use a word, it means just what I choose it to mean – neither more nor less',[6] but proponents of this type of natural law theory insist that it is not simply up to the users of a language to determine what its terms mean. Thus, the messages sent out by physical actions, although there may be some differences between cultures, are not infinitely malleable. We would be in an odd society indeed if it was normal to use a handshake to express extreme disapproval of somebody or to give them a slap round the face as a greeting. Similarly, the act of sexual intercourse speaks of total self-giving. As Mattison puts it, 'sex is an embodied form of communication that has an inherent meaning, and that meaning is exclusive and permanent love'.[7] Whether it is intended to or not, sexual intercourse unites two people with one another, as Saint Paul reminds members of the Corinthian church when he tells them that 'whoever is united to a prostitute becomes one body with her ... "The two shall become one flesh"' (1 Cor. 6.16; cf. Gen. 2.24). Thus, two people who have casual sex with one another, with no intention that the unitive language they speak with their bodies should be matched by lifelong commitment, are, as it were, contradicting themselves. They are speaking an incoherent and incomprehensible language, and sending out mixed and conflicting messages.

More controversially, reflection of this sort will often follow Paul VI in arguing that not only does sex have an inherently unitive meaning, but also an inherently procreative one and that this too must be honoured for the same reason: that openness to new life, like permanent and exclusive union, is an integral part of the language that sexual intercourse always and unavoidably speaks:

> The two meanings of sexual union blend into one another. An act of sexual union which truly and honestly expresses total and life-long and exclusive union between a man and a woman is also an act which is open to new life in a child. If the act is deliberately prevented from being open to new life, this can only be by the introduction of some barrier or separation into the life-giving act. But deliberately to introduce separation into an act which intends and says total union is a failure in truth.[8]

---

5 This section particularly draws on Mattison (2008), pp. 344–51 and the statement of the Irish Catholic Bishops' Conference, *Love is for Life* (1985).

6 Lewis Carroll, *Through the Looking Glass*, chapter 6. This section also draws on Moore (2003), pp. 273–80.

7 Mattison (2008), p. 345.

8 *Love is for Life*, 12. A contrasting view is expressed by Gareth Moore: 'Just as the meanings of words change over time in the same society, as people come to use words in changing ways, so the meanings of human acts can change with changing institutions and

Personalist approaches

Exponents of personalist approaches to natural law, such as Joseph Boyle (1942–), John Finnis (1940–), Germain Grisez (1929–) and William May often have considerable sympathy with the more physicalist approaches to natural law that have been outlined so far, but their own work on this subject tends to start in a somewhat different place: by considering the nature of the human good. For example, in his book *Natural Law and Natural Rights* (1980), Finnis, in a passage that was discussed in the previous chapter, follows Aquinas in seeking to identify the basic and self-evident human goods, which constitute the building blocks of ethical reflection – though he goes further than Aquinas in his somewhat bold assertion that his list of basic human goods is complete and exhaustive.[9] Finnis writes:

> All human societies show a concern for the value of human life; in all, self-preservation is generally accepted as a proper motive for action, and in none is the killing of other human beings permitted without some fairly definite justification. All human societies regard the procreation of a new human life as in itself a good unless there are special circumstances. No human society fails to restrict sexual activity; in all societies there is some prohibition of incest, some opposition to boundless promiscuity and to rape, some favour for stability and permanence in sexual relations. All human societies display a concern for truth, through education of the young in matters not only practical (e.g. avoidance of dangers) but also speculative or theoretical (e.g. religion). Human beings who can survive infancy only by nurture, live in or on the margins of some society which invariably extends beyond the nuclear family, and all societies display a favour for the values of cooperation, of common over individual good, of obligation between individuals, and of justice within groups. All know friendship. All have some conception of *meum* and *tuum*, title or property, and of reciprocity. All value play, serious and formalized, or relaxed and recreational. All treat the bodies of dead members of the group in some traditional and ritual fashion different from their procedures for rubbish disposal. All display a concern for powers or principles which are to be respected as supra-human; in one form or another, religion is universal.[10]

As this passage indicates, the basic goods as Finnis identifies them are seven-fold: life, knowledge, play, aesthetic experience, sociability, practical

---

habits ... Sex is no exception to this common phenomenon. People can and do fight over what sex means, and so where and when sex is appropriate; the Christian churches are party to this struggle'. Moore (2003), p. 278.

9 See Finnis (1980), pp. 90–2.
10 Finnis (1980), pp. 83–4.

reasonableness and religion. Such goods are 'basic' because none of them can be reduced to any of the others, and because they are held to be good by people from virtually all cultures and societies.

How do we discover that these are the basic human goods? They are, Finnis argues, self-evident: 'they are obvious ... to anyone who has experience of inquiry into matters of fact or of theoretical (including historical and philosophical) judgment'.[11] They are obvious not because they are somehow innate, 'inscribed on the mind at birth',[12] nor because we happen to feel very certain about them,[13] nor because we observe them in the world around us or within us, but because we presuppose them in everything we think and do. For example, take the good of knowledge: clearly babies are not born with an idea of the importance of knowledge already implanted in their minds, but once a child starts to find out things, he or she presupposes in doing so that it is better to know something than not to know it, hence that knowledge is preferable to ignorance. Similarly, once a child starts playing with friends, he or she presupposes by doing so the goods of play and sociability. It is in this sense that the human goods are self-evident: they are values that we simply assume before we get on with the various plans and projects we undertake.

Example: Is knowledge a basic human good?

Sarah would like to explain to her friend Jane why knowledge is a good thing.

Scenario 1: Jane sits down to listen to Sarah, lapping up her every word.
Scenario 2: Jane does not think that Sarah has anything interesting to say about this subject, and believes she can find out more about it elsewhere.
Scenario 3: Jane is uninterested in this sort of talk – she tells Sarah that it doesn't get you anywhere and that it's more helpful to concentrate on practical matters.

In each of the three scenarios, Jane assumes that knowledge is a good. In scenario 1, it is clear that she thinks this, but even when she distrusts Sarah (scenario 2), or eschews philosophy altogether (scenario 3), she still presupposes that it is good to know things – even if the thing that she believes she knows is that speculation about knowledge is useless.

Since the human goods are self-evident, it is, paradoxically as it might at first seem, impossible to prove that they are good, because 'they are presupposed

---

11 Finnis (1980), p. 69.
12 Finnis (1980), p. 65.
13 Cf. Finnis (1980), p. 69.

or deployed in anything that would count as a demonstration'.[14] It cannot be proved that the human goods are good: they just are. We can only say that any particular basic good 'is a good, in itself, don't you think?' For example, Finnis writes of the good of friendship that 'to be in a relationship of friendship with at least one other person is a fundamental form of good, is it not?'[15]

The basic human goods that Finnis identifies, like their very similar counterparts in Aquinas's writing (education of offspring, living in society, etc.), are 'pre-moral': they do not tell us how to act or not to act, but simply describe the things that human beings value. However, the basic goods do establish the bedrock for ethical action: once we recognize those things that are fundamentally and inherently good, then we are obliged to take them seriously and work from them. A morally good life will always honour the basic human goods. But Finnis retains Aquinas's insistence on the need for flexibility: there is no one way in which such participation must happen. The human goods do not constrict us, nor do they give us a blueprint for the form that a good life should always take. Rather, each of the human goods 'can be participated in, and promoted, in an inexhaustible variety of ways and with an inexhaustible variety of combinations of emphasis, concentration and specialization'.[16]

Advocates of this type of approach to natural law are often aware of the way in which Christian (and in particular Catholic) moral teaching has often been experienced simply as a set of prohibitions. Finnis notes that the danger of interpreting natural law 'in strict negative principles', so that it essentially amounts to declaring a succession of things to be wrong, such as 'killing of the innocent, any anti-procreative sexual acts, and lying and blasphemy'.[17] By contrast, the personalist approach emphasizes that the aim of leading a life that participates in the human goods is that human beings should be happy, and should flourish as the creatures that God has created and destined them to be. Recalling the concepts of *eudamonia*, and its fuller Christian counterpart of beatitude that were discussed in chapter 5, this approach sees the aim of the Christian moral life as 'integral human fulfilment', or, as Finnis terms it 'inclusive, all-round flourishing or well-being'.[18]

Environmentalist approaches

In order to appreciate something of the range of natural law theories, we can finally consider a rather different approach suggested by Michael Northcott,

---

14 Finnis (1980), p. 69.
15 Finnis (1980), p. 88.
16 Finnis (1980), p. 100.
17 Finnis (1980), p. 124.
18 Finnis (1980), p. 103.

an Anglican theologian who primarily writes about environmental ethics.[19] Once again following Paul in the letter to the Romans, Northcott emphasizes the way in which the creative hand of God can be discerned in all that he has made, and he particularly argues that this must include both God's human and non-human creation. The inherent goodness of creation, which comes into being through the agency of God's Word and his Spirit, is subsequently reaffirmed in the incarnation of the Word as Jesus Christ, and again by Christ's subsequent bodily resurrection. Thus, 'matter itself, as well as humans, plants and animals, is revealed as the object of the ordering and creative power of the creator'.[20] Moreover, the eschatological hope expressed by the New Testament, is not so much for the salvation of individual human souls, as for the renewal of the entire creation (see Rom. 8.18–25).

Northcott's approach to natural law shares with physicalist theories a sense of God's purposive ordering of creation, and with personalist theories, a belief that it is possible to arrive at a rational and objective understanding of the good. However, both these approaches to natural law are vulnerable to environmentalist critique, primarily because both tend to concentrate on one part of the natural world (the human part) at the expense of all the others. For example, physicalist theories, such as that encountered in *Humanae Vitae*, can be applauded for recognizing the intrinsic connection between human sexuality and childbirth. However, the insistence that every expression of human sexuality must be open to reproduction risks creating an overpopulated planet in which every species will find it difficult to do what, according to natural law theories, it is natural and good that they should do: preserve themselves. Similarly, personalist versions of the natural law, such as that of Finnis, while they provide a commendable account of different aspects of the *human* good, identify the natural law too closely with the structures of rational reflection, and thus fail to do justice to the more holistic vision of Aquinas in which 'natural' as well as 'intelligent' agents (animals and human beings) both pursue good ends, albeit in different ways. In fact, Northcott argues, these ways are not always so very different: some of the goods that Finnis seems to assume are exclusively human are in fact shared by many other animals, since they also respect the lives of members of their own species, co-operate with one another to achieve shared objectives, nurture and educate their young, and enjoy play and sociability. Northcott acknowledges that, although Aquinas believed animals and plants to be fundamentally ordered to human ends, nonetheless Aquinas's understanding of natural law provides a strong conceptual base within the Christian tradition for ecological ethics, since in his view not only human beings, but also animals and indeed inanimate objects participate in the natural law in their own particular ways: 'each and every creature tends

---

19 See Northcott (1996), chapters 6 and 7.
20 Northcott (1996), p. 206.

toward this – that it may participate in the Creator and be assimilated to the Creator insofar as it is able'.[21] Northcott writes that:

> [The natural law tradition] affirms that the natural order is a moral order, even though subject to elements of moral ambiguity arising at least partly from the Fall, that this order is determinative for human society and morality, that human goods are interdependent with the goods of the non-human world, that this order is represented in each human person by the powers of conscience and reason and that this naturally located morality is found in every human culture.[22]

Evaluation of natural law theories

Natural law and the Bible

Advocates of natural law ethics will often commend it for its ability to shed light on pressing moral questions that are raised by developments in science and society about which the Bible says nothing. As Timothy Renick somewhat polemically puts it, 'Many modern Protestants ... fall silent in the face of "new" moral issues – issues unmentioned and seemingly unanticipated in the Bible. Others are far from silent but are able to offer only questionable biblical footing for their strong opinions on these topics.'[23] Natural law thinking can be used to ground theological thought about subjects such as the just war, human rights and the common good which, although it may accord with the teaching of the Bible, could not explicitly be found in its pages.

Exercise

Consider what you think might be a natural law approach to any of the following topics:

  Fox-hunting
  Genetic engineering
  Climate change

However, allied with this strength comes what many regard as a crucial weakness of natural law ethics, and one to which Protestant theologians have often drawn attention: that natural law thinking plays down the need

---

21 Aquinas, *Summa Theologica* 1. 103.2; cf. Northcott (1996), p. 227.
22 Northcott (1996), p. 232.
23 Renick (2002), p. 73.

for the revelation of God in Scripture. Chapter 2, for example, discussed the way in which Aquinas believed it possible for those who are wise to work out the demands of the moral law without having recourse to the Bible. By contrast, for many of those coming from the Reformed traditions, it is *sola scriptura*, 'by Scripture alone', that we can know what are, as Aquinas terms them, the goods to be done and the evils to be avoided. Drawing on its strong legacy of thought from Augustine, Protestant theology has characteristically stressed the limitations of fallen human beings' capacity to discern the truth when they are unaided by revelation, especially since the world they are observing has itself fallen, and now only partially reflects God's original purposes for it.

In the modern period, the Swiss theologian Karl Barth (1886–1968) provides the most colourful example of such criticisms. For Barth, in his massive *Church Dogmatics*, the starting point for all ethical reflection, and indeed for the Christian life itself, must be found in, and only in, God's revelation of himself in Christ. To the argument of his contemporary Emil Brunner, in his work *Nature and Grace*, that human beings must have some sort of inbuilt consciousness of God otherwise the word of God could not reach us, Barth notoriously wrote a response which he simply entitled *Nein!* For Barth, Christian ethical reflection must take its cue from the revelation of God in Christ, and not from general philosophical reflections on the natural law.

For Barth, the revelation of God through Christ and his command addressed to us through the Bible must always precede our own reflections on moral questions. We might look to such reflections to fulfil the ancillary function of illustrating or amplifying God's own revelation of himself through Scripture, but they can certainly never displace it. In fact, the word of God firmly and finally displaces them in the same way that, in a somewhat unsettling comparison, the people of Israel displaced the original inhabitants of Cana in the Old Testament and radically diminished their status:

> We have to realize how far-reaching is this change in the conception of ethics. From the point of view of the general history of ethics, it means an annexation of the kind that took place on the entry of the children of Israel into Palestine. Other peoples had for a long time maintained that they had a very old, if not the highest right of domicile in this country. But, according to Josh 9.27, they could now at best exist only as hewers of wood and drawers of water. On no account had the Israelites to adopt or take part in their culture … the Word of God, and in its faithful proclamation the preaching of the Church, and with preaching dogmatics, and at the head of dogmatics the Christian doctrine of God is always the aggressor in relation to everything else, to general human thinking and language. When they enter the field of ethical reflection and interpretation they must not be surprised at the contradiction of the so-called (but only so-called) original inhabitants of this land. They cannot regard them as an

authority before which they have to exculpate themselves, and to whose arrangements they must in some way conform.[24]

In Barth's view, moreover, if we are really to be true to the ethics that we find in the Bible, we will not simply find there a 'proclamation of general precepts and rules',[25] which we then go on to apply to individual cases in the way that, for example, rabbinical scholars would do with the text of the Torah.[26] Rather, just as in the narrative of Scripture, God addresses his word directly to his people, so in each of our own particular sets of circumstances, God addresses his word to us through Scripture and calls us joyfully to submit and obey. God does not, therefore, give us a set of principles out of which we might, in the style of Aquinas, draw primary and remote conclusions, but rather 'a specific prescription and norm for each individual case', so that 'in every visible or invisible detail He wills of us precisely one thing and nothing else, and measures and judges us precisely by whether we do or do not do with the same precision the one thing He so precisely wills.'[27] Thus, along with a condemnation of natural law as a source of moral guidance goes a condemnation of the practice of casuistry discussed at the end of chapter 5, in which moral rules are applied in particular situations.

One question, however, that arises from Barth's analysis of this subject is whether it is in fact possible to rely so entirely on the command of God that natural reasoning is excluded altogether? In practice, the choices and decisions that we face are often unclear and murky. If we are confronted with a dilemma or difficult decision, and thus do not have a vivid sense of what is the 'one thing that [God] … precisely wills', or perhaps even if we do, but feel the need to check whether our intuitions are correct, then we may find ourselves thrown back on casuistry as we try as faithfully as possible to work out the right thing to do in our particular situation.

Richard B. Hays argues that this problem affects Barth himself in some of his own writing on the subject of war. On the one hand, for Barth, the commandment 'Thou shalt not kill' sets a strongly pacifist tone for the whole witness of the Bible on the subject of war and killing. And yet, God's absolute freedom – a fundamental theme of Barth's theology – includes the freedom to command war. So, Barth goes on to argue that there are certain specifiable circumstances in which recourse to war may be understood as the command of God.[28] For example, he claims that an exception may be made to the overall rule of pacifism when independent nation states find that their

---

24 K. Barth (1946), *Church Dogmatics* II/2, trans. G. Bromiley et al. (Edinburgh: T&T Clark), pp. 518–20. This section draws on the discussion of Barth's ethics in Hays (1996), pp. 225–39.

25 Barth, *Church Dogmatics* II/2, pp. 663–78.

26 Barth, *Church Dogmatics* III/4, pp. 7–8; cf. Biggar (1993), p. 40.

27 Barth, *Church Dogmatics* II/2, pp. 663–4.

28 See Hays (1996), p. 234. This section draws on Hays (1996), pp. 230–9.

'existence and autonomy are menaced and attacked'. An example of this would arise 'if there were any attack on the independence, neutrality and territorial integrity of the Swiss Confederation'.[29] Barth's views here look not only like a case of special pleading for his native land but also an exercise in natural law and casuistry in which, as Hays puts it, 'his christocentric hermeneutic recedes into the background, while nonscriptural factors, such as the independence and integrity of the nation-state, come surprisingly to the fore as warrants for exceptions to the rule prohibiting killing'.[30] Hays comments that 'human reason and experience cannot be summarily dismissed as factors in theological and ethical discourse. When one seeks to banish them, they tend to sneak in through the back door, unacknowledged.'[31] Barth's views on this subject thus raise a practical question about whether theological ethicists will actually find it possible to escape from natural law-type reflections on the nature of reality and the human good, or from natural law-type patterns of reasoning from first principles to conclusions, even when they have firmly decided that it is desirable to do so.

In his book *Resurrection and Moral Order*, Oliver O'Donovan suggests a more nuanced way through some of these difficulties, which maintains the Protestant insistence on the primacy of Scripture in ethical reflection, while at the same time affirming some important features of natural law theories. O'Donovan emphasizes the distinction between the *ontological* (to do with being) and the *epistemological* (to do with knowing) aspects of natural law. On an ontological level, O'Donovan argues that Christian ethics must have the strong concept of God's creative ordering that natural law theories traditionally presuppose: 'the order of things that God has made is *there*,' he writes, 'it is objective, and mankind has a place within it'.[32] However, on the epistemological level, natural law thinking is more problematic. Created in God's image as intelligent creatures, human beings have a basic capacity for thought, reason and discernment and yet, because we are fallen creatures and our minds are clouded by sin, it follows that our 'knowledge is not that communion with the truth of things that it should be, but misknowledge, confusion and deception'.[33] The unaided reflections of men and women about the way that the world appears to them to be ordered cannot, O'Donovan argues, provide a firm foundation upon which to arrive at moral knowledge.[34] If we are truly to understand the nature of the world God has created, and our own obligations within it, then we cannot do without God's revelation, which will show us the reality that is in front of us more clearly than we could ever work it out for ourselves.

---

29 Barth, *Church Dogmatics* III/4, p. 462.
30 Hays (1996), p. 238.
31 Hays (1996), p. 238.
32 O'Donovan (1994), p. 17 (quoted above).
33 O'Donovan (1994), p. 82.
34 See O'Donovan (1994), p. 89.

Natural law and the search for common ground

In a theme that was explored in chapter 2, for advocates of natural law, moral standards and values are not arbitrary or accidental, but are woven into the fabric of the universe as God has made it. As Stephen Holmgren writes, 'the world of nature possesses meanings of its own that have been placed there by the creator and precede any meanings we might want to give it'.[35] According to natural law theories, ethics are neither the arbitrary decrees of God, nor the subjective construction of human minds, but rather they are an expression of the way the universe is, because God in his wisdom has made it so. Recalling Euthyphro's dilemma, God commands actions because they are right or forbids them because they are wrong. They are not made right or wrong simply by divine command. Thus, for example, murder, is not just deemed to be wrong just because God (or human societies) have decided that it should be, so as to spoil our fun. Rather, murder is wrong because it contradicts a fundamental truth about the way that human beings have been made: that we are sociable creatures who flourish when we rely on and co-operate with other people.

Natural law theories, then, suggest that since the world is not morally neutral, but permeated with signs of God's creative design, Christians can expect to find widely shared understanding of what are the goods to be promoted and evils to be avoided. As Quash puts it, 'Ethics based on Natural Law ... looks at the world in the hopeful expectation that some sense can be made of it, insists that fundamentally human moral behaviour is recognizably consistent and appeals to widely held resources of rationality, common sense and good will.'[36] On a practical level, natural law thinking enables Christians to join together with others who do not share their theological beliefs, in efforts to promote, for example, a more just society or beneficial local projects, based on a common apprehension of the good that is evident in the reality that lies around and within us.

The encyclicals or circular letters sent out by successive popes since the end of the nineteenth century repeatedly emphasize this capacity of natural law to generate a shared understanding of the good, and provide a case study for the strengths and weaknesses of this aspect of natural law ethics. Although the papal encyclicals have primarily addressed the Catholic faithful, they characteristically also address not just Catholics, but 'all people of good will',[37] as their authors seek to commend Catholic teaching to a wider audience on the basis of a common perception of the good made possible by the existence and universality of the natural law. Pope Leo XIII provides an early example of this in his encyclical of 1891, *Rerum Novarum (Of the*

---

35 Holmgren (2000), p. 55.

36 B. Quash (2001), Ethics module for the Southern Theological Education and Training Scheme (Salisbury: STETS).

37 See Paul VI, *Humanae Vitae* 31.

New Things), a key text in Catholic social teaching. In the encyclical, Leo argues that two balanced points may be derived from natural law: on the one hand, that 'every man has *by nature* the right to possess property as his own',[38] but, on the other, that natural law gives to workers the right to be appropriately paid for what they do: 'there underlies a dictate of *natural justice* more imperious and ancient than any bargain between man and man, namely, that wages ought not to be insufficient to support a frugal and well-behaved wage-earner'.[39] As we would expect, Leo believes that these two guiding insights may also be derived from Scripture: the right to possess private property is implied by the biblical commandment not to covet what others own,[40] whereas any number of biblical texts can be drawn upon to support the view that the poor should be treated justly.[41] The fact that these insights about social justice can be derived from natural law demonstrates that social teachings derived from the Scriptures are not like the *recherché* views of some Gnostic sect, but that they correspond to the wisdom that is ingrained in the universe, and thus that all men and women can have access to them because they chime in with their deepest sense of what is right and just.

In a similar way, Leo's successor Benedict XVI argues that ethical thought founded in natural law has the capacity to appeal to those who do not explicitly share Catholic beliefs. In an address on 1 January 2007 for the celebration of the World Day of Peace entitled *The Human Person, the Heart of Peace*, Benedict invokes the words of John Paul II that 'we do not live in an irrational or meaningless world ... there is a moral logic which is built into human life and which makes possible dialogue between individuals and peoples'. Hence, there is, Benedict argues, a universal 'grammar', a body of rules for actions and relationships that are written by God on the hearts of all people and which everyone should therefore respect and uphold. On the basis of this, Christians and non-Christians can come together in pursuit of shared moral values:

> From this standpoint, the norms of the natural law should not be viewed as externally imposed decrees, as restraints upon human freedom. Rather, they should be welcomed as a call to carry out faithfully the universal divine plan inscribed in the nature of human beings. Guided by these norms, all peoples—within their respective cultures—can draw near to the greatest mystery, which is the mystery of God. Today too, recognition and respect for natural law represents the foundation for a dialogue

---

38 Leo XIII, *Rerum Novarum* 6 (my italics).

39 Leo XIII, *Rerum Novarum* 45 (my italics); for a further discussion, see Pope in Gill (2001), p. 87.

40 Deut. 5.21; cf. Leo XIII, *Rerum Novarum* 11.

41 For example Jas. 5.4; Luke 6.24–25; Matt. 25.40; cf. Leo XIII, *Rerum Novarum* 22.

between the followers of the different religions and between believers and non-believers. As a great *point of convergence*, this is also a fundamental presupposition for authentic peace.[42]

In the same address, Benedict reflects on the 1948 *Universal Declaration of Human Rights*, adopted by the General Assembly of the United Nations in the aftermath of the Second World War. While the *Universal Declaration* does not offer an explicit conceptual basis for the idea of human rights, Benedict XVI contends that the warrant for them is located in 'the natural law upon which the equality of all human beings is grounded and by which it is guaranteed'.[43] The human rights codified in the Declaration 'are held to be based not simply on the decisions of the assembly that approved them, but on man's very nature and his inalienable dignity as a person created by God'.[44]

Some questions, however, arise from such attempts to make common ground with a wider audience on the basis of shared perception of the natural law. First of all, simply because the exponent of an argument claims that what he or she says is grounded in natural law provides no guarantee that others will accept that it is. For example, it is arguable whether some papal encyclicals have in fact established common ground with non-Christians as successfully as their authors hoped they would. Pope Paul VI appears in retrospect to have been unrealistic in *Humanae Vitae*, when he expresses the belief that because his teaching about the inadmissibility of 'artificial' contraception was based upon natural law, his contemporaries would have little difficulty in seeing how reasonable it was.[45] Banner comments that:

> certain of the papal encyclicals of the nineteenth and twentieth centuries ... represent the most vaunting claims for the power of unaided reason ... holding as they do that, amongst other things, abortion, divorce, contraception, dueling, homosexuality, and euthanasia are all contrary to the natural law, and that they are known to be wrong on the basis of reason alone.[46]

Moreover, even if appeals to natural law were always successful in establishing common ground with non-Christians, other commentators would argue that such a state of affairs is not necessarily desirable. This criticism of natural law thinking is strenuously made by Stanley Hauerwas, who argues precisely that Christians ought *not* to be seeking to establish common ground with others, but rather to emphasize the distinctive nature of

---

42 Benedict XVI (2006), *The Human Person, the Heart of Peace*, p. 3.
43 Speech of Benedict XVI, 1 February, 2010.
44 Benedict XVI (2006), *The Human Person, the Heart of Peace*, p. 13.
45 See Paul VI, *Humanae Vitae* 12.
46 Banner (2009), p. 47.

the Church as a community that lives by a particular story, and whose life is shaped by a particular set of practices that are not universally shared. In his book *The Peaceable Kingdom*, and elsewhere in his writing, Hauerwas criticizes the natural law inspired view that 'Christian ethics is human ethics', and that the fundamental ethical command is simply to 'be human'.[47] In his view, ethics that emphasize the importance of values that are in principle available to anyone detract from the distinctiveness of the Christian story and tend to make 'the events and actions of Jesus' life seem accidental'.[48] While Hauerwas agrees with O'Donovan that, on an ontological level, we can talk about a natural order that really does exist, on an epistemological level, he contends that the right path to knowledge of it must be through the community of the Christian Church and its Scriptures: 'while the way of life taught by Christ is meant to be an ethic for all people, it does not follow that we can know what such an ethic involves "objectively" by looking at the human'.[49] Commending the approach of Karl Barth to this subject, Hauerwas further criticizes the absence of Christology that he detects in much natural theology, 'the truth that is Jesus Christ is ... not one truth among others ... [but] Christ is the truth by which all other truth is to be judged'.[50]

For Hauerwas, whose ethics are deeply permeated by his pacifist convictions, the apparently open-minded quest of natural law ethicists to establish common ground with non-Christians has a sinister dimension. Referring back to the origins of natural law in the work of the early Christian Apologists and later in Augustine, he notes that 'the power of natural law as a systematic idea was developed in and for the Roman imperium and then for "Christendom"'.[51] In other words, it came into being at a time when, as Hauerwas would see it, Christianity was moving from its pacifist origins towards a fateful accommodation with an inherently violent Roman state. True to its origins, natural law ethics can, Hauerwas argues, be used to underwrite violence because if moral truths are essentially self-evident to all people of good will, then those who do not recognize them may be judged to be wilful or obtuse, and corrected accordingly, if necessary by force. Hauerwas comments that:

> when Christians assume that their particular moral convictions are independent of narrative, that they are justified by some universal standpoint free of history, they are tempted to imagine that those who do not share

---

47 Hauerwas (1983), p. 56; cf. Paul VI: 'a human and Christian doctrine of marriage', *Humanae Vitae* 14.

48 Hauerwas (1983), p. 57.

49 Hauerwas (1983), p. 58.

50 Hauerwas (2001), *With the Grain of the Universe* (London: SCM Press), pp. 162–3.

51 Hauerwas (1983), p. 51.

such an ethic must be particularly perverse and should be coerced to do what we know on universal grounds they really should want to do.[52]

Alexander Lucie-Smith neatly summarizes the point: 'a universalist morality gives those in power an extra stick – that of sweet reason – with which to beat the dissenter'.[53]

Case study

Louise is a committed and practising Christian. As she sees it, her baptism and church membership should not confine her to the aims of, for example, trying to make other people into Christians or teaching them the faith, but as also pursuing wider human values such as education and trying to build a better society. Louise decides to accept an invitation to become a governor of a primary school in her area. She does not find this experience altogether easy, because in her discussions with her fellow governors, she sometimes disagrees with some of their assumptions. One governor, for example, argues strongly that the school is simply there to allow children to 'discover their own values' and that there is no right or wrong value system that could or should be imposed on them. Louise believes that a key aim of schooling is that children should be opened up to a sense of wonder at the world that God has made. She realizes that this aim would not be shared by many of her fellow governors, but their joint belief in the fundamental importance of education gives sufficient common ground for her to work co-operatively with them.

Questions for discussion

In what way do Louise's views compare with natural law thinking?

What do you see as the strengths and weaknesses of her approach?

How do you think that commentators who were unsympathetic to natural law ethics might want her to act in her role as a school governor?

Natural law, culture, history and power

Towards the end of his section on natural law in the *Summa Theologica*, Aquinas considers the questions of 'whether the natural law can be changed?' and 'whether the natural law can be abolished from the heart of man?'[54] He

---

52 Hauerwas (1983), p. 61.
53 Lucie-Smith (2007), p. 43.
54 Aquinas, *Summa Theologica* 1-2. 94.5–6.

concludes that although there may be some rare cases in which proximate conclusions about what it requires may vary, the natural law itself in its first principles endures for ever and applies at all times and in all places. In the words of the twelfth-century canon lawyer Gratian, one of the authorities he quotes on this point, 'the natural law dates from the creation of the rational creature. It does not vary according to time, but remains fixed and unchangeable.'[55]

Aquinas's claim that natural law extends across all places and human societies is called into question by cultural relativism, an approach which was discussed in the previous chapter. Cultural relativists emphasize the extent to which societal norms and variations in language shape different people's approaches to morality. In the words of the anthropologist Franz Boas (1858–1942), 'civilization is not something absolute, but ... is relative, and ... our ideas and conceptions are true only so far as our civilization goes'. In addition to cultural differences, Darwinian science has discovered some of the ways in which human beings, like other animals, evolve over generations. If we accept that human beings themselves are evolving and changing, then it may seem unreasonable to hold to a fixed and unchanging idea of natural law and the human good.

Feminist writers have, in particular, drawn attention to the way in which historically conditioned understandings of human and, in particular, female identity have been regarded as written into the laws of nature. Susan F. Parsons writes that:

> feminists have helped to shatter the illusion that there is some realm of nature apart from history that underlies all that we do. They have deconstructed this so-called reality, as yet another pretentious construction of culture. It is exposed as a lie, told by the powerful to subdue and silence the powerless.[56]

Stephen Pope agrees with this assessment:

> knowledge of history enables us to see as cultural what was once assumed to be 'natural' – the inferiority of women, the double standard for males and females in sexual morality, the disgracefulness of long hair on men, the enslavement of captives of war.[57]

As Pope and Parsons suggest, modern commentators on such subjects tend to be particularly aware of the power dynamics that may be at play when particular human characteristics or norms of behaviour are understood and

---

55 Gratian, *Decretum* I, quoted in Aquinas, *Summa Theologica* 1-2. 94.5.
56 Parsons in Hoose (1998), p. 145.
57 Pope in Gill (2001), p. 92.

described as 'natural'. Putting it crudely, they have asked 'who gets to define what is natural?'

There is perhaps some room for a position that mediates between the two sides of this argument. On the one hand, it is clearly important to be attentive and sensitive to the wide differences that undoubtedly do exist between cultures, including on some important and sometimes intractable ethical questions. On the other hand, however, the passage quoted (p. 122 above) from Finnis's *Natural Law and Natural Rights* about the universality of certain human values insists strongly that even societies that are far separated in place and time show striking similarities in their underlying values and understandings of the good. Advocates of natural law need not insist that all cultural differences are non-existent, nor that they have no ethical significance, but can make the rather more modest claim that there is sufficient commonality between societies to be able to draw limited but important trans-cultural conclusions about what are the goods to be done and evils to be avoided. As Cessario puts it:

> human nature is sufficiently invariant across cultures and types of social organization to be taken as a premiss in arguments seeking to justify particular courses for human behaviour, and, moreoever, that fixed elements of human nature provide substantial enough input to function in this role.[58]

Thus, while acknowledging the importance that different cultures and historical periods play in shaping the values and judgements of those who live in them, it is still possible for advocates of natural law ethics to insist that we can detect quite a number of stable characteristics of human nature and the human good that underlie these.

Natural law and the movement from is to ought

Oliver O'Donovan writes: 'the way the universe *is*, determines how man *ought* to behave himself in it'.[59] His statement reflects the general shape of much natural law thinking, which is often described as a movement from is to ought; from facts about the world to moral values which appear to be suggested by those facts. In other words, natural law theories characteristically start from an understanding of the nature of the God-given reality as it truly exists, and work from this towards an account of how men and women should conduct their lives within this reality. This procedure, however, is open to question for a number of reasons.

---

58 Cessario (2001), p. 87.
59 O'Donovan (1994), p. 17.

The first problem with the movement from is to ought was unintentionally encapsulated by President Bill Clinton during his 1998 grand jury testimony on the Monica Lewinsky affair. In a somewhat evasive answer, Clinton responded to one question with the remark that, 'It depends on what the meaning of the words "is" is.' Thus, as has been suggested above, natural law theorists need to ask themselves whether they can really be confident enough in the reality of what they observe (the *is*) to be able to draw from this the conclusions about right and wrong moral action that such a reality would seem to suggest (the *ought*). Many would concur with the view of Michael Banner that 'what is known as natural cannot, as a matter of fact, be securely naturally known'.[60]

However, a further problem concerns not just knowledge of the is, but the actual movement of thought from is to ought. A long line of philosophers, including figures such as David Hume (1711–76) and G. E. Moore (1873–1958) have criticized what is often called the naturalistic fallacy: the entire belief that it is possible to derive a set of moral rules from a description of how things are in the world. Thus, even if it were possible to be completely confident that we understand the facts, Hume argues that is it impossible to go on and derive a moral value out of them. In his influential *Treatise of Human Nature* (1739), Hume argues that descriptive language (which concerns facts and what is) in fact differs fundamentally from moral language (which concerns values and what ought to be), and that care should be taken not to conflate the two.

Echoing Hume's point, Finnis trenchantly insists that personalist versions of natural law theory, based on the 'self-evident' human goods do not in fact rely on the observation of how things are, and thus do not move from is to ought. Rather, the basic human goods are self-evident, derived from our basic grasp of what is good for us. The basic goods, Finnis writes:

> are not inferred from facts [nor from] ... metaphysical propositions about human nature, or about the nature of good and evil, or about 'the function of a human being', nor are they inferred from a teleological conception of nature or any other conception of nature. They are not inferred or derived from anything. They are underived (though not innate).[61]

However, most proponents of natural law theories in theological ethics would admit that precisely because moral rules and values are not arbitrary but built into the structure of the universe, nature must in some sense be capable of being used as a moral source, even if only an ancillary one. God

---

60 Banner (1999), p. 271.

61 Finnis (1980), pp. 33–4. Northcott questions Finnis's consistency on this point: 'His use of ... empirical studies of the character of the good in different societies demonstrates that in practice it is almost impossible to avoid making statements about what human societies normally and naturally do', Northcott (1996), p. 246.

has created all things through his Word and his Spirit, and so all things bear witness to his loving purposes, even if we do not always have eyes capable of discerning how they do so.

As a final comment, however, the title of O'Donovan's book *Resurrection and Moral Order* reminds us that natural law ethics should look not only to the current state of the world, but also to the eschatological future that God has in store for the whole of creation: a future of which Jesus' resurrection and the sending of the Holy Spirit at Pentecost are the 'first fruits' (see 1 Cor. 15; Acts 2). This eschatological future will, according to the New Testament writers, vindicate but also transform God's original creation: 'Christian ethics ... looks backwards and forwards, to the origin and to the end of the created order. It respects the natural structures of life in the world, while looking forward to their transformation.'[62] Thus, the movement from *is* to *ought* needs to be held in an eschatological perspective and can perhaps more accurately be described as a movement from *will be* to *ought* (when what *will be* is understood as what currently *is* when this has been transformed in the light of the Kingdom of God). Those who seek, as proponents of natural law ethics do, to emphasize that morality arises naturally from the reality that God has given, must take account not only of reality as it currently appears to be, but of the new reality that God begins to inaugurate at Easter and Pentecost: a reality that will be redeemed, re-pristinated, re-oriented and re-described, so that it once again truly reflects God's creative intentions:

> The resurrection of Jesus Christ opens the way for the Christian hope that God will one day renew and transform the created reality that we now experience, but this renewal and transformation will be not the negation of the created order, but its fulfilment and re-affirmation. In the new and more truly natural order to which the resurrection points us, 'origin and end are inseparably united'.[63]

Questions for discussion

Can you think of other places in the Bible, or more widely in Christian theology, in which the concept of natural law seems to feature?

What contribution do you think natural law theories might have to make to current debates in the Church or, more widely, in society?

What seem to you to be the most important strengths and weaknesses of natural law theories?

---

62 O'Donovan (1994), p. 58.
63 O'Donovan (1994), p. 57.

8

Further Perspectives on Conscience

Conscience must be followed, but conscience must also be educated.[1]

The discussion of conscience in chapter 4 suggested that this provided a good summary of the attitude to conscience that comes across from the Bible and from the wider Christian moral tradition. This chapter will discuss three relatively recent critiques of the way that conscience can be understood, and seek to explore how these shed light on this important but elusive concept.

Conscience and subjectivism

The first of these critiques comes from Pope John Paul II (1920–2005) in his encyclical of 1993, *Veritatis Splendor* (*The Splendour of Truth*), which has been discussed in various contexts in previous chapters. John Paul II, a charismatic leader of the Roman Catholic Church, was widely credited with having helped to bring about an end to Communism in his native country of Poland, and indeed throughout much the Eastern Bloc. During his papacy, he also, perhaps with less obvious success, mounted a sustained critique of the individualism that seemed to him endemic in the modern Western world. John Paul II articulated many of his moral teachings in this encyclical, whose core message is encapsulated in Jesus' words in John's Gospel, 'you will know the truth and the truth will make you free' (John 8.32). John Paul's alignment of freedom and truth contrasts with a widespread modern assumption that the assertion of moral truth by religious authorities is likely to conflict with the freedom of the individual. John Paul argues, on the other hand, that 'patterned on God's freedom, man's freedom is not negated by his obedience to the divine law; indeed, only through this obedience does it abide in truth and conform to human dignity'.[2] In a theme that was discussed in chapter 1, he argues that true freedom is not freedom *from* the truth, but freedom *in* the truth:[3] 'man's genuine moral autonomy in no way means the rejection, but rather the acceptance of the moral law,

---

1 Holmgren (2000), p. 126.
2 John Paul II, *Veritatis Splendor* 42.1.
3 John Paul II, *Veritatis Splendor* 64.2.

of God's command'.[4] For human beings to live in accordance with truth is thus truly to be free and to flourish.

In line with Aquinas and Newman, whose thought on the subject was discussed in chapter 4, John Paul II's specific teaching on the subject of conscience affirms its imperative character: 'man must act in accordance with it'.[5] He shares the view that it must be right to do those things that, in our heart of hearts, we believe we should do, and that it must also be right to refrain from doing something that in our heart of hearts we sincerely believe would be wrong. However, the fact that individuals have this obligation to follow their consciences does not mean that their consciences are always right in their discernment. Indeed, John Paul II strongly criticizes the subjectivist view that all moral viewpoints are true for those who hold them. He argues that we should reject the idea 'that one's moral judgement is true merely by the fact that it has its origin in conscience'.[6] Drawing on Romans 2, John Paul II reiterates Saint Paul's point that conscience itself does not independently generate morality, but rather that its role is to bear witness to objective truth, and to 'apply the universal knowledge of the good in a specific situation'.[7] Conscience 'does not *establish* the law; rather it *bears witness* to the authority of the natural law and of the practical reason with reference to the supreme good, whose attractiveness the human person perceives and whose commandment he accepts'.[8] Conscience, as the term *syneidesis* implies, is necessarily a dialogue, a 'knowing together with', but it must not simply be 'a dialogue of man with himself'. It must also be 'a dialogue of man with God, the author of the law, the primordial image and final end of man'.[9]

John Paul II argues that the objective truths of morality, to which conscience bears witness, are not alien impositions on us, but derive from natural law, and so they are ingrained in our deepest nature, even if we do not realize it (a position that for some people, of course, is controversial). Thus, the task of the Church's teaching authority, as he sees it, is not to inflict new and arbitrary rules upon the consciences of Christians, but rather to keep on reminding them of those truths which, because they arise from natural law, we should already be able to recognize: 'the Magisterium does not bring to the Christian conscience truths which are extraneous to it; rather it brings to light the truths which it ought already to possess'.[10] However, since, because of our fallen human nature, we tend to forget such

---

4 John Paul II, *Veritatis Splendor* 41.1.
5 John Paul II, *Veritatis Splendor* 60.
6 John Paul II, *Veritatis Splendor* 32.1.
7 John Paul II, *Veritatis Splendor* 32.2.
8 John Paul II, *Veritatis Splendor* 60; my italics.
9 John Paul II, *Veritatis Splendor* 58.
10 John Paul II, *Veritatis Splendor* 64.2.

truths, our consciences require continual education, formation and conversion to what is good and true.

Many commentators at the time of the encyclical were quick to point out that one particular issue that was near the surface of the Pope's concerns in *Veritatis Splendor* was the use by many Catholics of 'artificial' methods of contraception, in disobedience to the teaching most famously articulated by Pope Paul VI, in *Humanae Vitae*. Many Catholics who use contraception have justified their decision on the grounds that it was made in good conscience, and that the Church taught that conscience should be followed. Such people seem an obvious target of John Paul II's criticisms of those who set freedom against truth, and their own consciences against the objective, God-given moral law. In part because of this contentious debate, polarized reactions to *Veritatis Splendor* were expressed, both within and outside Roman Catholicism. Some agreed with the Pope's attack on apparently inflated understandings of conscience, and believed that *Veritatis Splendor* provided a timely reassertion of the objectivity of moral truth in a society dominated by individualism and subjectivism. Others saw the encyclical as an unwelcome and unnecessary intrusion into freedom and indeed the privacy of individual couples.[11] To the Pope's contention that the individual conscience is not 'a supreme tribunal of moral judgment which hands down categorical and infallible decisions about good and evil',[12] some of his critics tended to argue that this was a role that John Paul preferred to reserve for himself. The Catholic moral theologian Bernard Häring commented that the encyclical was 'directed, above all, towards one goal: to endorse total assent and submission to all utterances of the Pope'.[13]

At the time of its publication and subsequently, controversy surrounding the reception of *Veritatis Splendor* sometimes obscured the importance of the wider points about conscience that John Paul makes in the encyclical. One of these concerns the essentially rational nature of the exercise of conscience. The judgement of *synderesis* is based on the '*rational* conviction that one must love and do good and avoid evil',[14] and the working of *syneidesis* also is a reasoned application of basic moral insights to concrete situations. In line with this, conscience is defined in the *Catechism of the Catholic Church* as 'a judgment of reason whereby the human person recognizes the moral quality of a concrete act that he is going to perform, is in the process of performing, or has already completed'.[15] This is not to say that emotions have no role to play in moral decision making but, to return to a theme that

---

11 A selection of these views may be found in J. Wilkins (1994) (ed.), *Considering Veritatis Splendor* (Cleveland: Pilgrim Press); see also Banner (2009), pp. 107–13.

12 John Paul II, *Veritatis Splendor* 32.1.

13 Quoted in J. Cornwell (2001), *Breaking Faith* (London: Viking), p. 211; see also Mahoney (1987), pp. 289–94.

14 John Paul II, *Veritatis Splendor* 59.2 (my italics).

15 *Catechism of the Catholic Church* 1778.

was discussed in chapter 6, it does call into question the emotivist tendency to use conscience as a sort of ethical conversation-stopper, able to trump all rational arguments on the grounds that no one can really question what I happen to feel my conscience is telling me about how to act in a particular situation.

In his book *Changing Values*, David Attwood writes about the role accorded to conscience when men and women are being conscripted into military service in times of war. Attwood points out that democratic societies normally respect the consciences of individuals who believe that it is wrong under all circumstances to fight and kill. However, before they are excused their military service, conscientious objectors are required to lay out carefully the reasons why they hold their particular beliefs. Attwood writes that 'in valuing freedom of conscience very highly, we ask that those who conscientiously dissent from those in authority engage critically and rationally, giving good reasons for their dissent'.[16] Attwood's comments provide a helpful example of how conscience can be given the very greatest respect, and yet at the same time held rationally accountable.

Discussion point

During the Second World War, those who wanted to register as conscientious objectors in the United States because of their religious beliefs received a DSS 47 form with ten questions

1. Describe the nature of your belief which is the basis of your claim.

2. Explain how, when, and from whom or from what source you received the training and acquired the belief which is the basis of your claim.

3. Give the name and present address of the individual upon whom you rely most for religious guidance.

4. Under what circumstances, if any, do you believe in the use of force?

5. Describe the actions and behavior in your life which in your opinion most conspicuously demonstrate the consistency and depth of your religious convictions.

6. Have you ever given public expression, written or oral, to the views herein expressed as the basis for your claim made above? If so, specify when and where.

---

16 Attwood (1998), p. 178.

7. Have you ever been a member of any military organization or establishment? If so, state the name and address of same and give reasons why you became a member.

8. Are you a member of a religious sect or organization?

9. Describe carefully the creed or official statements of said religious sect or organization as it relates to participation in war.

10. Describe your relationships with and activities in all organizations with which you are or have been affiliated other than religious or military.

Can you think of other areas in which people today might want to make a conscientious objection?

What questions should they be asked under such circumstances?

Conscience and prudence

Previous chapters have discussed the way in which contemporary Catholic theologians such as Servais Pinckaers (1925–2008) and Romanus Cessario (1944–) have been concerned to reorientate moral theology towards themes such as human flourishing, beatitude, grace and virtue, and away from a heavy stress on obligation and law. By so doing, such writers have sought to reach back to the tradition of Aquinas, Augustine, Paul and indeed Jesus himself, and to correct the excessive legalism that they perceive in the so-called 'manuals' of moral theology, whose approach had predominated in the Roman Catholic Church since the Council of Trent in the mid-sixteenth century.[17] Writers of the manuals provided much systematic reflection on the subject of conscience, making strenuous efforts, for example, to describe in detail the state of the conscience as it related to decision making. An individual's conscience could be judged with great precision to be, for example, true or false; certain or doubtful; perplexed, scrupulous or lax. It was from this tradition also that the important distinction between formal and material sin was formulated.

---

17 See Pinckaers (2005), chapters 16 and 17.

Formal and material sins

Material sins are actions that are objectively speaking wrong, but are not known to be so by the person who commits them. A person who drives at 40 miles per hour on a particular stretch of road, unaware of the fact that there is a speed limit of 30 would be committing a material sin.

Formal sins are sins that are committed in the knowledge that they are sins. A person who drives at 40 in the full knowledge that they should not be going above 30 would be guilty of one of these.

In both cases, the person has done something that is wrong, but there is clearly a distinction to be drawn between them. 'Formal' sins are more culpable because, if a person knows that something is wrong, but deliberately does it nonetheless, they will thereby have ignored their conscience.

However, for all its detail and seriousness of purpose, this tradition of reflection on conscience had, in Pinckaers's view, some serious shortcomings. In a graphic image, he compares conscience in the tradition of the manuals with an arbitrator between two competing landowners arguing over a field. The two landowners stand for freedom and law, and the field stands for the human person.[18] On the one hand, freedom would like to claim the land: we would like to do whatever we want, entirely unconstrained by any rules. On the other hand, moral law stakes a claim on us: it would like to stop us doing what we want. Conscience, by applying the rules in our situation, will adjudicate whether, in a particular instance, freedom wins, in which case we can get away with acting as we want to, or whether law wins, in which case we must submit to the limitations that it places on our freedom and our fun.

For Pinckaers, this view is inadequate on many fronts. Echoing the approach of Augustine to this subject,[19] Pinckaers argues that it is an impoverished view of freedom to see it simply as the ability to do whatever we want, unconstrained by anyone else. The truly free person is the one who is liberated to fulfil the potential of his or her created nature, and to be happy in the fullest and widest sense – the sense that Jesus describes in the Beatitudes. Similarly, the view of law that this analogy presents is also inadequate, because the moral instructions contained in the Bible are, in Kantian style, viewed primarily as a set of constraining obligations ('Thou shalt nots'); obligations that we would rather did not exist. This attitude may be contrasted with the joyful and open attitude to God's law expressed, for example, by the psalmist, for whom God's statutes and ordinances are a

---

18 See Pinckaers (2005), pp. 343–4.
19 See chapter 1 and the discussion at the start of this chapter.

continual source of inspiration and happiness. Most pertinently for the subject of this chapter, the analogy presents an inadequate view of conscience, relegating it to the legalistic role of policing boundary disputes between what is forbidden and what is permissible. Thus, conscience loses what was described in chapter 4 as its 'transcendent' dimension of revealing human beings to themselves and drawing them forwards towards everlasting happiness with God. Pinckaers commends the writing of Newman for recapturing that transcendent sense of conscience. For Newman, he writes:

> the term 'conscience' has been able to recoup ... all that is best in the moral lives of many Christians. It no longer designates the awareness of a law that obliges and constrains, but rather the knowledge of a law that appeals to the heart and touches it.[20]

However, if the tradition of the manuals led on the one hand to a reductive understanding of conscience as a legalistic process of adjudicating between freedom and law, Pinckaers also criticizes it for, in another sense, fostering an inflated view of conscience as an exercise not just of judgement, but also of the will which enables us to act in a particular way. In a sort of mirror image of John Paul II's criticisms of the way that conscience has been extended *backwards* to become the source of moral knowledge, so Pinckaers criticizes the way in which conscience has been extended *forwards* to be seen as the motor of our actions and choices. But, while we can use our conscience to apply moral principles to particular cases, the conscience itself does not, in Pinckaers's view, enable us to act well. If this were so, then we would always act in accordance with the dictates of our conscience, but in fact we often do not do so. As Cessario notes, 'the view that conscience by itself provides the faculty for translating moral knowledge into actual practice ... runs counter to the evidentiary fact that, sometimes even over a long period of time, people act against the deepest instincts of conscience'.[21] Through the working of conscience then, we may be able to know the good, but as Saint Paul reminds us in Romans 7, or Augustine in his dispute with Pelagius, knowing the good does not necessarily enable us to do it.

Commentators such as Pinckaers and Cessario insist therefore that, in order to be a person who acts well we need not only a properly working conscience, able to apply moral principles in particular situations, but also a particular set of personal characteristics; in other words, a virtue. Traditionally, the virtue in question is that of prudence, which 'concerns itself with translating moral wisdom into practical action, into actually doing something concrete about engaging with the good'.[22] Prudence, then, takes up where conscience leaves off. Pinckaers writes that 'prudence ... is not

20 Pinckaers (2005), p. 337.
21 Cessario (2001), p. 133.
22 Cessario (2001), p. 134.

content to deliberate, to counsel, or to judge in the abstract. Its distinctive action is the command, that is, the decision to act.'[23] The prudent person will accept the guidance of his or her conscience, but then be able to put this into practice. Prudence, like the other virtues, is built up through habit and training, effort and virtuous example. But crucially, in its specifically Christian sense, it becomes, like the theological virtues, 'infused' and not simply an 'acquired' virtue, animated by grace and, like the other virtues, finding its true direction in the love of God and neighbour. The diagram below is a thumbnail sketch of how, according to some of the ideas we have considered, we might understand good actions being made, from their origins in the eternal law of God, known through natural law and revelation, through the workings of conscience, and on into concrete action. As the diagram indicates, conscience plays an important but limited part in the process.

1. God's eternal law	→	2. *synderesis*	→	3. *syneidesis*	→	4. virtuous action
'How God knows the world to be' (Cessario)		Our awareness of 1.		Our application of 2. in a specific case		Our putting of 3. into action in love of God and neighbour
Requires understanding of natural law and Scripture	**= Conscience**					*Requires prudence*

Conscience and responsibility

A final and very different critique of conscience comes from the German Lutheran theologian Dietrich Bonhoeffer (1906–45). Bonhoeffer was a theologian and pastor of the Confessing Church in Germany who was imprisoned in 1943 for participating in a plot to assassinate Adolf Hitler, and executed with his fellow-conspirators in April 1945, only a matter of days before Hitler himself committed suicide. Bonhoeffer's *Ethics* is a late work, largely written in the heat of controversy, and only collated in its present form after the author's death.

The book begins with a radical critique of all ethics, which Bonhoeffer argues is itself a fallen discipline – a sign of our fundamental disunity with God, caused by original sin. Bonhoeffer writes that 'man at his origin knows only one thing: God',[24] with whom he is entirely united. However, as a

23 Pinckaers (2005), p. 352.
24 Bonhoeffer (1949), p. 3.

result of the Fall, human beings start to know good and evil, and hence to become like God, although simultaneously estranged from him (Gen. 3.5, 22). Morality, as human beings now understand it, has lost its moorings in God's eternal will, and become 'the good and evil of man's own choosing, in opposition to the eternal election of God'.[25] Thus, moral knowledge 'now means the establishment of the relationship to oneself; it means the recognition in all things of oneself and of oneself in all things'.[26]

For Bonhoeffer, the conscience, as we normally consider it, follows this fallen trajectory, because conscience inevitably seeks to establish unity of human beings with themselves, rather than engaging in the more important task of establishing the unity with God lost by the Fall. Conscience makes us want to ensure that our judgements and ultimately our actions are consistent with our most deeply held principles so that, as in the diagram above, each stage will flow smoothly on from the one before. Thus, despite what might be intended, the consistency of moral agents with themselves becomes the primary benchmark for virtuous action. For Bonhoeffer, then, the judgements of conscience, the sifting of good and evil, the concern for personal integrity, the attempt to resolve inner conflicts and tensions – all of these are signs not, as we might think, of good character, but rather of our fallen nature; of our striving for autonomy and self-sufficiency, and of our desire to be at union with ourselves, while being radically disunited from God: 'the call of conscience has its origin and its goal in the autonomy of a man's own ego'.[27] Unsurprisingly, we discover that conscience buys us this self-consistency at a very high price, because when our primary objective is to act in accordance with our own theoretical ethical codes and 'categorical imperatives', then we inevitably downgrade those things that are really important for moral action: the call of God in the here and now, and the concrete reality of the needs of our neighbour. The ultimate absurdity of pursuing moral consistency for its own sake is evident from Kant's 'grotesque conclusion that I must return an honest "yes" to the enquiry of the murderer who breaks into my house and asks whether my friend whom he is pursuing has taken refuge there'.[28]

By contrast, 'responsible' moral agents will sometimes be inconsistent for the sake of God and neighbour, willing to act on occasion against conscience, and sacrifice even their most deeply held principles for the sake of others. This 'bearing guilt for the sake of our neighbour'[29] itself reflects Jesus' own actions who, Bonhoeffer argues, 'enters into the fellowship of human guilt',[30] by breaking Sabbath regulations, eating with sinners and

---

25 Bonhoeffer (1949), p. 5.
26 Bonhoeffer (1949), p. 11.
27 Bonhoeffer (1949), p. 212.
28 Bonhoeffer (1949), pp. 213–14; see chapter 6 for further details.
29 Bonhoeffer (1949), p. 213.
30 Bonhoeffer (1949), p. 213.

outcasts and, ultimately, dying on the cross so as to set the human conscience free for the service of God and neighbour:

> When a man takes guilt upon himself in responsibility, and no responsible man can avoid this, he imputes this guilt to himself and to no one else; he answers for it; he accepts responsibility for it. He does not do this in the insolent presumptuousness of his own power, but he does it in the knowledge that this liberty is forced upon him and that in this liberty he is dependent upon grace. Before other men the man of free responsibility is justified by necessity; before himself he is acquitted by his conscience; but before God he hopes only for mercy.[31]

Bonhoeffer's writing on this subject has an unmistakeably autobiographical ring to it. Commenting in an earlier work, *The Cost of Discipleship*, on Jesus' teaching about 'an eye for an eye and a tooth for a tooth' (see Matt. 5.38–42), he had argued that 'the only way to overcome evil is to let it run itself to a standstill because it does not find the resistance it is looking for'.[32] In view of this, Bonhoeffer's depiction of the form that responsible action might take bears obvious comparison with his own decision to lay aside his own pacifist principles, and become involved in the plot to assassinate Hitler. The self-consistency that conscience seeks to ensure is a theoretical good which, Bonhoeffer argues, we should be prepared to sacrifice for the actual needs of our neighbour – in his own case, those suffering throughout the world because of the actions of Hitler. By contrast, then, with the smooth progression that is suggested in the diagram above, Bonhoeffer leaves us with the disturbing, and perhaps characteristically Protestant, insight that, in a fallen world, the exercise of true Christian conscience may not always follow a smooth path from principles to practice, but may sometimes appear to involve rupture and discontinuity.

Questions for discussion

Is it always authoritarian to want to limit the role of the individual conscience?

Are Bonhoeffer's comments on conscience helpful, or are they simply a case of special pleading?

---

31 Bonhoeffer (1949), p. 216.
32 Bonhoeffer (1937), p. 127.

9

Further Perspectives on Virtue

The revival of virtue ethics

Despite its importance in the classical and Christian traditions, virtue has had a sad story over the last 500 years. For reasons that were discussed in more detail in chapter 5, theologians in the Protestant tradition have traditionally been suspicious of Aquinas's understanding of virtue, because it appeared to give some quarter to the idea of justification by works. Strongly influenced by Augustine's insistence in the Pelagian controversy that human beings cannot improve themselves out of their own moral resources (see chapter 1), Luther in particular condemned the idea that we can become better people through acquiring good habits. In a characteristically colourful passage, he describes the group of Parisian theologians who had espoused this teaching as

> [an] impure and foul whore which has declared that Aristotle's teachings on morals are not in conflict with the teachings of Christ, since he teaches nothing other than that virtue is acquired by works, saying 'By doing good we become good'. The Christian conscience curses this statement as bilge water of hell and says, 'By believing in Christ who is good, I, even I, am made good: his goodness is mine also, for it is a gift from him and is not my work.'[1]

Luther's suspicion of virtue persists to this day in the somewhat defensive note that modern Protestant theologians can strike, when they are seeking (as several now do) to commend virtue ethics to their readership. 'The very mention of virtue', writes N. T. Wright, 'will make many Christians stiffen in alarm. They have been taught, quite rightly that we are not justified by our works, but only by our faith.'[2]

Given the enduring importance of Thomas Aquinas and the huge amount of attention that he devotes to the theme of virtue, it is perhaps more surprising that virtue has also been downplayed in the Catholic tradition. In

---

1 J. J. Pelikan, H. C. Oswald and H. T. Lehmann (1966) (eds), *Luther's Works*, vol. 44 (Philadelphia: Fortress Press), p. 300, quoted in Tomlin (2006), p. 91.

2 Wright (2010), p. 51; cf. Tomlin (2006), p. 89.

part as a counterblast against the Reformation emphasis on justification by faith, the moral theology which grew out of the sixteenth-century Council of Trent tended to emphasize the importance of obeying rules and fulfilling obligations based on natural law. This emphasis on rules tended to crowd out the more subtle analysis, made possible by reflection on the virtues, of the way in which Christian moral character is formed over time through grace and the development of good habits. Moreover, the all-important practice of confession tended to lead both priests and penitents to assume that the key challenge of the Christian moral life was to avoid sin. The complementary challenge to do the good, and to pursue those things that lead to human flourishing (again, key concerns in reflection upon the virtues) was often relegated to spirituality and ascetical theology. The twentieth-century moral theologian Thomas Slater (1855–1928) wrote the following grim summary of the aims of manuals for confessors such as his own:

> They are not intended for edification, nor do they hold up a high ideal of Christian perfection for the imitation of the faithful. They deal with what is of obligation under the pain of sin, they are books of moral pathology.[3]

More recent years, however, have seen a revival of interest in virtue both in philosophical and theological circles. This has been influenced by the writing of, among others, two contemporary moral philosophers, both of whom, although converts to Roman Catholicism, nonetheless, write in a primarily philosophical rather than theological register. The philosopher with the greatest claim to have initiated modern virtue ethics is G. E. M. (Elizabeth) Anscombe (1919–2001),[4] who, in an essay entitled *Modern Moral Philosophy*, written in 1958, launched a fierce attack on the approaches to ethics that she found among her contemporaries. Anscombe criticized advocates of deontological ethics for, among other things, espousing what seems to her an 'absurd' idea that human beings can accurately identify the maxims (the underlying principles) of their own actions, and then legislate about these for themselves. She further criticized the 'shallow philosophy' that the rightness or otherwise of actions could be assessed solely on those actions' expected consequences. The moral judgements of consequentialists would, she argued, inevitably be held captive to fashionable ethical standards. What is needed, Anscombe argues is 'an account of human nature, human action, the type of characteristic a virtue is, and above all of human "flourishing"'.[5]

A second powerful influence has been that of the Scottish philosopher

---

3 Thomas Slater, *A Manual of Moral Theology*, p. 6, quoted in Keenan (2010), p. 11. This section draws on Keenan (2010), chapter 2.

4 Reprinted in Crisp and Slote (1997), chapter 1.

5 Anscombe in Crisp and Slote (1997), p. 44.

Alasdair MacIntyre (1929–), whose book *After Virtue* was first published in 1981, and who expressed a similarly gloomy verdict on the state of modern ethical thought.[6] MacIntyre argues that the Enlightenment project, represented by Kant, Bentham and others, of attempting to construct a universal morality upon which all could agree, was one that 'had to fail'. The supposed resources of human rationality, upon which such philosophers based their ethics, could not provide a secure enough mooring for moral judgements, when these judgements were not also anchored in a wider sense of the overall purpose or *telos* of human life (the sort of purpose provided by Aristotle's understanding of *eudaimonia*, or Aquinas's of *beatitudo*).[7] The failure of the Enlightenment project led to a breakdown of moral conversation and the sort of interminable ethical arguments between consequentialists and deontologists that are all too familiar in Western countries over subjects such as abortion.

Eventually, MacIntyre argues, the failure of rationalist approaches to ethics inevitably led to the rise of emotivist thinking, which (hopelessly) eschewed rationality altogether, seeing all moral judgements as the exercise only of feelings and personal preferences.

Another well-known writer in this field, and one on whom this chapter will particularly focus, is the colourful Texan ethicist Stanley Hauerwas (1940–). Declared 'America's best theologian' by *Time* magazine in 2001, Hauerwas has sought to explore the theological implications of the insights on virtue provided by Anscombe, MacIntyre and other philosophers working in this field. Hauerwas is an ecclesial hybrid who, at the time that this book is being written worships in an Episcopal (Anglican) church, but he remains deeply influenced by his native Methodism, as well as by Roman Catholicism and the Anabaptist traditions, with which he has had extensive contact.

Definitions

Quandary	a state of perplexity or doubt
Dilemma	a choice between unattractive alternatives

Key shifts in virtue ethics

Moral action $\rightarrow$ Moral agent

Reflection on quandary/decision/dilemma $\rightarrow$ Reflection on character

---

6 For summaries, see Vardy and Grosch (1994), chapter 8; Wells and Quash (2010), pp. 184–6.

7 See MacIntyre (1984), chapter 5.

At the forefront of Hauerwas's critique is his contention that thinkers strongly influenced by the Enlightenment, whether they are deontological or consequentialist are, for all their differences, united in a common tendency to focus too sharply on moral dilemmas and quandaries, and how to resolve these. Indeed, influenced by such thinkers, many people often simply assume that ethics as a discipline is primarily about how to move forward when faced with an apparently impossible decision.[8] By contrast, Hauerwas emphasizes the importance of looking beyond individual moments of crisis and decision, and concentrating instead on the character of the men and women who make them. 'Christian ethics,' writes Hauerwas, 'is more concerned with who we are than what we do.'[9] Echoing such views, the Catholic virtue ethicist James Keenan summarizes this approach to moral questions:

> We are not primarily interested in particular actions. We do not ask 'Is this action right?' 'What are the circumstances around an action?' or 'What are the consequences of an action?' We are simply interested in persons. We believe that the real discussion of ethics is not the question 'What should I do?' but 'Who should I become?'[10]

Virtue ethicists thus stress that the moral life of any man or woman should be viewed as a continuous film, rather than as a succession of disconnected stills. It is not only the decisions that we take on the relatively rare occasions in which we are caught in a crisis that are morally significant. Even more important are our on-going, habitual, and often unconscious patterns of action. It is these that primarily shape what we are likely to do at any given moment. Virtuous people will act virtuously even when they are unaware that they are doing so. They simply do what appears to come naturally. An anecdote from Robert Spaemann encapsulates this point.

> More good actions, actions which are good in an unqualified way, actually do happen than we generally believe. I do not mean heroic examples, but simple things like when I asked a young man how to get somewhere which turned out not to be all that easy to find. He stopped whatever he was doing and walked with me for five minutes, to show me the way. This was a small incident, hardly worth talking about, but it was a fine thing to do, and that can be said without qualification. Actions like that make life worthwhile. The young man did not indulge in any great moral reflections, he simply did what occurred to him to do; and this occurred to him because of the sort of person he was.[11]

---

8 See Wells (1998), pp. 16–18.
9 Hauerwas (1983), p. 33.
10 Hoose (1998), p. 84.
11 Spaemann (1989), p. 76.

Although the movement towards a renewed emphasis on virtue is far from being an exclusively Christian or even religious phenomenon, nonetheless there are clearly reasons why Christians in particular might warm to virtue ethicists' shift of focus from actions to agents. The New Testament authors frequently stress the importance not just of individual actions, but of inward issues of character. Paul, for example, writes of the importance of being 'transformed by the renewing of your minds' (Rom. 12.2). Similarly, Jesus himself tells the disciples that actions, both good and evil, come from the heart – in Jewish thought, the seat of the human personality. The ways in which the hearts of men and women are disposed, rather than the minutiae of their individual actions carries decisive importance (see, for example, Matt. 15.18–20).

Themes in virtue ethics

In the first chapter of *A Community of Character*, entitled *A Story-Formed Community*, Stanley Hauerwas uses Richard Adams' novel *Watership Down* to illustrate some of the key themes in the type of virtue ethics that he and other similar commentators seek to promote.[12] *Watership Down* describes the adventures of a group of rabbits who, after escaping from a warren that one of their number correctly intuits is about to become dangerous (it is in fact due to be turned into a building site), embark on a series of adventures as they look for a new place in which they can settle down and flourish.

Central to Adams' depiction of rabbits is the theme of narrative. Rabbits are storytelling creatures, indeed a rabbit 'can no more refuse to tell a story than an Irishman can refuse to fight'.[13] The stories primarily concern the founder and prince of rabbit history, El-ahrairah, and it is these stories that enable them to find meaning in their lives. As their adventures bring them into contact with rabbits from other warrens, it becomes clear that 'the crux of any society in *Watership Down* is whether it is organized so as to provide for authentic retelling of the stories of ... El-ahrairah'.[14] To their surprise, the rabbits discover that not all rabbit societies acknowledge the importance of these seminal stories: members of one warren, whose attitudes broadly reflect liberal societies, dismiss them as charming fairy tales, while members of the sinister Efrafa warren, modelled on a totalitarian society, and led by the fearsome dog-like rabbit, General Woundwort, brutally suppress them.

The rabbits' central practice of continually telling and retelling the stories of El-ahrairah instils in them virtues such as fortitude and hope that they need to survive in a hostile world. Equipped by these stories, they are able

---

12 See Hauerwas (1981), pp. 9–35.

13 R. Adams (1972), *Watership Down* (London: Penguin), p. 99, quoted in Hauerwas (1981), p. 15.

14 Hauerwas (1981), p. 14.

throughout the novel, to find ways of life appropriate to their circumstances; to rise to new challenges, and to make the right decisions at the right times. Moreover, the stories of El-ahrairah and the habits of life that arise from their commitment to these stories binds this group of rabbits together as a community. They are able to rely on one another in the face of danger, and to respond to leadership, without being cowed or coerced by it. Formed as a community by these stories, and committed to the practice of telling them, the rabbits are able to understand that life is a gift, and to approach it as a journey and an adventure. They are also able finally to face death with courage and equanimity.

Narrative

Samuel Wells, an Anglican theologian closely associated with Stanley Hauerwas, draws a helpful distinction between two distinct types of narrative, which he terms 'narrative from below' and 'narrative from above'.[15] In relation to narrative from below, Wells and other writers point out that people of all ages and cultures, like Adams' rabbits, tend to appreciate stories, and to see their lives reflected in them. In the words of Alasdair MacIntyre, 'man is in his actions and practice, as well as in his fictions, essentially a story-telling animal'.[16] Indeed, from the earliest days of reflection on morality, human beings have learned about virtuous behaviour from stories, such as originally the heroic myths of ancient Greece and Rome. As MacIntyre indicates, our own lives, as individuals and as communities, have a storylike quality with, in most cases, a beginning, middle and an end.[17] Thus, truly to understand human lives, and in particular the moral choices that men and women make, it is necessary to know something about the stories that have brought them to where they currently are. Such stories might include the background from which they come; the hand that 'luck' has dealt them; the ways in which they have interacted with other people, and so on. Although, in the view of Hauerwas and others, such attention to the relationship between the narratives of individual men and women and their ethical decision making has often been overlooked by ethicists, wedded to more abstract utilitarian and deontological forms of thought, it is the stock in trade of fictional authors. For example, the novels of eighteenth and nineteenth-century British authors, such as Jane Austen, George Eliot and Anthony Trollope, provide richly textured illustrations of how virtues such as constancy and forgiveness are displayed in real human lives.[18] A lower

---

15 This section draws in particular on Wells (1998), chapters 3–4.

16 MacIntyre (1984), p. 201.

17 Hauerwas points out in his book *Naming the Silences* that an exception to this is a child who suffers an early death.

18 See S. Hauerwas (1994), *Dispatches from the Front: Theological Engagements with the Secular* (Durham, NC, and London: Duke University Press), pp. 31–57.

brow example may be found in one well-known genre of British national entertainment: the soap opera which, at its best, is able to explore complex moral issues by placing them in the three-dimensional narrative context of characters' lives.

EastEnders

In the 1990s and early 2000s, the long-running BBC serial, *EastEnders* depicted a period of 13 years between the diagnosis of Mark Fowler with HIV, and his eventual death of an AIDS-related illness. By contrast with tabloid newspapers' descriptions of life afflicted by what one described as the 'Gay Plague', the ongoing narrative of Mark's life in *EastEnders* enabled a more subtle and truthful exploration of the moral, social and practical issues surrounding the illness. The actor Todd Carty, who played Mark Fowler, commented that 'it showed someone living with HIV, as opposed to dying of it'.

Wells uses the term 'narrative from above' to describe the most specifically theological aspect of this type of virtue ethics: the way in which particular stories told about God in different religious traditions train and shape the character of those who tell them and hear them. In particular, Judaism and Christianity rest not on abstract philosophical principles, but on stories: 'God has revealed himself narratively in the history of Israel and in the life of Jesus.'[19] Thus, the Bible itself can essentially be understood as a narrative: 'a loosely structured, non-fiction novel',[20] full of sub-plots and diversions, which takes the reader through the great sweep of the creation of the world, the exodus from Egypt, the kingdom and the exile, and forwards into the life, death and resurrection of Jesus and the sending of the Holy Spirit on the Church. For sure, intertwined with the central sweep of this story are a number of sub-plots, and indeed non-narrative genres of writing, such as poetry and philosophy, and yet all of these contribute to the overall thrust of the narrative.

In the Christian moral life, the narratives from above and from below correspond with one another: the small-scale narratives of individual human beings and their communities find their true context in the wider narrative that is given in Scripture, and in the ongoing history of the Church. As Sallie TeSelle writes,

> We recognize our own pilgrimages from here to there in a good story; we feel its movement in our bones and know it is 'right'. We love stories,

---

19 Hauerwas (1983), p. 29.
20 Wells (1998), p. 64.

then, because our lives are stories and in the attempts of others to move, temporally and painfully, we recognize our own story. For the Christian, the story of Jesus is *the* story par excellence. That God should be with us in the story of a human life could be seen as a happy accident, but it makes more sense to see it as God's way of always being with human beings as they are, as the concrete, temporal beings who have a beginning and an end – who are, in other words, stories themselves.[21]

For such writers, then, it is stories rather than rules or laws that fundamentally shape the character of moral agents and their communities. Rules and laws may be important, but they are secondary to the narrative, and derive their authority from it. The passage below from the book of Deuteronomy, for example, indicates that it is the story of God's deliverance of his people that most fundamentally shapes their identity. The narrative provides the basis for the commandments which, although crucial, are secondary to it.

When your children ask you in time to come, 'What is the meaning of the decrees and the statutes and the ordinances that the Lord our God has commanded you?' then you shall say to your children, 'We were Pharaoh's slaves in Egypt, but the Lord brought us out of Egypt with a mighty hand. The Lord displayed before our eyes great and awesome signs and wonders against Egypt, against Pharaoh and all his household. He brought us out from there in order to bring us in, to give us the land that he promised on oath to our ancestors. Then the Lord commanded us to observe all these statutes, to fear the Lord our God, for our lasting good, so as to keep us alive, as is now the case. If we diligently observe this entire commandment before the Lord our God, as he has commanded us, we will be in the right. (Deut 6:20–25)[22]

For Hauerwas, Wells and others, then, the Bible's central place in ethical reflection is not so much as a dictionary or text book, to which we can refer to find answers to difficult moral questions. Rather, its central role is to be the repository of the foundational stories that the Christian community must tell and retell in order to remain true to its basic identity. Virtuous Christian living is shaped by seeing the narrative of our lives within the wider narrative. The Church's pastors and theologians have the particular task of keeping this narrative before the eyes of the people of God, and of helping them to locate their own particular stories within the wider story of God's dealings with his people that its pages relate, so that they can, in

---

21 Quoted in S. Hauerwas (1977), *Truthfulness and Tragedy* (Indiana: Notre Dame Press), p. 72.

22 See Lucie-Smith (2007), p. 34.

the words of Nicholas Lash, 'perform the scriptures'.[23] Eventually, then, the lives of individual Christians and their communities can themselves become part of the story that God continues to tell to the world.

MacIntyre, Hauerwas and others argue that members of modern liberal societies characteristically assume that they have broken free of all stories, and thus that they make their moral choices in a calm, detached way, unaffected by sectional interests. As Graham Tomlin writes, 'today ... we value the ability to distance ourselves from our own culture or history. We are all taught to stand autonomously outside our own tradition and history and to critique it, question it, and even think we live outside "stories" altogether.'[24] This, however, Hauerwas and others argue is a myth of liberal society, for liberalism does in fact have its own guiding narratives, whether these are acknowledged or not: 'where did we Americans get the story that our lives are our possessions, to make up whatever story we like and then to live that?'[25] Historically, such writers argue that liberalism in fact does have a story, since it has its roots in developments that took place in European societies in the late Middle Ages and thereafter. Such developments included the Renaissance rediscovery of the classical appreciation of the power of human thought; the discovery of societies in the 'new world' that had been hitherto untouched by Christianity and its values; and the chaos and confusion caused by religiously inspired wars between Catholics and Protestants in the aftermath of the Reformation, in particular, the Thirty Years' War of 1618–48.[26] Such developments encouraged Enlightenment philosophers, most prominently Kant, to look for a supposedly neutral, narrative-free, non-religious ground on which ethics could be based (see chapter 6), and yet the very wish to do this was itself shaped by the narrative of a particular historical period. Thus, what Hauerwas terms the 'story that we have no story' is not only, as its name implies, self-contradictory, but it also does not stand up to historical scrutiny.

Community

We are 'storied people' because the God that sustains us is a 'storied God', whom we come to know only by having our character formed appropriate to God's character. The formation of such character is not an isolated event but requires the existence of a corresponding society – a 'storied society'.[27]

---

23 See N. Lash (1986), *Theology on the Way to Emmaus* (London: SCM), pp. 37–46.
24 Tomlin (2006), p. 49.
25 Hauerwas and Willimon (1996), p. 82.
26 See Banner (2009), p. 72.
27 Hauerwas (1981), p. 91.

A second, and connected, theme in the version of virtue ethics proposed by MacIntyre, Hauerwas and other similar writers is that of community. The title of one of Hauerwas's best-known books, *A Community of Character*, indicates that one of his central insights is that formation in virtue primarily happens in communities. Communities teach their members to see and respond to the world in particular ways and thus all communities, including churches, schools, businesses and nation states, are schools of moral formation, shaping the character of their individual members for good (or for ill), and inculcating in them particular virtues (or vices).

To give an illustration of this, for a number of years, I had the good fortune to teach at a theological college or seminary whose primary task was to train candidates for ordination. The life of this residential community gave its members an intense experience of studying, praying, eating, drinking and living together over a period normally of two or three years. The life of this community formed deeply ingrained habits of thinking and acting in the men and women who trained there and eventually emerged from it. Even those students who felt distinctly ambivalent about their experience of the institution would admit they had been deeply changed by it. Indeed, one well-known saying about such experiences is that 'you can take the boy out of the seminary, but you can't take the seminary out of the boy'.

MacIntyre, Hauerwas and others argue that the moral incoherence they see in modern societies can only be rectified by the construction of communities, whose members foster virtuous patterns of behaviour within a common life, and transmit these patterns to new members. An important historical inspiration for this line of thought is Saint Benedict of Nursia (480–547) whose *Rule* guides members of his monasteries in their daily task of living in community with God and neighbour.[28] Arguing at the end of his book that modern society needs 'another – and doubtless very different – St Benedict', MacIntyre writes that 'what matters at this stage is the construction of local forms of community within which civility and the intellectual and moral life can be sustained through the new dark ages which are already upon us'.[29] A similar insight is expressed by the Lutheran theologian Gilbert Meilaender (1946–), in his book *The Theory and Practice of Virtue*:

> Each should help his children and friends strive for virtue as we fashion our smaller communities of belief and seek to transmit the vision which inspires us ... And perhaps out of such sectarianism there will arise some smaller communities whose vision is so powerful and persuasive that new moral consensus will be achieved among us.[30]

---

28 See Banner (2009), pp. 10–22.
29 MacIntyre (1984), p. 263.
30 Meilaender (1984), p. 98.

The strongly communitarian approach of many virtue ethicists to the moral life provides a further point of contrast with the individualism that tends to characterize the approach of consequentialist and deontological ethicists. Bentham indeed can go so far as to say that 'the community is a fictitious body, composed of the individual persons who are considered as constituting as it were its members.'[31] The proponents of such views thus tend to present men and women as ethical lone-rangers, who must make their own moral decisions for themselves on strictly rational grounds, and for whom the advice that others might give is potentially a damaging distraction.

One way in which communities can particularly contribute to moral formation is by providing role models. In the context of the Church, this particularly means men and women whose lives exemplify Christian virtue. Hauerwas and his sometime colleague and co-writer, William Willimon (1946–) write that:

> Christian ethics is, in the Aristotelian sense, an aristocratic ethic ... a primary way of learning to be disciples is by being in contact with others who are disciples ... an essential role of the church is to put us in contact with those ethical aristocrats who are good at living the Christian faith.[32]

Such ethical aristocrats are most obviously to be found among the communion of saints. As Cessario puts it, 'in their way, holy persons as much as sound doctrines reveal moral truth',[33] and indeed Christians have traditionally derived far more moral formation from reading and hearing about the lives of the saints than they have from reading books about ethics. Moreover, examples of virtue may also be found among the living: in almost every church there are particular individuals, some of them very unlikely characters, towards whom the community naturally looks to find the skills that are necessary for living well.[34]

The vocation of the Christian Church is primarily, then, as Hauerwas and his collaborators would see it, to be a community at local level whose common life of worship, witness and service shapes the lives of its members in virtue. They argue that the Christian Church in the West now lives in the era of 'post-Christendom': one in which the long-standing partnership between Church and State inaugurated by the Emperor Constantine's declaration of Christianity as the official religion of the Roman Empire has finally come to an end. Superficially, the collapse of the Church–State partnership appears to leave the Church in a far weaker position than it had previously occupied. And yet, in this weakness is its strength. Now that the Church is no longer

---

31 Bentham (1780), p. 3.
32 Hauerwas and Willimon (1989), p. 102.
33 Cessario (2001), p. 17.
34 See Hauerwas and Willimon (1989), pp. 93–111.

tied to the controlling and, as Hauerwas would see it, inherently violent nation state, it is free at last truly to become a community of character: a community that fosters and transmits authentically Christian virtues, and not only those pseudo-virtues that are officially approved by the governing authorities.

> Here we show the world a manner of life the world can never achieve through social coercion or governmental action. We serve the world by showing it something that it is not, namely, a place where God is forming a family out of strangers.[35]

Practices

The third in the triad of virtue-forming themes espoused by MacIntyre, Hauerwas and others is practices. As the emphasis of virtue ethicists on narrative reminds us of the role of classical myths in virtue formation, and as the emphasis on community takes up ancient thinking about the importance of community life, so virtue ethicists' emphasis on practices echoes the thought of both Aristotle and Aquinas about the key role that habits have to play in moral formation.

So, what counts as a practice? In his analysis of the nature of virtue, MacIntyre defines this concept in the following ways:

- *Practices are complex:* simple activities such as throwing a football or singing a hymn are not practices, but habitually playing football or going to church services are. 'Bricklaying is not a practice; architecture is.'[36]
- *Practices are social:* they are established within communities. The virtues they foster cannot be acquired by individuals on their own and, indeed, 'no practices can survive for any length of time unsustained by institutions'.[37]
- *Practices are valuable for their own sake:* they enable us to realize specific goods, internal to them: goods that we can only realize by engaging in them. To use an example of MacIntyre's, a child may play chess in order to receive sweets or money, but these are external goods, because they could be obtained in ways other than playing chess. On the other hand, there are other goods, such as the ability to engage in a particular kind of analysis and strategic thought that are internal to the practice of chess, and could not be acquired in any other way.[38]

---

35 Hauerwas and Willimon (1989), p. 83.

36 MacIntyre (1984), p. 187; On this point Hauerwas disagrees. In his autobiography, Hauerwas describes how his father, who was a bricklayer, inducted his son into the Texan bricklaying community, with its distinctive set of skills and practices. See S. Hauerwas (2010), *Hannah's Child* (London: SCM), pp. 27–33.

37 MacIntyre (1984), p. 194.

38 See MacIntyre (1984), p. 188.

- *Practices are character-forming*: engagement in virtuous practices by individuals and communities fosters virtuous living in a more general sense; because such practices train us to achieve human excellences of different kinds.

This emphasis that virtue ethicists lay on the importance of practices in the moral life contrasts with that laid on 'values' in much modern moral discourse. Hauerwas and Willimon indeed state that 'by focusing on practices we are trying to find ways to help one another resist the tendency for Christianity to become a matter of belief, of values'.[39]

Virtues and values

Virtue ethics questions the assumption that ethics and values are simply identical to one another, in much the same way that, in former years, ethics might have been assumed simply, in Kantian style, to be about obeying rules. For example, the introduction to a Social Work degree at the Open University asserts simply that 'Ethics is one aspect of values', and this equation of ethics with values is often echoed by politicians and other people in public life. The former prime minister Gordon Brown, when he became leader of the Labour Party in 2007, told his audience that 'I joined this party as a teenager because I believed in (its) values. They guide my work, they are my moral compass. This is who I am.'

While the language of 'values' can be useful in moral discourse, because it helps to clarify the wider approach that underlies particular rules or norms, such language can also be very vague, since it essentially relates to activity that takes place within our heads. By contrast, habits and practices do not exist only on a cerebral level, but are embodied in the daily activity of people's everyday lives. The language of values also tends to be subjectivist since, as Attwood notes, it normally 'belongs to an outlook where morality is decided upon, and chosen, rather than reasoned'.[40] Indeed, the very term 'values' suggests that these can be traded for something of greater worth if the need arises. Virtuous patterns of behaviour, on the other hand, formed within men and women by repeated and consistent practice, and indeed by God's grace, shape their core identity as moral beings. By contrast with 'values', those endowed with them do not simply have control of them, but carry them, as part of themselves, into every new situation they face. Virtues shape us as much as we shape them: a person who only believed in honesty as a value might be willing to commit an act of dishonesty, if this

---

39 Hauerwas and Willimon (1996), p. 20.
40 Attwood (1998), p. 13.

would bring permanent financial security to himself and his family. By contrast, somebody who, through a lifetime of training, had become an honest person through and through (that is, somebody endowed with the virtue of honesty) would find it much more difficult to do this.

The church and the gym

The Evangelical Anglican writer Graham Tomlin in his book *Spiritual Fitness, Christian Character in a Consumer Culture* recounts being struck by the difference between much church life and his experience of joining a local gym. By contrast with the somewhat passive language of 'attending' services that is often used, people who opt for a fitness programme at the gym expect that they will become habituated to the rigorous programme of disciplined training that is offered, and that this will change their lives. The gym, Tomlin writes, 'is the new asceticism. And it promises change.'[41] Setting Tomlin's point in the context of the present discussion, gym members believe that the 'value' of fitness is not enough to make them fit, but that it can only become real if it is embodied in a particular set of practices. They also, Tomlin notes, believe the story that the gym will change their lives, and they form a community with other gym users.[42]

It is perhaps supremely in the Christian Eucharist that the triad of narrative, community and practices are drawn most closely together. Many people would be surprised to discover that it was possible to make any connections between liturgy and ethics. They seem to be two different subjects, operating in entirely disparate spheres: the former concerned with church services, and the latter with making tough decisions and choices in real life. However, for some of the writers we have been considering in this chapter worship, and in particular the celebration of the Eucharist, is at the centre of moral formation, because it is above all in the distinctive practice of celebrating the Eucharist that the church comes together as a community to tell and begin to live out its particular narrative. Wells elaborates on this subject in detail in his book *God's Companions*. Analysing each part of the Eucharist, he highlights the ways in which the Eucharist continually keeps the central narrative of the Christian faith before the eyes of the community, whose members hear its central stories read and expounded in the biblical readings, the sermon, the recitation of the Creed and the Eucharistic Prayer. Similarly, those who participate in the Eucharist are trained, Wells argues, in a particular set of practices. The practice of listening to Scripture, for example, trains the community to listen not only to God, but to other

---

41 Tomlin (2006), p. 28.
42 See Tomlin (2006), chapter 8.

people.[43] The practice of sharing the Peace trains members of the community in practices of peace-making and reconciliation,[44] and the sharing of bread and wine trains them to make just and wise use of God's abundant provision in creation.[45] These, and a large number of similar examples, give vivid and concrete expression to the precise ways in which 'the Eucharist makes the Church'.[46]

Issues in virtue ethics

Stanley Hauerwas's writing on the subjects of medicine and medical ethics provides an example of his version of virtue ethics applied to a particular set of ethical issues in a striking and, on first acquaintance, somewhat surprising way. In his work in this area, Hauerwas challenges what he sees as the widespread assumption that medicine is essentially about the application of (increasingly sophisticated) medical technology to people's illnesses in order to try and get them to be well again. Instead, he argues that medicine is not primarily about curing diseases with the aid of scientific discoveries, but about caring for people in the context of sympathetic human relationships. As a biblical example of this, he cites Job's (otherwise problematic) three friends, whose initial response to Job's having lost his entire household and family was that 'they sat with him on the ground seven days and seven nights, and no one spoke a word to him, for they saw that his suffering was very great' (Job 2.13). The primary calling of the physician, he argues, is to embody this kind of presence to those who are sick and, similarly, the basic function of a hospital is, precisely as its name suggests, to be a 'house of hospitality', which assures people that, just because they are sick, they will not therefore be excluded from the human community. Of course, a fortunate by-product of the care that people receive in a hospital may, in some cases, be that they actually recover from their illnesses, but the most important aspect of their treatment is that other people continue to be there for them in their suffering. The palliative care offered by hospices to people who are not expected to recover is thus a paradigm of medical care rather than, as it is sometimes viewed, a slightly eccentric sideline.

In line with this analysis, Hauerwas questions the preoccupation of much mainstream medical ethics with the dilemmas and quandaries of medical care. Such quandaries might include, for example, the circumstances under which a patient should be allowed to refuse treatment, or a doctor could

---

43 See Wells (2006), pp. 163–5.

44 See Wells (2006), pp. 184–91.

45 See Wells (2006), pp. 210–14.

46 This expression is used by Paul McPartlan in his writing on Henri de Lubac (1896–1991); see P. McPartlan (1995), *Sacrament of Salvation* (London: T&T Clark), chapter 1.

justify the decision to switch off a life support machine, or to withhold expensive drugs from somebody who was dying. Clearly such issues are important, but they are secondary to the prior challenge of being able to be present to the sick. This shift of the spotlight away from actions considered in the abstract, and towards agents – those people endowed with the necessary personal qualities (virtues) that will enable them to be present to those who are sick is, as we have seen, highly characteristic of virtue ethics. Characteristic also is Hauerwas's insistence that the formation of agents who are equal to the task of being present to sick people will require the training and support of communities: 'If medicine,' he writes, 'can be rightly understood as an activity that trains some [people] to know how to be present to those in pain, then something very much like a church is needed to sustain that presence day in and day out.'[47] Christians, in Hauerwas's view, cannot and should not try to offer a 'solution' to the problem of human suffering, but what they can do is form 'a community of care that has made it possible to absorb the destructive terror of evil that constantly threatens to destroy all human relations'.[48]

In order to be such a community of care, the Church is able to draw on her central narratives, and her reflection upon these. The Bible contains, for example, the psalms of lament in the Old Testament and (supremely) accounts of the passion, death and resurrection of Jesus in the New. Such passages speak of a God who does not offer his people a pain-free existence, or a premature release from suffering, but who holds out to them a hope for the future and, in Christ, comes to share that suffering with them. These central narratives, along with the daily experience of upholding one another day after day in a myriad of ways, equip members of the Church to develop what Hauerwas calls the necessary 'habits of care' for those who are suffering:

> for what does our God require of us other than our unfailing presence in the midst of the world's sin and pain? Thus our willingness to be ill and to ask for help, as well as our willingness to be present with the ill, is no special or extraordinary activity but a form of the Christian obligation to be present to one another in and out of pain.[49]

A further example of the insights of virtue ethics being applied in practice concerns the controversial subject of abortion. In modern Western societies, the moral debate about abortion tends to focus upon the decision that an individual woman might make to terminate her pregnancy, and whether

---

47 Hauerwas in Berkman and Cartwright (2001), p. 542.

48 S. Hauerwas (1990), *Naming the Silences: God, Medicine and the Problem of Suffering* (Edinburgh: T & T Clark), p. 53.

49 Hauerwas in Berkman and Cartwright (2001), p. 542.

such a decision can ever be morally justified.[50] Hauerwas's first move is to resist seeing the issue in the hackneyed and polarized terms of an argument between those who are 'pro-life', and those who are 'pro-choice'. Rather, he argues that the true moral question concerns the kind of moral character that people will need to have if they are to be capable of welcoming children into the world. Abortion, he argues, is an issue for church communities, and not just for individual pregnant women, because the Church is called to be a community that knows how to welcome children, and how to support those of its members who face the challenges of pregnancy and child-rearing. If the Church hopes (as Hauerwas does) that women will make the decision to carry their pregnancies to full term, then the Church must also take responsibility for supporting them in their decision to do this, especially when they face adverse circumstances. Such support might even extend to church members being willing to bring up the children of biological parents who are unable to look after them.

The Church is strengthened in this task by its central narrative of a God who holds the future in his hand. Having children, as Hauerwas describes it, is first and foremost an act of Christian witness to the eschatological hope of the New Testament: 'we are able to have children because our hope is in God, who makes it possible to do the absurd thing of having children'. And the welcoming of children is something that the Church is called to embody in the ongoing practices of her common life. Small practices in the life of a local church such as providing worship and activities for children will embody the message that children are welcome and so, supremely, does the practice of infant baptism: 'we are a baptizing people ready to welcome new life into our communities'. A community whose members are schooled in this narrative, and shaped by these practices will be able to welcome children into the world, and thus find a whole new perspective on the quandaries and dilemmas that the easy availability of abortion presents to modern society.

A final example comes from business ethics: a field which in recent years has seen considerable interest in virtue ethics, not least because of some examples of apparently *un*ethical behaviour in the run-up to the financial crisis of the early twenty-first century. In an article on this subject, the economist John Dobson argues that, although stringent rules and regulations may be necessary for contracts to work, such rules are not sufficient to create a good and flourishing business environment. This requires not just regulatory frameworks, but good people, who are able 'to pursue excellence through virtuous acts'. Dobson quotes with approval Michael Pritchard's view that 'beyond discussing codes of ethics, principles of right and wrong, dilemmas … and moral disaster stories, we need stories of a different sort – *stories of good professionals whose lives might inspire emulation*'. Making what will by now be a familiar virtue ethics point, Dobson argues that the production

---

50 See Hauerwas in Berkman and Cartwright (2001), pp. 603–22.

of virtuous businessmen and women is community dependent: 'an individual, whether finance professional or otherwise, cannot be ethical in a vacuum ... [but] must be educated in the virtues by a nurturing community, and by the guidance of exemplars'.[51]

Virtue ethics: some questions

Has virtue ethics got anything to do with the Bible?

In his book *Understanding Old Testament Ethics*, John Barton explores what might seem to be the somewhat tenuous connection between the Bible and virtue ethics.[52] On the one hand, Barton argues that the Old Testament contains little comment on virtues that both the Old Testament authors and modern readers would have found morally relevant, such as humility, gentleness or forbearance, and indeed that the Old Testament writers sometimes seem to commend actions that would not appear virtuous to us, such as implacable revenge, polygamy, resort to prostitutes and material acquisitiveness. Moreover, the Bible seems to present us with a different account of moral agency to that presented by virtue ethics. The Aristotelian sense that virtuous living can be derived from studying and distilling the virtuous actions of human beings is entirely absent. Rather, Old Testament texts such as Psalms 19 and 119 indicate a primary emphasis upon the sufficiency and perfection of divine law, and the responsibility of human beings simply to obey it. Similarly, themes such as growth and development in the moral life that are integral to virtue ethics seem to be largely absent from both Old and New Testaments. In the Old Testament Saul, for example, 'begins good, and then becomes bad';[53] while, by contrast, in the New Testament, Paul begins bad and becomes good. Rather than moral growth coming through a process of ongoing change and development, 'ethical choice is a once-for-all affair which sets one's feet either on the way to life or on the way to death: there are no half-measures'.[54] The moral emphasis is placed upon conversion rather than formation: the prophet Ezekiel's advice to his people is simply 'Turn, and live' (Ezek. 18.32).

However, despite these reservations, Barton does not see the Old Testament, or indeed the rest of the Bible as inimical to the virtue ethicists' overall project. He acknowledges that, while we certainly cannot find a fully articulated theory of virtue ethics (or indeed of any other kind of ethics) in the Bible, nevertheless we can discover some important pointers towards it. And Barton further notes that even if there is little or no virtue ethics in the Bible,

---

51 J. Dobson, 'Applying Virtue Ethics to Business: The Agent-Based Approach', in the *Electronic Journal of Business Ethics and Organization Studies*, 12 November 2007.

52 This section draws on Barton (2003), pp. 65–74.

53 Barton (2003), p. 68.

54 Barton (2003), p. 67.

nonetheless, the Bible can be 'used constructively by those who are trying to achieve what virtue ethics puts forward as the great aim of human life: the achievement of stable and good moral character'.[55]

For an illustration of the first of these points, we might look to the way in which, as discussed above, virtue ethics have been characterized as 'aristocratic', emphasizing the extent to which moral behaviour is primarily learned from the example of other people. To use a catchphrase of the author's grandmother, 'manners, morals and ethics are caught, not taught'.

In his study of New Testament ethics, Richard B. Hays writes about the different modes in which the Bible speaks about moral questions. Hays argues that, contrary to what is often assumed, the ethical teaching of the Bible is not only delivered in the mode of rules and prohibitions but is rather conveyed through a variety of different modes. Hays identifies these as:

- *Rules*: direct commands or prohibitions, e.g. Ten Commandments (Exod. 20)
- *Principles*: general frameworks of moral considerations, e.g. the golden rule (Matt. 7.12)
- *Paradigms*: accounts of characters who model exemplary conduct
- *Symbolic world*: frameworks for interpreting reality and the moral life, such as Paul's depiction of the fallen human condition (Rom. 1.18–32).[56]

Hays's third mode of moral instruction: that of paradigms, is particularly significant in this context. Both Old and New Testaments hold before us particular characters who act as virtuous examples to be followed. To take some obvious examples, we might think of Job as a paradigm of fortitude and hope in suffering; of the Good Samaritan as a paradigm of prudence and charity, of Mary as a paradigm of temperance and faith. Paul suggests his own behaviour in relation to food sacrificed to idols might be seen as a paradigm for other Christians to follow: 'be imitators of me, as I am of Christ' (1 Cor. 11.1). Supremely, of course, the New Testament encourages us to look on Jesus himself as a paradigm of the virtues: 'let the same mind be in you that was in Christ Jesus' (Phil. 2.5). Further examples of 'negative paradigms' do a similar work in reverse, by providing us with examples *not* to be followed. These might include, for example, Jezebel in the first and second books of Kings, or Ananias and Sapphira in the Acts of the Apostles (Acts 5.1–11).

Finally, a small number of biblical characters might be seen as paradigms in a somewhat different sense, by holding before us some of the difficulties and complexities of the moral life. The lives of such individuals as they are described in the Bible portray in narrative form a point that many of the psalms also indicate: that human beings, affected by conflicting emotions

---

55 Barton (2003), p. 73.
56 Hays (1996), p. 209, adapted.

do not always find it easy either to perceive, or to do what is right and good in a fallen world. Such stories offer us hope that, through grace, such difficulties can be overcome, even though they are not capable of easy resolution. Examples of characters who wrestle with such problems might again include Job and also the apostle Peter, but perhaps the most obvious is that of David, the great king of Israel in the Old Testament. The very complexity of David's career, the strengths and weaknesses of his personality, and the particular challenges that he faced make him a paradigm for human beings whose lives are also complex and challenging. Barton comments that:

> The story of David handles human anger, lust, ambition and disloyalty without ever commenting explicitly on these things but by telling its tale in such a way that the reader is obliged to look them in the face and to recognize his or her affinity with the characters in whom they are exemplified.[57]

To return to Barton's second point about the constructive use of the Bible in virtue ethics, it has been noted that virtue ethics has brought renewed attention to the importance of liturgy for the shaping of moral character. Ideally, the daily and weekly cycle of readings to which Christians are exposed in the liturgy should slowly and over a period of time begin to form their moral landscape. Augustine speaks eloquently in a sermon about the ability of the psalms both to reflect and to shape the life of his congregation. Members of the community that sing the psalms day by day and week by week in their worship bring the narrative of their own lives into a reciprocal relationship with the biblical text:

> If the psalm is praying, pray yourselves; if it is groaning, you groan too; if it is happy, rejoice; if it is crying out in hope, you hope as well; if it expresses fear, be afraid. Everything written here is like a mirror held up to us.[58]

Viewed in this way, the Bible is not so much an ethical dictionary or reference book which an individual scholar may consult, but rather the script of a play, or a musical score which Christian communities enact in their liturgy and then, even more importantly, in the everyday lives of their members. In an essay entitled *Performing the Scriptures*, Nicholas Lash writes that 'the fundamental form of the Christian interpretation of scripture is the life, activity and organization of the Christian community, construed as the performance of the biblical text'.[59]

A by-product of this is that the entire Bible, and not just those texts that

---

57 Barton (2003), p. 73.
58 Augustine, *Exposition* 4 of Psalm 30.
59 N. Lash (1986), *Theology on the Way to Emmaus* (London: SCM), p. 45.

are thought to be specifically related to ethics, can help to frame and shape the moral life of communities and individuals. This more holistic view was familiar to the Church Fathers for whom Scripture was so entirely interconnected that every passage within it, even those that seemed initially the least promising, was potentially morally and spiritually formative. By contrast, Pinckaers laments the way that ethicists from the late Middle Ages until the modern period often fixed upon the more narrowly moral and legal passages of Scripture, and lost sight of the ability of texts of all kinds to contribute to flourishing Christian life. Pinckaers comments that 'when a modern ethicist consults Scripture, he is looking for normative texts, laws, commands and prohibitions in which the divine will expresses its authority. The results are rather meagre; he normally falls back on the Decalogue.'[60]

Case study: Samaritans

The passage below describes the foundation of the Samaritans, a 24-hour support service for distressed people which today has branches throughout the United Kingdom.

Samaritans was started in 1953 in London by a young vicar named Chad Varah, then incumbent of St Stephen Walbrook. Through his work in a number of different parishes in the City he had seen the range and extent of the distress experienced by people everywhere, every day. During his career he had offered counselling to his parishioners, and he increasingly wanted to do something specific to help people in distress who had no one to turn to. He makes reference to one example of a girl aged 14, whom he had buried – in unconsecrated ground. She had started her periods, but having no one to talk to believed that she had a sexually transmitted disease and took her own life.

He says, 'I might have dedicated myself to suicide prevention then and there, providing a network of people you could "ask" about anything, however embarrassing, but I didn't come to that until later.'

When he was offered charge of the parish of St Stephen Walbrook, in the summer of 1953, he knew that the time was right for him to launch what he called a '999 for the suicidal'. At the time, suicide was still illegal in the UK and so many people who were in difficult situations and who felt suicidal were unable to talk to anyone about it without worrying about the consequences. A confidential emergency service for people 'in distress who need spiritual aid' was what Chad felt was needed to address the problems he saw around him. He was, in his own words, 'a man willing to listen, with a base and an emergency telephone'.[61]

---

60 Pinckaers (1995), p. 199.
61 Taken from the website of St Stephen Walbrook.

Questions for discussion

Nicholas Lash writes that 'the performance of scripture is the life of the church'. Does the setting up of the Samaritans by Chad Varah provide a good example of 'performing the Scriptures'?

Can you think of other examples of the Scriptures being performed by communities?

Is virtue ethics any practical use?

It has already been noted that a central theme of virtue ethics has been to question the central role that is often assigned to difficult decisions and choices in the moral life. The Good Samaritan, for example, does not seem to make a decision to help the injured man on the road to Jericho, but just does what he sees needs to be done. Saint Maximilian Kolbe did not decide to take the place of a stranger in Auschwitz. He was used to offering his life for other people and now did so again in a different context. 'Thomas More,' Hauerwas notes, 'did not choose to die at the hands of Henry VIII ... He simply did what he had to do.'[62] In each of these examples, the people concerned appeared to do what came naturally to them, and thus the language of dilemmas, quandaries and decision making fails to describe actions that flowed naturally from their character. If, as in Herbert McCabe's provocative description, 'Ethics is entirely concerned with doing what you want',[63] then ongoing ethical training: the shaping of our desires and our character, rather than concentration on the more dramatic moments of choice, will be a more practical way of ensuring that people act well. Stanley Hauerwas writes that 'morally the most important things about us are those matters about which we never have to make a "decision"'.[64]

Nevertheless, dilemmas and quandaries frequently do arise in the lives of individuals and communities, and surely ethical reflection should equip us to face them. We might, for example, need to know whether in a particular set of circumstances, it would be right to smack a child, or to blow the whistle on the corrupt practices of a work colleague, or to tell a lie to a dying relative about their condition. In each of these situations, we might well feel the need for more concrete guidance that virtue ethics are able to provide. Further quandaries arise when it comes to public policy, such as in the field of health-care; when is it permissible to give drugs to a dying patient that will both make them comfortable but also kill them? Should

---

62 Hauerwas (1983), p. 129.
63 H. McCabe (2003), *Law, Love and Language* (London: Continuum), p. 61.
64 Hauerwas (1983), p. 125.

money be spent on an expensive treatment that will save the lives of a very small number of people, or should it be spread around more widely to benefit a larger number? Faced with such situations, it might seem that virtue ethicists offer vague platitudes rather than specific practical guidance.

In a theme that was discussed in earlier chapters, traditional reflection on the virtues acknowledges the importance and reality of difficult decisions by giving special status among the virtues to the key virtue of prudence, which guides us to apply practical reason about things to be done. The prudent person is one who, among other qualities, has developed the necessary skills to make difficult choices when these arise. Thus, virtue ethics does not claim that quandaries and dilemmas are unimportant, but simply that the Christian moral life cannot be reduced to them, and that they can rarely be satisfactorily addressed in an abstract way that does not pay attention to the character of those involved.

Moreover, virtue ethicists who share Hauerwas's interest in narrative emphasize that the way in which we see and describe situations that present moral difficulty will radically affect the choices that seem to be available to us within them. As Hauerwas puts it, 'the description under which the decision is proposed is as important as the decision itself ... the description frames the decision'.[65] A worked example explores the following dilemma: 'What would you do if you saw a psychopathic killer attacking your child? Surely you would kill him rather than allowing him to kill your child?'[66] Hauerwas, who draws here on the work of the Mennonite theologian John Howard Yoder, argues that in such a situation, a number of different options are in fact open to us. These options are set out in the table below:

Option one	Allow myself to be killed	
Option two	Look for a way out	This might be: a) 'natural' (a loving gesture might disarm the attacker emotionally) b) 'providential' (an escape route might be provided)
Option three	Positively accept martyrdom and suffering as Jesus did	The martyrdom might be of: a) the intended victim b) myself
Option four	Kill the attacker	An attempt to do this might: a) succeed b) fail

---

65 Hauerwas (1983), p. 124.
66 See Hauerwas (1983), pp. 124–6.

The analysis of Hauerwas and Yoder indicates that, although the way in which the dilemma was originally stated envisages only options 1 and 4a as possible outcomes, this is in fact an oversimplification. More careful description of such a situation opens up various further possibilities. Option 2 alerts us to the need for careful attention to the actual situation, as there are almost certainly more possible outcomes than we might anticipate. Option 3 reminds us that, if we are to describe a situation accurately, then the particular histories, beliefs and commitments of those involved must form part of our description. For, although to many people, option 3 would look very similar to option 1, Christians will have a different perception of it since, as Yoder puts it, 'a believer's death for a reason relating to God's will and His way is part of His victory over evil within this world'.[67] Dilemmas, therefore, are rarely as simple as they might appear, and questions of narrative, character and community are integral and not incidental to the way we understand and thus begin to address them.

What counts as a virtue anyway?

A further question concerns what the virtues actually are, given that, from the earliest days of reflection upon virtue, we encounter some different accounts of them. MacIntyre traces the ways in which the ancient Greek virtues that were highly prized in heroic societies, such as the physical strength to win battles and the cunning needed to hatch plots and plan defences, evolved over time into somewhat different ones that were more appropriate to life in the city state of Athens, such as fortitude and wisdom.[68] Further unclarity is evident in the Christian tradition when Augustine in the *City of God* comments that the virtues of pagans 'are really themselves vices, and not virtues at all, if they do not have reference to God'.[69] Echoing Augustine in the modern period, John Milbank argues that the classical virtues are flawed because they rest on an inherently violent and unchristian view of the world in which 'to be' is 'to be antagonistic'.[70] Among modern writers on the subject, James Keenan argues that the traditional virtues lay too great an emphasis on justice, seeing the other virtues as auxiliary to the central aim of treating everyone equally.[71] Arguing that we need virtues that help us to take more account of the particular relationships that we have with others, and indeed with ourselves, Keenan proposes that we re-conceive the cardinal virtues as justice in our relationships with people generally; fidelity in our relationships with friends and family members and self-care in our relation-

---

67 Quoted in Hauerwas (1983), p. 126.
68 See MacIntyre (1984), chapters 10 and 11.
69 Augustine, *City of God* 19.26.
70 For a summary of Milbank's thought on this subject, see Wells and Quash (2010), pp. 186–8.
71 See Keenan in Hoose (ed.) (1998), pp. 91–3.

ship with ourselves. In another strand of Christian virtue ethics, Hauerwas largely bypasses the traditional lists of virtues, concentrating instead on virtues such as peacefulness, truthfulness and fidelity, while Graham Tomlin can write an entire book on the subject of virtue and the development of Christian character without mentioning the cardinal and theological virtues at all.[72]

Such continuing discussion about the exact nature of the virtues may in fact be a strength rather than a weakness. Virtue ethics, rather than providing a rigid blueprint for right action in every conceivable area, is flexible enough to allow for a range of contrasting visions of the good life, since 'the path of virtue is never laid out in advance'.[73] However, for all the benefits of retaining some flexibility in this area, there seem to be strong arguments for insisting that the traditional theological and moral virtues should be included somewhere in the mix.

So far as the theological virtues of faith, hope and love are concerned, these are so integral to Christianity that it is impossible to imagine a truly Christian life that does not give them a central place. Moreover, experience tends to suggest that Christian communities in which any or all of them are absent invariably founder and fail. This having been said, writers such as Hauerwas are at pains to remind us that these qualities can become very abstract, and that we need the narratives provided in the Bible to give them their fullest and most specific display. For example, we will understand the virtue of faith much better if we have the story of Abraham to embody it (see Rom. 4), or hope if we are regularly reminded of Simeon and Anna (see Luke 2.25–38). Similarly, we will learn most about love not by treating it as an abstraction, but by reflection upon Jesus at the last supper and upon the cross.

Moreover, just as it is impossible to conceive of a truly Christian life without the theological virtues, so it scarcely seems possible to conceive of a truly moral life without the cardinal virtues either. For the very concept of virtue seems to require that all of these virtues should in some way be present and working together in interconnected ways. It appears integral to any idea of virtue that it must include treating others appropriately (justice); having the determination to endure setbacks (fortitude); not being so overcome by our desires that we find ourselves unable to act (temperance); and possessing the ability to assess situations and take appropriate actions (prudence). Even if we have quite different views of the good life, and believed many other human qualities to be virtuous, it is very difficult to conceive of a virtuous person who lacked such qualities.

---

72 See Tomlin (2006).
73 G. H. von Wright, quoted in Meilaender (1984), p. 8.

Is virtue ethics divisive?

It has already been noted that the solution to contemporary moral break-down that is proposed by thinkers such as MacIntyre and Hauerwas is 'the construction of new forms of community within which the moral life could be sustained so that both morality and civility might survive the coming ages of barbarism and darkness'.[74] The vision of society held out by such commentators might seem to be one in which separate communities each tell their own story, pursue their own goods, engage in their own practices, and consequently look on each other with mutual hostility and incomprehension. Hauerwas is indeed often accused of advocating a tribalistic, sectarian version of Christianity, in which the Church becomes a highly distinct pacifist sub-group within society, somewhat similar to the Anabaptists or even the Amish.

In their book *Resident Aliens*, Hauerwas and Willimon fiercely rebut the charge of sectarianism and tribalism, arguing that it is not the Church, extended throughout the world, and serving God rather than political power, that can justly be accused of being divisive, but the modern institution of the nation state: 'tribalism is the United States of America, which sets up artificial boundaries and defends them with murderous intensity'.[75] Hauerwas and Willimon claim that their belief that the Church should be a distinctive community living by its own set of narratives and practices should not be interpreted as a call for Christians to retreat into a ghetto, cut off from the rest of society. Christians, they argue, should engage in social and political life, but they should do so unapologetically *as Christians*, modelling to the world a particular style of life, and a particular set of moral commitments.

However, although communities rightly live out of their own particular traditions and practices, they do not necessarily need to do this in a way that is defensive and closed off to others. A tradition that is, as MacIntyre terms it, in 'good order', in other words healthy and thriving, is one that will be open to discussion and debate among its own members, and also to dialogue with those on the outside, about the goods that it seeks to pursue. Indeed, a tradition in good order does not simply permit argument and discussion over the goods that it holds but actually '*is* an historically extended, socially embodied argument ... about the goods which constitute that tradition'.[76]

Finally, the fact that a community such as the Church draws life from its own foundational narratives in the Scriptures and the Creeds does not necessarily need to close it off from all other groups that do not share the same story. The emphasis of some virtue ethicists on narrative might seem to be 'a barrier to those outside the exclave, shutting them out of the charmed

---

74 MacIntyre (1984), p. 263.
75 Hauerwas and Willimon (1989), p. 42.
76 MacIntyre (1984), p. 222 (my italics).

circle of the story-telling and story-listening church'.[77] However, the Catholic theologian and novelist Alexander Lucie-Smith argues that while stories are, by their nature, particular and local, the best of them (Augustine's *Confessions*, for example, and, in particular the Gospels) are capable of being infinitely widened out. From humble beginnings, events that happened 'once upon a time' are capable of leading those who engage with them towards a universal horizon which transcends the story's original form, and which leads us towards truths that are valid for all times and places: 'behind the story looms the infinite background'.[78] Stories themselves do not arise out of nowhere, but can only be told in the first place because their authors have a wider horizon of meaning from which to draw their narrative. Far from erecting barriers between groups of people, the sharing of stories can draw people together more effectively perhaps than, say, a discussion of the categorical imperative. And stories have a particular role to play in ethical reflection, because they can articulate universal moral truths and values by embodying these and making them comprehensible within a narrative framework:

> The narrative provides the language with which to express moral concepts and to talk about them. The narrative gives us something to point to when we wish to express what we mean by good. The narrative brings the question of the good and moral obligation 'down' to the realms of that which can be discussed.[79]

Questions for discussion

What seem to you to be the most important strengths and weaknesses of virtue ethics?

Which do you think are the most important virtues?

How might virtue ethics contribute to the following areas of ethical reflection: sexual ethics, the ethics of war, the ethics of punishment?

---

77 Lucie-Smith (2007), p. 174.
78 Lucie-Smith (2007), p. 191.
79 Lucie-Smith (2007), p. 216.

10

Love and the Moral Life

All you need is love, love
Or, failing that, alcohol.

Wendy Cope, 'Variation on a Lennon and McCartney Song'

Love in the Bible

'Love' is one of the most frequently used (and perhaps misused) words in the English language, but it stands at the heart of the Christian moral life. In the Bible, both Old and New Testaments have a range of Hebrew and Greek words that are translated 'love', and this chapter will begin by exploring some of these.

Old Testament

One of the most powerful and evocative Hebrew terms for 'love' in the Old Testament is *hesed*, translated, among other ways, as 'loving kindness', 'mercy' or 'steadfast love'.[1] *Hesed* is evident in human interactions such as those between, for example, Sarah and Abraham (Gen. 20.13) or Jacob and Joseph (Gen. 47.29), but it comes into its own as a theological term, expressing God's relationship to Israel – his solemn commitment to his people, and his provision for their need. Far from the vengeful and capricious caricature that is sometimes depicted, the Old Testament writers understand the God of the covenant to be 'merciful and gracious, slow to anger, and abounding in steadfast love (*hesed*) and faithfulness, keeping steadfast love (*hesed*) for the thousandth generation, forgiving iniquity and transgression' (Exod. 34.6–7). Reflection on God's *hesed* becomes a cornerstone of Israel's devotional life: the psalms frequently reflect upon the way that it is manifested in his forgiveness, sustenance, faithfulness and forgiveness. As the

---

1 This section draws in particular on Attwood (1998), chapter 3 and the articles by K. D. Sakenfeld and W. Klassen in D. N. Freedman, et al. (eds) (1992), *The Anchor Yale Bible Dictionary*, vol. 4 (New York: Doubleday), pp. 375–96 and the article on Love by D. H. Field in Atkinson and Field (1995), pp. 9–15.

repeated refrain to Psalm 136 has it, 'his steadfast love [*hesed*] endures for ever'.

Mutuality and reciprocity between those who give and those who receive love are central to the concept of *hesed*. God's people, as the recipients of his *hesed*, are called upon to keep the law, and to do what they can to maintain the covenant relationship: to respond to God's love with an answering love of their own, both for God and for others. The prophet Hosea insists that God desires from his people 'steadfast love [*hesed*], and not sacrifice, the knowledge of God rather than burnt offerings' (Hos. 6.6), and Micah declares that the Lord's essential requirements are to 'do justice, love kindness [*hesed*] and to walk humbly with your God' (Micah 6.8). While God may command such a response (Deut. 6.5), he ultimately cannot coerce it, and so it is ultimately up to human beings, aware of what God has done for them, to offer love back to him freely and willingly.

Micah's famous words quoted above draw attention to a further dimension of love in the Old Testament. In the Old Testament, both *hesed* and another important Hebrew term for love, *aheb*, have a strongly practical dimension to them. In their own patterns of action and behaviour, human beings are called upon to reflect the love that God himself shows to the weak and those who need it most: to Hebrew slaves suffering under bondage in Egypt, to widows, orphans and the destitute. Assistance to the needy is also commanded when the Israelites are told: 'you shall love your neighbour as yourself (Lev. 19.18), and when the definition of 'neighbour' is widened out to include even strangers living in the midst of Israel, since God's people were themselves once strangers in the land of Egypt (Lev. 19.34). The practical nature of this love; its steadfast and enduring quality underline the fact that love in its biblical context is not primarily understood to be about emotions and feelings, but it is also a matter of the will.[2] Love does, of course, in the Bible as elsewhere, have a strongly emotional element, but the truly loving person will also display a consistently self-giving approach to life, the ability to go beyond selfish concerns and will the good of another, and his or her happiness, whether he or she feels like doing so or not.

New Testament

The Greek noun *agapē* (a rendering of *aheb*, which also encompasses much of the sense of *hesed*) is by far the most common New Testament word for love. *Agapē* describes that love which flows from God to human beings and makes us, in the words of Saint Paul 'more than conquerors' (Rom. 8.37). The New Testament writers, like their Old Testament counterparts, frequently indicate that the love of human beings for God and for one another should reflect the nature of the God who himself is love (1 John 4.16). The actions of God in Jesus Christ provide a model or standard for human

---

2 See Mattison (2008), pp. 297–9.

behaviour: God's command about the loving way in which human beings should act is often based upon the loving way that God himself has acted, is acting or will act. This is often described as an *imperative* (that is a command) based on an *indicative* (a factual statement):

'So if I, your Lord and Teacher, have washed your feet, you also ought to wash one another's feet.'

John 13.14

Be kind to one another, tender-hearted, forgiving one another as God in Christ has forgiven you.

Ephesians 4.32

We know love by this, that he laid down his life for us – and we ought to lay down our lives for one another.

1 John 3.16

In this is love, not that we loved God but that he loved us and sent his Son to be the atoning sacrifice for our sins. Beloved, since God loved us so much, we also ought to love one another.

1 John 4.10–11

Love is, of course, a particular focus of Jesus' own teaching and, in particular, his combination of the central command of the Jewish law to 'love the Lord your God with all your heart and with all your soul and with all your might' (Deut. 6.5) with the less prominent Old Testament command to 'love your neighbour as yourself' (Lev. 19.18; cf. Matt. 22.37–40; Mark 12.29–31; Luke 10.26–28). The author of the first letter of John sees the two parts of Jesus' double commandment as integrally related to one another: 'those who do not love a brother or sister whom they have seen cannot love God whom they have not seen' (1 John 4.20). In Jesus' own teaching and lifestyle, the commandment to love your neighbour is, as in the Old Testament, stretched beyond what this term would normally include: strangers, outcasts and ultimately even enemies can all be regarded as neighbours (Matt. 5.44; Luke 6.27). Saint Paul teaches that such love for enemies is itself rooted in the prior action of God: 'while we were enemies, we were reconciled to God through the death of his Son' (Rom. 5.10). Augustine regarded the 'double commandment' of love for God and neighbour to be so central to the teaching of Jesus, and of the Bible in general that, in a somewhat postmodern moment, he argues that we should accept any interpretation of a scriptural passage that serves to build up the love of God and neighbour, even if the interpretation seems to vary from the author's original intention. Likewise, interpretations that fail to build people up in these loves should always be rejected as misunderstandings, however accurate they might seem to be on other grounds.[3]

Varieties of love

The exact connotations of the New Testament term *agapē* have been the subject of controversy in the twentieth century. The Swedish Lutheran theologian Anders Nygren (1890–1977) in an influential work entitled in its English translation *Agape and Eros* explores the relationship between these two Greek terms for love. Nygren draws attention to the way in which the New Testament writers, and in particular Saint Paul, took *agapē*, a formerly somewhat obscure term, from the Septuagint (the Greek translation of the Old Testament), and placed it at the centre both of their teaching about the nature of God and about Christian morality. By contrast, the more prominent Greek word *eros* (meaning intimate, but not necessarily sexual, love) is used only very infrequently in the Septuagint and not at all in the New Testament. This, Nygren argues, is because *agapē* love is a fundamentally Christian concept, and *eros* love is its antithesis: '*eros* and *agapē* belong originally to two entirely separate spiritual worlds, between which no direct communication is possible'.[4] Some of the distinctions that Nygren draws between the two kinds of love are summarized in the following table:[5]

Eros	Agape
Egocentric	Theocentric
Human beings strive to ascend to God	God descends in Christ to humanity
Desires to get and to possess	Gives sacrificially
Pursues the good of the self	Seeks the good of the other
Responds to the value of objects	'Loves and imparts value by loving'
Calculating, evoked, motivated	Spontaneous, overflowing, unmotivated[5]

Nygren develops his sharply contrasting depiction of *agapē* and *eros*, arguing that these two types of love have unhelpfully been confused in the Christian tradition, in particular by Augustine in his account of *caritas* (charity). The

---

3 Augustine, *De Doctrina Christiana* 1.36.40.

4 Nygren (1932), p. 31.

5 This chart draws on a similar one by Andrew Goddard, in his lecture notes from Wycliffe Hall, Oxford.

famous words from the start of Augustine's *Confessions* epitomize what Nygren regards as the problem: 'you [God] have made us for yourself, and our heart is unquiet until it rests in you'.[6] Augustine's words, influenced as they are by the idea of ascent to God in the writing of Neoplatonist philosophers such as Plotinus (AD 204–70), depict the human heart seeking, for its own spiritual satisfaction, to ascend to God. Such a wish to ascend to God may in some respects be commendable, but its self-seeking quality makes it fundamentally different from the downward-moving, self-emptying love of God in Jesus Christ, which seeks nothing for itself, but only the good of the other. In Nygren's analysis, human love, in the sense of *agapē*, occurs when men and women allow themselves to become 'possessed' by God's love, which drives out all natural, self-seeking loves and replaces these with divine love which works through them. An individual who loves in such a way is free of any egocentricity, or anything he can attribute to his own agency: 'God's *agapē* ... has "chosen" him and made him a slave of God.'[7]

In his influential work *The Four Loves*, C. S. Lewis sets out a contrasting approach to the subject, analysing four of the principal Greek terms that are translated 'love' in English, so as to bring out some of their distinctive qualities:

- *storge* (pronounced store-gay): affection, such as exists between family members, in particular the love of parents for their offspring
- *philia*: friendship, primarily as Lewis understands this between people of the same gender
- *eros*: love that longs for an emotional connection: in particular (though not exclusively) sexual love
- *charity* (*agapē*): 'Gift-love', in particular that which comes by God's grace, and inspires in the hearts of Christians.

Any of the first three loves, based upon natural human desires and instincts has, as Lewis analyses them, the potential to go wrong. *Storge* and *philia* can, for example, become inward-looking, claustrophobic and exclusive, while people inflamed by *eros* can easily destroy one another. However, God's charity or *agapē*, while it channels, corrects, transforms and ultimately perfects the other human loves, does not, as in Nygren's account, destroy or negate them. Ultimately, the pattern for this is the incarnation of Christ, in whom the human and the divine go together and do not exclude one another: 'as Christ is perfect God and perfect Man, the natural loves are called to become perfect Charity and also perfect natural loves'.[8]

A similar point is made by Pope Benedict XVI in his encyclical of 2006, *Deus Caritas Est* (*God is Love*), where he, like Lewis, argues that, although

6 Augustine, *Confessions* 1.1.1, trans. H. Chadwick (1991).
7 Nygren (1932/1953), p. 94.
8 Lewis (1960), *The Four Loves* (London: Fount), p. 162.

agapē is the primary and characteristic New Testament term for love, none-theless descending love and ascending love (*agapē* and *eros*) must be held together. Benedict points out that to view God's love exclusively as *agapē* hardly does justice to the way in which it is described by the biblical writers, notably Hosea and Ezekiel, who write of God's love for Israel using 'boldly erotic images' of sexual love and marriage. God's love for Israel is tender, personal and jealous of other lovers, but at the same time entirely self-giving, forbearing and forgiving: 'God's *eros* for man is also totally *agapē*.'[9] Without *agapē*, *eros* indeed becomes covetous and self-seeking, but without *eros*, *agapē* potentially becomes entirely other-worldly, separated from the love that we experience in normal human relationships:

> *eros* and *agape* – ascending love and descending love – can never be completely separated. The more the two, in their different aspects, find a proper unity in the one reality of love, the more the true nature of love in general is realized. Even if *eros* is at first mainly covetous and ascending, a fascination for the great promise of happiness, in drawing near to the other, it is less and less concerned with itself, increasingly seeks the happi-ness of the other, is concerned more and more with the beloved, bestows itself and wants to 'be there for' the other. The element of *agape* thus enters into this love, for otherwise *eros* is impoverished and even loses its own nature. On the other hand, man cannot live by oblative, descending love alone. He cannot always give, he must also receive. Anyone who wishes to give love must also receive love as a gift. Certainly, as the Lord tells us, one can become a source from which rivers of living water flow (cf. John 7:37–38). Yet to become such a source, one must constantly drink anew from the original source, which is Jesus Christ, from whose pierced heart flows the love of God (cf. John 19:34).[10]

This apparently abstract discussion of the meaning of *eros* and *agapē* has some important repercussions for theological ethics, and for the entire way in which we consider the Christian moral life. The insistence of C. S. Lewis and Benedict XVI that *agapē*/charity does not negate other types of love but transforms and perfects them, recalls the discussion in chapter 3 of Aquinas's view of charity as the 'form' of all the other virtues. Christian love does not exist on some remote and rarefied plain. It does not invali-date other types of love, nor is it detached from other human qualities and activities. Rather, charity has the potential to infuse all of these with its own distinctive dynamic of self-giving, directing them along towards their ultimate end in God.[11]

---

9 Benedict XVI, *Deus Caritas Est* 13.
10 Benedict XVI, *Deus Caritas Est* 10–11.
11 See Mattison (2008), p. 303.

In one particular area of ethics, the approach to *eros* that Lewis and Benedict XVI outline supplies a helpful corrective. Chapter 1 discussed the way in which the Christian tradition, influenced in part by Augustine's teaching on the subject, tended to view sexual and bodily life as always being to some extent affected by concupiscence or immoderate desire. In the light of the more positive approach to *eros* that has been explored in this chapter, sexual desire can be viewed in a different light. For sure, erotic love, like the other loves, needs to be transformed and purified by divine love. Repentance, forgiveness and healing will be needed in men's and women's sexual lives as much as in any other sphere of human activity. But according to this account of them, physical desires and erotic love are not in themselves sinful, and thus outside the ambit of what can be redeemed by God's *agapē* love. Rather, *eros* is capable of being united with God's *agapē*; of being renewed and transformed by it.

Love, rules and the human good

Sexual intercourse began
In nineteen sixty-three
(Which was rather late for me) –
Between the end of the Chatterley ban/And the Beatles' first LP.

Philip Larkin, 'Annus Mirabilis'

Situation ethics

It was in the radical and subversive atmosphere of the 1960s, three years after Larkin's supposed date for the start of sexual intercourse, that Joseph Fletcher (1905–91) wrote his notorious work, *Situation Ethics*, in which he attempted to reassert the priority of love in Christian ethics over and against those who emphasized laws, duties and moral rules. Near the start of the book, Fletcher highlights three contrasting approaches to morality:

- *Legalism*: this, in Fletcher's view, is the attitude of the major Western traditions, including Judaism, Catholicism and Protestantism, in which morality has been guided primarily by rigid rules and laws.
- *Antinomianism*: the polar opposite of legalism, encountered in, for example, citizens of first century Corinth or twentieth-century existentialists, who reject all moral principles and see moral decision making as unconnected with reality, thus rendering moral decision making as 'random, unpredictable, erratic (and) anomalous'.
- *Situationism*: Fletcher's own approach is that the ethical maxims and rules of a community should be taken seriously, but that Christian moral decision making should primarily be guided by Christ's law of love:

Christian situation ethics has only one norm or principle or law ... that is binding and unexceptionable, always good and right regardless of the circumstances. That is 'love' – the *agapé* of the summary commandment to love God and the neighbour. Everything else, without exception, all laws and rules and principles and ideals and norms, are only *contingent*, only valid *if they happen* to serve love in any situation.[12]

For Fletcher, then, morality and the human good are not given, objective entities, but always hypothetical and contingent. Only the commandment to love is categorically good in itself; all other actions are only good insofar as they serve love. If, to return to a theme from chapter 5, casuistry involves applying moral rules in different situations, situation ethics seeks to apply love in different situations.[13] Fletcher argues that such an approach is evident in Jesus' own teaching and ministry. He cites, for example, Jesus' words to the Pharisees when they question him about his disciples plucking and eating grain on the Sabbath. Jesus commends the actions of David, when he and his companions were hungry in entering the temple and eating the bread of the presence (see Matt. 12.1–8; Mark 2.23–28; Luke 6.1–5).

Case study

The following case study is offered by Fletcher himself in Situation Ethics. *Outline what might be in Fletcher's terms the legalist, antinomian and situationist approaches to this case, and try to assess the strengths and weaknesses of each of these. Fletcher's own analysis may be found on pages 37–39 of his book.*

In 1962 a patient in a state mental hospital raped a fellow patient, an unmarried girl ill with a radical schizophrenic psychosis. The victim's father, learning what had happened, charged the hospital with culpable negligence and requested that an abortion to end the unwanted pregnancy be performed at once, in an early stage of the embryo. The staff and administrators of the hospital refused to do so, on the ground that the criminal law forbids all abortion except 'therapeutic' ones when the mother's life is at stake – because the moral law, it is supposed, holds that any interference with an embryo after fertilization is murder, i.e., taking of an innocent human being's life.

---

12 Fletcher, p. 30.

13 I owe this point to Professor Nigel Biggar, from his lectures on 'Christian Moral Reasoning' at the University of Oxford in 2007.

Criticisms of Situation ethics

Fletcher's approach must surely be commended for its insistence that Christian ethical reflection must always be 'rooted and grounded in love' (Eph. 3.17–18), and that good moral decision making will not simply involve reaching for off-the-peg rules and solutions in a mechanical and unthinking way. However, it has been criticized on a number of counts. One of these is that Fletcher draws, far more sharply than the Bible itself, a sharp juxtaposition between rules and love. In the Old Testament, God's love is seen, as D. H. Field puts it, as 'both the expression of his love and the explanation of what loving relationships meant in practice'.[14] And, in the New Testament also, love and rules accompany and complement one another, as Jesus implies when he tells his disciples, 'if you love me, you will keep my commandments' (John 14.15).

For sure, obeying moral rules for their own sake cannot be at the heart of Christian morality, nor can rules themselves motivate us to act well. And yet, rules can encapsulate an indispensable set of minimum standards to which loving action will always adhere. For example, the commandment, 'you shall not commit murder' (Exod. 20.13), although it does not necessarily prohibit all forms of killing, clearly shows that murder – the unlawful killing of another person with deliberate malice – can never be a loving action. It would be nonsensical to think that sitting light to the commandment not to murder could somehow help us to act in a more loving way. All murder crosses a line that love will never want to cross. Reflecting this more positive appreciation of the role of moral rules for demarcating loving action, many proponents of love-based ethics have rejected act agapaism, as espoused by Fletcher, which seeks to work out how to act lovingly in each situation on a case by case basis, and instead favoured rule agapaism, espoused by ethicists such as the American Methodist, Paul Ramsey (1913–88). This approach, rather than downplaying the importance of rules, tries to frame them carefully, so that they can point the way towards love.

A further criticism of situation ethics returns to a theme that was covered in the previous chapter, in the analysis of the narrative-based virtue ethics of writers such as Stanley Hauerwas. Such theologians point to the fact that Christianity is rooted in a set of narratives about God and his dealings with the world, as these are recounted in the story of Israel, Jesus and the Church, primarily encountered in the Scriptures. Through their incorporation in the Church, Christians become part of the community that tells this story, and understands its life in the light of it. For those who hold this view, ethical systems oriented around themes such as, for example, 'love', 'justice' or

---

14 D. H. Field (1995) (ed.), *New Dictionary of Christian Ethics and Pastoral Theology* (Leicester: InterVarsity Press), p. 13.

'inclusivity' run the risk of becoming vague and abstract.[15] Such themes are important, but should not be allowed to lose their toe-hold in the overall story that gives them their particular context and meaning.

A third, somewhat contrasting, critique of situation ethics takes us back to chapter 2, and to the insights that natural law offers into the nature of the human good. Commentators from this perspective would point out that, while love can move us to want what is good for the beloved, love itself cannot tell us what that good actually is. As Mattison writes, 'if love is seeking the good and happiness of another, doing so requires that we have a sense of what is the true good of the person we love, and how we can pursue it effectively. Having such a grasp gives a distinctive shape to how we love'.[16] Thus, for example, a parent bringing up a child may love the child very much, but this love, however strongly felt will be fairly useless if the parent does not understand what is good for the child, and know the specific things that he or she should do in order to foster the child's welfare. As the discussion of the biblical aspects of love indicated, love has a strongly practical dimension, and so if it is to be effective, those who love in any situation need a grasp of the reality of that situation in order to act lovingly. This is something that love, in and of itself, cannot supply. For this reason, and referring back to the discussion of the virtues in chapter 3, the virtue of charity needs prudence, regarded by classical writers as the 'charioteer of the virtues', since prudence gives to all the other virtues their proper direction and focus. The prudent person has the ability to see the world as it really is, and then to respond accordingly.

Love and grace

The first chapter of this book explored the disagreement between Augustine and Pelagius on the subject of grace and free will. This final section returns to that disagreement, with some further comments about the importance of love. In his mature years, Augustine reflected upon some of the issues in the Pelagian controversy in a series of sermons preached on Psalm 118 (119 in modern English translations). In these sermons, he continues to criticize the Pelagian view that, since God has given the commandments, the primary task for human beings should simply be to get on and obey them. Augustine reflects that a person who obeys the law only out of fear of the consequences is not truly united to it. To such a person, the law is a hindrance and an obstacle from doing what they really desire to do: 'a person controlled by this kind of fear would like to do what the law forbids and is peeved because

---

15 See Hauerwas (1983), pp. 22–4.

16 This point draws on Mattison (2008), pp. 300–3 and Professor Nigel Biggar's lectures on 'Christian Moral Reasoning'.

it is forbidden'.[17] Far different from this grudging attitude is the love of the law that permeates, for example, the words of the psalmist, who sees God's law not as a set of lifeless obligations that he is commanded to obey, but rather as a source of joy and inspiration:

> Oh, how I love your law!
> It is my meditation all day long.
>
> Psalm 119.97

To the question of whether love brings about the keeping of the commandments, or whether keeping of the commandments brings about love, Augustine replies emphatically, 'who can doubt that love comes first? For the one who does not love has no reason for keeping the commandments'.[18] Just as historically, God's love, supremely shown in Jesus Christ, inspires and evokes human love in response, so also existentially, God's love empowers and animates men and women's capacity to live moral lives. Without such love, adherence to the commandments becomes a lifeless imitation of real virtue: 'what is done for fear of punishment or for any carnal reason, and not with reference to that charity which the Holy Spirit pours into our hearts, is not yet being done as it should be done, although it seems to be being done'.[19] This is especially so, given that the most important of all the commandments are themselves commandments to love: only love itself can inspire us to keep a commandment to love. As Burnaby writes:

> The paradox of the command to love is that if it be obeyed because it is commanded, it is not obeyed ... To delight in the law of God is to delight in God, and in that delight to be free ... The law of love is the law of liberty: it is the very presence of the Holy Spirit, the finger of God, writing His Law in our hearts, spreading abroad in them the love which is the fulfilling of the law.[20]

As these words indicate, the source of the love that animates men and women is the Holy Spirit: 'it is God the Holy Spirit, proceeding from God who fires man to the love of God and neighbour when he has been given to him, and he himself is love'.[21] A crucial verse for Augustine is Romans 5.5: 'the love of God has been poured into our hearts by the Holy Spirit who has been given to us', and for him, our ability, such as we have it, to keep God's commandments is entirely the work of the Spirit who pours love into our

---

17 Augustine, *Exposition of Psalm* 118.25.7.
18 Augustine, *Tractates on the Gospel of John* 82.6.
19 Augustine, *Enchiridion* 32.121.
20 Burnaby (1938), p. 234.
21 Augustine, *De Trinitate* 15.31.

hearts: 'how are we to keep ... (the law) unless the life-giving Spirit grants us the power and comes to our help? '[22] Inspired and renewed by the love that the Spirit brings, development in the Christian life can be not the grim determination to follow a set of rules but, as the biblical writers suggest, a joyful and freely willed response to the love that God has given, and continues to pour out to all eternity.

---

22 Augustine, *Exposition of Psalm* 118.16.2.

Bibliography

Atkinson, D. H. and Field, D. J. (eds) (1995), *New Dictionary of Christian Ethics and Pastoral Theology* (Leicester: InterVarsity Press).

Attwood, D. (1998), *Changing Values: How to Find Moral Truth in Modern Times* (Carlisle: Paternoster Press).

Augustine of Hippo, *Confessions*, trans. M. Boulding (1996) (New York: New City Press).

— *Expositions of the Psalms* (6 vols) trans. M. Boulding (2000–4) (New York: New City Press).

— *Teaching Christianity*, trans. E. Hill (1996) (New York: New City Press).[1]

Ayer, A. J. (1936), *Language, Truth and Logic* (London: Penguin).

Banner, M. (1999), *Christian Ethics and Contemporary Moral Problems* (Cambridge: Cambridge University Press).

— (2009), *Christian Ethics, A Brief History* (Oxford: Wiley Blackwell).

Barton, J. (2002) (2nd ed.), *Ethics and the Old Testament* (London: SCM Press).

— (2003), *Understanding Old Testament Ethics* (Louisville, Kentucky: Westminster John Knox Press).

Bentham, J. (1780), *An Introduction to the Principles of Morals and Legislation* (Mineola, New York: Dover Publications).

Berkman, J. and M. Cartwright (2001) (eds), *The Hauerwas Reader* (Durham, NC, and London: Duke University Press).

Biggar, N. (1993), *The Hastening that Waits: Karl Barth's Ethics* (Oxford: Clarendon Press).

Bonhoeffer (1937), *The Cost of Discipleship*, trans. R. H. Fuller (London: SCM Press).

— (1949), *Ethics*, trans. N. H. Smith (London: SCM Press).

Bonner, G. (1986) (rev. ed.), *St Augustine of Hippo, Life and Controversies* (Norwich: Canterbury Press).

Brown, P. (1967), *Augustine of Hippo: A Biography* (London: Faber and Faber).

Burnaby, J. (1938), *Amor Dei, A Study in the Religion of Saint Augustine* (London: Hodder and Stoughton).

Cessario, R. (2001), *Introduction to Moral Theology* (Washington DC: The Catholic University of America Press).

Chadwick, H. (1986), *Augustine* (Oxford: Oxford University Press).

---

1 Other citations from Augustine come from the translations in the Nicene and Post Nicene Fathers series.

Childress, J. F. and Macquarrie, J. (eds) (1986), *The Westminster Dictionary of Christian Ethics* (Philadelphia: Westminster Press).

Cosgrove, C. H. (2002), *Appealing to Scripture in Moral Debate: Five Hermeneutical Rules* (Grand Rapids, MI: Eerdmans).

Crisp, R. and M. Slote (1997) (eds), *Virtue Ethics* (Oxford: Oxford University Press).

Finnis, J. (1980), *Natural Law and Natural Rights* (Oxford: Clarendon Press).

Fletcher, J. (1966), *Situation Ethics* (Louisville, KY: Westminster John Knox Press).

Freedman, D. N. (1992) (ed.), *The Anchor Bible Dictionary* (New Haven and London: Yale University Press).

George, R. P. (1992) (ed.), *Natural Law Theory* (Oxford: Oxford University Press).

Gill, R. (2001) (ed.), *The Cambridge Companion to Christian Ethics* (Cambridge: Cambridge University Press).

Gustafson, J. F. (1978), *Protestant and Roman Catholic Ethics: Prospects for Rapprochement* (Chicago: University of Chicago Press).

Harrison, C. (2000), *Augustine: Christian Truth and Fractured Humanity* (Oxford: Oxford University Press).

Hauerwas, S. (1981), *A Community of Character: Toward a Constructive Christian Social Ethic* (Notre Dame, IN: University of Notre Dame Press).

— (1983), *The Peaceable Kingdom: A Primer in Christian Ethics* (Notre Dame, IN: University of Notre Dame Press).

— (1993), *Naming the Silences: God, Medicine and the Problem of Suffering* (Edinburgh: T&T Clark).

Hauerwas, S. and S. Wells (2004), *The Blackwell Companion to Christian Ethics* (Oxford: Blackwell Publishing).

Hauerwas, S. and W. Willimon (1989), *Resident Aliens: Life in the Christian Colony* (Nashville: Abingdon Press).

— (1996), *Where Resident Aliens Live: Exercises for Christian Practice* (Nashville: Abingdon Press).

Hays, R. B. (1996), *The Moral Vision of the New Testament: A Contemporary Introduction to New Testament Ethics* (Edinburgh: T&T Clark).

Holmgren, S. (2000), *Ethics after Easter* (Cambridge, Massachusetts: Cowley Publications).

Hoose, B. (1998) (ed.), *Christian Ethics: An Introduction* (London and New York: Continuum).

Kant, I. (1785), *Groundwork of the Metaphysics of Morals*, trans. H. J. Paton as *The Moral Law* (London: Routledge).

Keating, J. (2000) (ed.), *Spirituality and Moral Theology: Essays from a Pastoral Perspective* (Mahwah, New Jersey: Paulist Press).

Keenan, J. F. (2010), *A History of Catholic Moral Theology in the Twentieth Century* (New York: Continuum).

Kerr, F. (2002), *After Aquinas: Versions of Thomism* (Oxford: Blackwell Publishing).

Kierkegaard, S. (1843), *Fear and Trembling*, trans. A. Hannay (London: Penguin).

Kreeft, P. (1990), *A Summa of the Summa: The Essential Philosophical Passages of St Thomas Aquinas' Summa Theologica Edited and Explained for Beginners* (San Francisco: Ignatius Press).

Lewis, C. S. (1960), *The Four Loves* (London: Harper Collins).
Lucie-Smith, A. (2007), *Narrative Theology and Moral Theology: the Infinite Horizon* (Aldershot: Ashgate).
Luther, M. (1520), *A Treatise on Christian Liberty*, trans. W. A. Lambert, rev. H. J. Grimm (Philadelphia: Fortress Press).

MacIntyre, A. (1984) (2nd ed.), *After Virtue: A Study in Moral Theory* (Notre Dame, Indiana: University of Notre Dame Press).
Macquarrie, J. (1970), *Three Issues in Ethics* (London: SCM Press).
Mahoney (1987), *The Making of Moral Theology: A Study of the Roman Catholic Tradition* (Oxford: Clarendon Press).
Mattison, W. C. (2008), *Introducing Moral Theology* (Grand Rapids, MI: Brazos Press).
May, W. E. (1991), *An Introduction to Moral Theology* (Huntingdon, IN: Our Sunday Visitor Publishing Division).
McCoy, A. (2004), *An Intelligent Person's Guide to Christian Ethics* (London: Continuum).
Meilaender, G. (1984), *The Theory and Practice of Virtue* (Notre Dame, Indiana: University of Notre Dame Press).
Moore, G. (2003), *A Question of Truth: Christianity and Homosexuality* (London: Continuum).

Northcott, M. (1996), *The Environment and Christian Ethics* (Cambridge: Cambridge University Press).
Nygren (1932), *Agape and Eros*, trans. P. Watson (London: SPCK).

O'Donnell, J. J. (2005), *Augustine, Sinner and Saint* (London: Profile Books).
O'Donovan, O. (1994) (2nd ed.), *Resurrection and Moral Order* (Grand Rapids, MI: Eerdmans).

Pieper, J. (1966), *The Four Cardinal Virtues*, trans. R. and C. Winston (Notre Dame, Indiana: University of Notre Dame Press).
— (1986), *Faith, Hope, Love*, trans. R. and C. Winston (Notre Dame, Indiana: University of Notre Dame Press).
— (1988), *A Brief Reader on the Virtues of the Human Heart*, trans. P. C. Duggan (San Francisco: Ignatius Press).
Pinckaers (1995), *The Sources of Christian Ethics*, trans. M. T. Noble (Edinburgh: T&T Clark).
— (2005), *The Pinckaers Reader: Renewing Thomistic Moral Theology*, trans. M. T. Noble, eds J. Berkman, C. T. Steven (Washington DC: The Catholic University of America Press).

Renick, T. M. (2002), *Aquinas for Armchair Theologians* (Louisville, KY: Westminster John Knox Press).

Rist, J. M. (1994), *Augustine* (Cambridge: Cambridge University Press).

Spaemann, R. (1989), *Basic Moral Concepts*, trans. T. J. Armstrong (London: Routledge).

Tarnas, R. (1991), *The Passion of the Western Mind* (London: Pimlico).

Taylor, J. (1660/1855), *Doctor Dubitantium or The Rule of Conscience in all her General Measures* (London: Longman).

Thomas Aquinas, *Summa Theologica*, translated by the Fathers of the English Dominican Province, 1920.[2]

Tomlin, G. (2006), *Spiritual Fitness: Christian Character in a Consumer Society* (London: Continuum).

Vardy, P. and P. Grosch (1994), *The Puzzle of Ethics* (London: Fount Paperbacks).

Wells, S. (1998), *Transforming Fate into Destiny: The Theological Ethics of Stanley Hauerwas* (Eugene, OR: Cascade Books).

— (2006), *God's Companions, Reimagining Christian Ethics* (Oxford: Blackwell).

Wells, S. and B. Quash (2010), *Introducing Christian Ethics* (Oxford: Wiley Blackwell).

Wright, N. T. (2010), *Virtue Reborn* (London: SPCK).

Ziesler, J. (1989), *Paul's Letter to the Romans* (London: SCM Press).

---

2 Some citations from Aquinas use the translation in Kreeft (1990).

Index

[Note: references to authors of secondary literature only appear if they are discussed in the text.]